THE BEST OF BRITISH PLUCK

THE BEST OF BRITISH PLUCK

The Boy's Own Paper

REVISITED BY

PHILIP WARNER

BOOK CLUB ASSOCIATES
LONDON

CONTENTS

My thanks are due to Mr R. B. Goodall for supplying all the photographic material which is reproduced in this book.

INTRODUCTION

On 18 January 1879 there appeared the first issue of a weekly magazine which described itself as 'pure and entertaining reading'. It was indeed both, although there were numerous recommendations in later issues for curing impure thoughts and – even worse – impure actions. Nearly a hundred years later, and nine years after the last issue ended its history, it is customary to see and hear comments such as 'It's like something out of the *Boy's Own Paper*' or 'He's a typical *Boy's Own Paper* hero.' Note that it was the '*Boy's*', not the '*Boys*'' – a significant difference and perhaps one that was fundamental to its success. It was read by thousands of boys, in generation after generation, but every single boy who read that paper sitting, standing, lying, lounging, knew that it was for him. It was for him, and about him, and the main character in every story was him as well.

Yet for everyone who has seen and read the *B.O.P.* (as it soon came to be called) there seem to be two or three more who have only heard of it. Nobody who has read it has tried to attack it. Perhaps there have been resourceful sociologists who have picked up copies with a view to denouncing it as an imperialistic, class-conscious, insidious publication, but having made the fatal mistake of starting to read it perhaps they became so immersed in the stories, often true and sometimes fiction based on fact, that they forgot their original purpose. How on earth could one compete with Mr Charles Waterton, who recalled in one issue:

Soon after this I had another battle, but single-handed, with a young coulacanara, only ten feet long. I saw he was not thick enough to break my arm in case he got twisted round it. I laid hold of his tail with the left hand, one knee being on the ground; with my right I took off my hat and held it as you would a shield for defence. The snake instantly turned and came on me, with his head about a yard from the ground as if to ask me what business I had to take liberties with his tail. I let him come, hissing and open-mouthed within two feet of my face, and then with all the force I was master of, I drove my fist, shielded by my hat, full in his jaws. He was stunned and confounded by the blow, and ere he could recover himself I had seized his throat with both hands, in such a position that he could not bite me. I then allowed him to coil himself around my body and marched off with him as my lawful prize.

Far-fetched, the modern reader might say – you could not possibly do that with a python or an anaconda. You and I perhaps could not, but jungle-dwellers do not stand much nonsense from snakes if they are edible. And Charles Waterton knew as much about snakes as natives did, and what was more G. A. Hutchison, the Editor, knew that he did.

For the *B.O.P.* had to satisfy severer critics than self-appointed social reformers. It had to satisfy boys. What its devoted readers said about it in misty retrospect, prime ministers, archbishops, dukes, generals, captains of industry though they may have been, was beside the point. The *B.O.P.* had to be worth a boy's penny once a week, and a penny in the early days of the *B.O.P.* was still a penny. You could do a lot with it in the period 1879–1914. You could buy twelve boxes of matches with it for a start, and you can have a lot of fun with twelve boxes of matches if you're a boy. And so you should. One penny was a whole week's pocket money for many boys. The *B.O.P.* was not just a rich boy's paper. The letters, the prizewinners and many of the references tell a very different story.

There is advice for lads who have to be at the factory at 6 a.m. Many of the hobby articles appear to be written for boys with very slender resources. Many of the stories are of boys who rose from destitution to fame. Others are of fall from wealth to the poorhouse. Even if you begin in Chapter I at an expensive public school you are as likely as not to be in a doss-house in Liverpool, starving and penniless, before the story has gone far. Snobbery about public schools had hardly begun before the First World War, and even in the 1930s, when school snobbery was probably at its zenith, the *B.O.P.* was publishing stories about grammar schools and gently indicating that schools were schools whatever their name or fame. Up until 1944 there were of course hundreds of fee-paying grammar schools, some with boarders, who bridged that extraordinary gap which now exists between boarding school and day school.

By 1939, after which the *B.O.P.* went into a slow decline, eighty million words had been published. Clearly in a book of some eighty thousand words one is not going to make much impact on eighty million, and the extracts here are merely samples, mainly chosen from the earlier years when the paper was at its most influential.

All this productivity resulted from a proposal in 1878 to the Religious Tract Society, who were already publishers of a popular magazine called *Leisure Hour*, that they should cater for an increasingly literate public by providing something better than the current 'penny dreadfuls' (weird fantasies of macabre violence) and something more gripping than uplifting literature. James Macaulay was the Religious Tract Society's General Editor but, as mentioned later, he was merely the nominal head of the *B.O.P.* G. A. Hutchison was aged 37 when he became the magazine's first editor, and he quickly had the circulation up to a quarter of a million. His ability at spotting talent was not limited to writers but covered artists as well. An attractive feature of all *B.O.P.*'s was the colour plate, often produced by such notable artists as R. Caton Woodville and Stanley Wood; Frank Brangwyn and Jack Nettleship (Augustus John's father-in-law) also drew for the *B.O.P.*

In 1914 weekly parts were discontinued and the magazine became a monthly. The price rose after 1916 and reached one shilling in 1918. Here it stuck until the Second World War. In 1913 A. L. Haydon had succeeded to the editorial chair; he was followed by G. R. Pocklington (1924–33), G. J. H. Northcroft (1933–35), and Robert Harding, who had been a frequent contributor, from 1935 up to the Second World War.

The paper must have exerted considerable influence. It reeked of sound commonsense. Many of its readers were clearly underprivileged, but self-pity was not encouraged; evidently they wished to be larger, cleverer, free of acne or blackheads; sometimes the letters indicated that they were seriously ill. Perhaps the *B.O.P.* was the only reliable, consistently cheerful factor in their lives.

Its long-term effects were curious, and no doubt varied with the individual. In the middle of 1943 the compiler of this book was a Japanese prisoner-of-war in Siam (Thailand), working on the infamous Bangkok-Moulmein railway of death. Food was inadequate and appalling; the work was heavy and exhausting; the Japanese and Korean guards seemed scarcely sane; malaria, dysentery, cholera, beri-beri, and a host of other diseases were rife. Sometimes it rained incessantly and there was no protection at night except for a few leaking tents or huts. Men died with steady regularity. Around was the jungle, hot, oppressive, menacing. There was really no hope of survival. Even if the Allies won the war it would take so long that we should all have long since been dead. I remember one day looking round at the scene and saying to myself: 'What an extraordinary situation! It's like some strange adventure in the *Boy's Own Paper*.' Suddenly it was less real, more bearable: after all, *B.O.P.* characters lived to tell the tale. Fantasy perhaps, but in certain conditions illusion may be more genuine than reality.

THE CONTRIBUTORS

The success of the *B.O.P.* was almost entirely due to the genius of one man. This was G. A. Hutchison, the editor who presided from 1879 to 1913; he died at work. He was not in fact the titular editor of the first volume; this honour belonged to James Macaulay, although Hutchison was already the master hand. By the second volume Macaulay had become a mere contributor. It seems that the fact that James Macaulay was M.A. and M.D. was more likely to commend the new magazine to parents and headmasters than the untitled G. A. Hutchison, who had begun his working life as a printer's apprentice and subsequently became editor of the *Social Science Review*, *The Sunday School World* and *The Baptist*.

Hutchison had a remarkable gift for knowing exactly what boys wanted to find in their magazine. With this went the equally valuable accomplishment of knowing where to find the right authors. The roll-call of these authors is impressive. Many of his discoveries were still writing for the paper a quarter of a century after he was dead. Even the lesser-known authors have a stamp of quality about them. Some, of course, are household names. Jules Verne did not appear till the second volume (a volume comprised the complete annual output of the paper), but once in he was one of the most regular contributors. 'The Cryptogram' appeared in serial form in Volume IV, 'The Clipper of the Clouds' in Volume IX, but these were only two of many of his stories. R. M. Ballantyne appeared in Volume II with 'The Red Man's Revenge', and thereafter was a regular contributor.

Other well-known names were W. H. G. Kingston, one of the most prolific writers of boys' stories, G. A. Henty, H. de Vere Stacpoole, Conan Doyle, Algernon Blackwood and Gunby Hadath. Talbot Baines Reed appeared on the very first page of the first issue but under the pen-name of 'An Old Boy'. 'The Adventures of a Three-Guinea Watch' appeared in 1881 and from then onwards almost every volume contained one of Reed's extraordinarily gripping school stories. A reader may never have heard of Talbot Baines Reed and may not like school stories, least of all those set in the late nineteenth century, but let him read a few paragraphs of Reed and he is away. Small wonder that many of Reed's titles have recently been reprinted.

Another writer who began in the Hutchison period was the highly consistent Captain (later Major) Charles Gilson. Ranks were rarely used in the *B.O.P.* after the first few numbers, but there was something about Captain Charles Gilson which set him apart from all the other thousands of captains. Gilson, like the majority of contributors, wrote from firsthand experience, and he had no lack of it. His heyday was the 1920s when his heroes discovered lost cities in the desert, lost worlds in the jungle, lost treasures in Peru and lost English boys in Chinese pirate ships. With Gilson, as indeed with many of the other authors, you were no hero. You were often very afraid. You remained very much yourself in those highly dangerous surroundings, and that meant you were often pretty scared. Never mind, you kept cool and alert and waited for the next instalment. Ultimately, on balance, you felt you were lucky to have survived.

ATTITUDES TO LIFE

Although G. A. Hutchison never spoke or wrote religion the undercurrent of Christian ethics clearly flowed strongly through the volumes. Later editors were less subtle and printed boring and priggish homilies 'By an Old Boy', which can have been seldom read except by the converted or by parents.

The motto of the *B.O.P.* was '*Quicquid agunt pueri nostri libelli farrago*'. The majority of the early readers, with their heavily classical education, probably translated it with ease, although 'farrago', which literally means 'mixed fodder for cattle', might have given them pause. The intended meaning was 'Whatever boys do makes up the mixture of this little book'.

Hutchison's understanding of boys did not extend to being gentle to them. Anyone who wrote to the Editor was liable to get a crisp and caustic reply. 'No one with your handwriting could hope to get a job in a bank. You would use up too much paper.' He replied in 1891 with what seems unnecessary brutality to George O. and others: 'The object of the medical examination is that the country should not be served by the deformed, the crippled and the weak. If you are not perfect in limb and health you are simply wasting your time. Is it likely that a lad with a broken leg and a hip growing out would make a desirable soldier?' He might have been surprised if he had ever known of some of the people who did succeed in passing. (The author knows of one successful soldier in the Second World War who had a collapsed lung.) But then the Victorians did not believe in giving unnecessary encouragement: 'Glandular scars will prevent you from being accepted for the Marines unless as an officer.'

There must have been a lot of letters seeking medical advice, for the Editor often dealt with them in batches. Personal replies were never sent even to those who hopefully enclosed stamped addressed envelopes.

MEDICAL (Nemo writes again) – Yes: we received your letter and replied under the heading 'Consult a doctor'. How could you expect our advice upon a case of deformity of the feet which we had not seen. We are ever willing to advise our readers in cases where self-doctoring is likely to be of any avail but not otherwise. We may tell you for your comfort, however, that deformities of nearly all kinds are amenable to treatment nowadays so lose no time.

That answer was immediately followed by:

TATTOO MARKS (Old Ipswichian) – Nothing certain but an operation, unless you care to run red-hot needles under the skin. You can't bleach them out.

And that by:

CATS HAVING KITTENS (Perseus) – As early as seven or eight months if not looked after.

Cats unfortunately had to be 'well looked after'. Unlike boys they could not be told to take cold baths, exercise vigorously with the dumb-bells, and stop visiting art galleries, if troubled by sexual thoughts. The scourge of youth was of course masturbation. It ruined health, concentration and looks, and led to imbecility and early death. Nowadays, with equal improbability, sociologists seem to think it is positively beneficial.

E. S. Turner, in his delightful book *Boys Will Be Boys*, thought that the Editor of *B.O.P.* was tetchy because he received so many ill-packed bird or beetle corpses for post-mortem diagnosis. As a medical adviser the Editor seems to have had more limitations than he may have guessed:

PROPORTIONS. Good if you are not fat. Fat makes duffers.

Girls also wrote for advice:

MAKING HAIR GROW (Haidée) – No, miss, it was only meant for moustaches. For eyebrows the following might be rubbed in morning and evening for a few weeks. Eau de Cologne, two ounces; tincture of cantharides, two drachms; oil of rosemary and oil of lavender, of each ten drops. It is also used for the cure and prevention of baldness.

An interesting recipe indeed!

Many of the enquiries were for the health of pets, which seemed to embrace every variety of animal and bird. Others – sometimes on behalf of 'a friend' – concerned eyes, knock-knees, chilblains, red noses, pigeon breasts, bandy legs, bunions, blackheads etc. Some boys did not grow enough, others found themselves growing too tall. 'Fifteen years old 6 feet 2 inches in height. Grows five inches a year, and that will do famously. In five years time you will be 8 feet and over. Try to grow broad also and try to grow good.' Some letters were mysterious: 'Getting on Nicely. We are so glad. As long as you do what you mention it will not hurt you. To some extent it is natural provided you keep pure and good.'

The attitude to corporal punishment was to treat it as a joke. That at least was the editorial view, and as boys continued to buy the paper they must have shared it. Corporal punishment has many aspects. The recipient may be discouraged from repeating the offence, although some might transgress again out of sheer bravado. It was preferable to a lengthy imposition. A boy's first beating was an initiation ceremony; you could not command any respect till you had taken six of the best (without flinching of course). In the same way a soldier is simply not a soldier till he has been on a 'charge' and duly punished. In Volume V (1883) there was an article entitled 'Swishing Anecdotes' which spoke of the more celebrated caners of the past. They included the tutors and deans of certain Oxford and Cambridge Colleges (it is said that John Milton was flogged at Christ's, Cambridge). Students were liable to be flogged for 'Hunting wild animals with dogs and visiting the exhibitions of rope-dancers, actors and sword-players'. The author seemed unaware of the enormous variety of physical punishment which was casually referred to in volume after volume of the *B.O.P.* It was as natural and considerably more regular than meal times. Much of it was administered by boys themselves (see the section on school stories on pages 11 and 12).

The Victorian attitude to boys was epitomised in everything which Gordon Stables, M.D., R.N., wrote. Stables was born in 1840 and qualified in medicine at Aberdeen. He served with the Royal Navy for about ten years and was then invalided out. He died in 1910. He wrote extensively for the *B.O.P.* in both story and article form. Apparently he spent most of his time touring the country in a caravan. In his 'New Year's Letter to Working Lads' he describes a time and motion study he had conducted to prove that a factory lad could have a cold bath before arriving at work at 6 a.m. The 'letter' is reproduced on page 96; perhaps its most notable feature is the staggering egoism of the nomadic doctor.

By this time the *B.O.P.* had given out a wealth of advice and pleasure. In 1899 it had a coming-of-age dinner at the Holborn Restaurant in London. The Chairman,

. . . who was the Archdeacon of London, made a speech. He reminded them that 'those who had to educate the youth of England knew full well the danger of immoral literature permeating and poisoning the minds of lads'. He was therefore exceptionally pleased that the *B.O.P.* was filling not only a literary but a national want and that it exercised a wonderful power for good in raising the moral tone of the youth of our nation, both at home and abroad.

Soon after, the Editor produced

A few amazing statistics. The *B.O.P.* had published 35,251,200 words. If all these words had been set out in a straight line they would have extended for 135 miles, or from London to Stafford. However, if all the pages had been spread out side by side they would have covered $2\frac{5}{8}$ square miles. They had, as well as their words, printed 17,472 illustrations. And if all the copies sold had been piled on end they would have made a column 63 miles high. Place them on the ground and they would cover the whole of Great Britain.

And that was after only 21 years.

At the Jubilee lunch held at the Connaught Rooms on 18 January 1929 (when a string band of St Anne's boys' school, composed entirely of elementary school boys, played before and during the meal) Stanley Baldwin made one of the speeches. He said: 'I rejoice to find in this age of progress this advertisement here today. "Stink bombs. Just drop one. 3d." And most mysterious of all with no illustration to its effect, "Itching powder, 3d." That shows, I think, that the boys who are nurtured on the *Boy's Own Paper* will turn out men and neither prudes nor prigs.' Baldwin was then Prime Minister, but his sentiments were echoed by Ramsay MacDonald, then leader of the Opposition, who contributed: 'Many a gorgeous hour of happiness came to me from the *Boy's Own Paper*.' Baldwin mentioned that he had taken it from the beginning. A penny a week, particularly if it went on the school bill, probably did not worry the young Harrovian, but Ramsay MacDonald would have had to make considerable sacrifices for his copy.

At this dinner G. R. Pocklington, the Editor, who usually put '(Rossall and Balliol)' after his name when it appeared, said he had recently had a letter from a boy 'whom I judged to be somewhere about ten years of age, who wanted to know if I could tell him the *lowest* cost of an expedition by aeroplane to either the North or the South Pole, for one man and his dog. I have the most profound admiration for that boy who was not going to leave his faithful hound behind even if it involved the additional cost of a dog ticket to the Polar regions.'

What no one seems to have remarked was that during the first thirty years of its life the *B.O.P.* was genuinely a paper for boys of all ages, even very old ones. There is nothing juvenile about it. Many of the early articles could easily have appeared in adult magazines. To some extent this remained true during the *B.O.P.*'s whole life as far as articles were concerned, but from about 1925 onwards the paper seemed to be catering principally for middle-class schoolboys. One can hardly imagine the 1886 article on 'Half Hours with Hard Workers: Scavengers' appearing in the 1930s. Nevertheless 'Death of a Famous Fire-horse' in Volume I would have aroused interest at any time.

Perhaps one of the most revealing tributes was that given in a letter printed in September 1903:

Dear Sir – I wish the *Boy's Own Paper* another 25 years of useful activity. Personally I owe it a debt of gratitude for it was one of the first papers which grew tired of returning my MSS and began to print them instead. With all good wishes, Yours truly,
Arthur Conan Doyle.

Hutchison had a genius for discovering authors who later became famous.

Even by the early 1900s the *B.O.P.* seemed to be drifting much more towards the middle-class boy. Ten years earlier the net had been flung wider – with success, both in age and in social status. In the Handwriting Competition for under-11s in 1890 no fewer than seventeen pupils from Harrow Green Board School, Leytonstone, had been awarded certificates. In the Music Competition set at the same time the joint first-prize winners were aged 23 and 24. In September 1892 prizes were won by: Lance-Corporal William Pitt, Norton Barracks, Worcester; Victor Chart of Bombay; Emanuel Misaelides of Smyrna; Alice Manders of Camden Town; Earnest Foderingham of Barbados; and Lenn Thomas of Tokyo. The oldest entrant in that competition was 65.

However, dealing with such a wide variety of people who were only too pleased to enter fairly simple competitions did not inhibit the Editor from corresponding with the more educationally advanced. 'You might get the job if you apply in person but they will think you insane if you write as you did to us on Cambridge Union paper,' he wrote in 1892.

In 1902 there appeared the first article by G. A. Wade, B.A. It was entitled 'When I was at school'. There were three articles in this series, but none of them disclosed the name of the school. It may well have been Harrow, for one of the writer's later references to that school seems particularly partisan. Wade was what might be described as a 'professional old boy'. His own schooldays had been in the early 1880s, but they were evergreen. He did not get into his stride immediately, for C. W. Alcock was writing, with illustrations, about 'Public Schools and their Football Captains', but in 1904 Wade was off with the series of articles on every conceivable aspect of public schools which kept him going for thirty years. He wrote on such subjects as:

Famous Schoolmasters in Caricature
Boys who Wrote
Playing Fields at Public Schools
Chapels at Public Schools
Songs of our Public Schools
Famous Schoolmasters in the Boat Race
Extraordinary Athletic Feats of Schoolboys
Swimming at the Chief Schools
Schools that originated Football
Famous Runs at Famous Schools
The Greatest Cricketing Family

By 1910 he was moving nicely:

The Greatest of Football Schools
Famous Schools with Coronation Rights

And so it went on, year after year:

Words Peculiar to the Public Schools
Round the Cloisters at our Public Schools.

In 1923 he was writing about 'War Memorials at Public Schools'. On and on he went, even writing about such unpromising subjects as 'Dining Halls at Public Schools'.

It is difficult to imagine who can have read these articles. Certainly as a schoolboy I scarcely gave them a glance. 'Who on earth' (in schoolboy vernacular) 'could want to read about someone else's rotten old dining hall?' Most schools ate by Houses, anyway. Unfortunately this relentless series of articles gave the impression that the *B.O.P.* was only for public schoolboys and some pretty limited public schoolboys at that. In the old days – even in the very issue in which Wade first wrote – there was an article on 'A Boy's Life in a Workhouse School', and before that pictures of Board (Primary) School football teams. After Hutchison's editorship poor boys only seemed to appear when they were the subject of public-school missions or performed some surprisingly honourable feat which may not have been expected from their background.

Nevertheless any ideas that schools were worse in the early 1900s than they had been in the previous century are probably wrong. The articles and stories in the early *B.O.P.*'s paint a picture which, though not as horrific as Dickens's Dotheboys Hall, showed that few schoolboys would regard time spent in school as the happiest days of their lives. In the very first Volume – 1879 – an anonymous writer describes in 'My Early Schooldays' his school life at a small boarding school in Oxford apparently in the period around 1820. He learnt little but was constantly being punished for one minor offence or other. Small wonder that boys were prepared to run away to sea and undergo hardships which now seem scarcely bearable for boys of their age.

LANGUAGE

Language, of course, is constantly changing and developing. Schoolboys, however, are great preservers of tradition and for that reason many expressions which were used by adults in the nineteenth century but discarded in the twentieth still lingered on in schoolboy or even schoolgirl life. Nobody except a few junior pupils would now use the expression 'getting into a jolly good row', but it was used in the Crimean War to describe a brisk skirmish with Cossack raiders.

Schoolboy slang fell into two distinct categories. There were words which were given a specialised meaning at certain schools; thus a 'tosh' was a bath at Rugby but elsewhere was a synonym for nonsense. Much slang was universal. Boys would get into a 'regular fix', have a jolly close shave from being nabbed, perhaps be sneaked on by a cad and a bounder but be saved by the intervention of a decent chap who was an absolute brick. 'Fagging', the system by which junior boys performed various menial services (running errands, cleaning muddy football boots, making toast) for senior boys, was a recognised custom well back in the nineteenth century and may be the origin of the expression 'a fag' for drudgery and 'fagged out' for exhausted.

Other words which were used in the *B.O.P.* have had a less happy development, and this gives some of the earlier titles a startling effect. An article entitled 'How to Stuff Birds' appeared in 1899, and the 1903 volume saw 'My Little Tits' and a story entitled 'Queer Mr Quern'. Even in 1928 it was possible to write an article entitled 'Getting to Know the Birds', although 'birds' was already being used for girls.

All these represent a fairly jocular outlook. Other words have changed meaning because of a determined policy. However, the policy rarely succeeds in its object – which is to add lustre and dignity to the activity to which it is applied. Thus a 'gay hussar' in the nineteenth century would be a cheerful, dashing cavalryman; however, no one today would assume that a supporter of 'gay lib' would be a cheerful dashing homosexual – merely a homosexual. However, the adoption of certain words gives a slightly humorous flavour to Victorian reading. 'Camp life suited him and especially with the OTC.' 'He did not want to work in a co-educational school but he did so for the sake of the jolly good screw he got there.'

SPORT AND HOBBIES

Sport was clearly a vital element in the *B.O.P.* The very first article printed was 'My First Football Match'. It contained the illuminating words: 'An officer in the Crimean War described his sensation in some of the battles there as precisely similar to those he had experienced when a boy on the football field at Rugby.' Rugby football in the nineteenth century was no game for the squeamish. Although legal 'hacking' (kicking your way to the ball) had been abolished in 1871 the game was still a very physical affair. All ten forwards formed a wedge by which they hoped to clear a path and enable their runners, 'the quarter backs', to race through and score. In an 1881 *B.O.P.* there was an article on 'Rugby Football, and How to Excel in it' by Dr Irvine, the Scottish Captain. Other sports were equally well placed. Captain Webb was advising on Channel swimming and the immortal Dr W. G. Grace on cricket. One of the most surprising articles was that in 1904 entitled 'Kings in the Cricket Field' by Harold Macfarlane; they included the Prince of Wales and Kings from various parts of the British Empire.

Athletics were mentioned, and there are interesting records of what were then considered outstanding performances, but serious articles on self-improvement in technique did not begin till the 1900s (except for a totally misleading article on hurdling by Gordon Stables in 1894). Then Percy Longhurst and later Captain F. A. M. Webster produced numerous highly informative pieces. The virtue of these articles lay in the stimulus they gave. No matter what the sport the young reader felt that success was within his grasp. In 1892 the name of E. H. D. Sewell is first mentioned. Sewell was a good athlete but his ideas were wildly unorthodox. At the end of each article full of irresponsible assumptions the Editor would print: '(Note – The views and criticisms expressed in this article are the author's and are not necessarily endorsed by the *B.O.P.* – Editor)'. Sewell covered both cricket and rugby football, with misleading zeal, right up into the 1930s.

In 1892 Somerville Gibney wrote a series called 'Public School Football and How to Play It'. It dealt with games like the Eton Wall Game and Harrow 'Footer' which the vast majority of *B.O.P.* readers would not have been able to play, even if they had wished to.

Lovers of statistics and records were always well catered for. In a reply to 'Henry Reader' in 1891 it was stated that:

There is a case on record of a hit for 13. It was at a cricket match at Tunbridge Wells in 1863. The ground is at the top of the hill and Mr Charles Payne hit the ball down the hill for 13. There was no overthrow. In 1865 Mr J. H. T. Roupell hit a 10, a 9, and an 8 on Parker's Piece at Cambridge in an innings of 97.

On 16 September 1899 there appeared a photograph of the immortal A. E. J. Collins. In the words of the entry:

A Hero of the moment is the fourteen year old boy A. E. J. Collins of Clifton who has made the record cricket score of 628 not out. His father, who was in the Indian Civil Service, died in Burmah last autumn.

Young Collins was born in India in August 1885, and joined the Junior School at Clifton two years ago where he has been taught cricket chiefly by Mr H. G. Barlow. He batted for seven hours.

The *B.O.P.* seemed to have no difficulty in acquiring the services of experts to write articles. Apart from W. G. Grace, such notables as G. L. Jessop, Wilfred Rhodes, Warwick Armstrong (the Australian Test captain), Jack Hobbs, and a host of other well-known cricketers contributed. No matter what the sport the best was always to be found in the *B.O.P.* In 1914 boys were instructed on 'How to Throw the Boomerang' and told how to play soccer by the renowned Steve Bloomer. Patsy Hendren, better known as a cricketer, also wrote on soccer. Rugby football produced a stream of literate experts, but no one reached the heights of G. H. Harnett, an international referee, who wrote in 1917 about 'Rugby Football: An Asset of Empire'. The article began: 'War, as we know, is the greatest game there is. But we want other more peaceful games, not only to fit us for the great game of war but also to prepare us physically and morally – remember that! – for the battle of life in which every one of us is predestined to take part.' Later he continued: 'For the average healthy British boy Rugby football is the king of games. Why, look at the fellows who play it and remark what manner of men they are! Rugby football – clean, straightforward, free from any taint, makes men.'

Soccer was not considered a socially inferior game. Eton, Westminster, Shrewsbury, Winchester and many other public schools played it (and still do). To belong to the Corinthian Football Club, which won the F.A. cup, was thought of as the pinnacle of sporting prestige. All sport was considered a valuable means of developing the manly virtues and a sense of fair play. Everybody in the country knew what the expression 'it isn't cricket' meant.

Where most of the articles on sport excelled was in teaching novices. Whether the sport was hockey, lawn tennis, boxing, fencing, chess or even mountaineering, the reader knew that if he followed the instructions he would attain at least a degree of proficiency. In the earlier volumes the range of games was much wider. Ancient forgotten games were described, such as 'trap ball', as also were games from other countries – such as Skhe and Tatti from Afghanistan.

Hobbies were legion. In the early years there were innumerable articles on pets of various sorts. The correspondence columns carried a quantity of advice and diagnosis.

Fishing, bee-keeping, poultry, rabbits, birds, aviary building, were all fully covered. There were regular series of unappetising articles on taxidermy of various kinds. Long before the end of the nineteenth century there were articles on making electric bells and home telephones. In the 1920s there was an excellent series of articles on building wireless sets. Later these tended to need too many expensive components, and set building became a costly hobby. But the author 'Adsum' (A. D. Stubbs) made an enormous contribution to contented boyhood with his numerous and lucid articles covering a much wider technical range than wireless sets. But the joy of building a set, putting on the headphones and switching on! Oh, the magic of hearing the tinny music!

In the 1920s and 1930s there were more expensive hobbies – motor cycling for one. But even these were interesting, although there might be no hope whatever of acquiring so expensive a habit.

ADVENTURE

Adventure came in two forms in the *B.O.P.* Either it reached you in blood-stirring stories with an authentic background, or it came in personal experiences which read like adventurous fiction. One of the latter variety began in the very first issue. This was Captain Webb's account of 'How I swam the Channel' and included much more than that famous first swim, for one of the author's various adventures included trying to rescue a man in a gale in the middle of the Atlantic. Webb's personal experiences were soon followed by many others. One writer was 'Wrecked on a Floe' (off Greenland), another was attacked by a tiger in northern India:

Suddenly my attention was arrested by what looked like two bright emeralds glittering in the moonlight. In another instant I perceived the body of a huge tiger, even then crouching to spring upon me. It was the dreaded 'man-eater' of whom I had heard the natives speaking during the day. With a wild despairing cry I started to my feet but before I had taken a step towards the hut the creature was upon me and I felt his cruel claws tearing my flesh.

Others did not have to go so far afield. In the East End of London a Bengal tiger which had just been imported broke loose: 'As soon as he got into the street a boy of about nine years of age put out his hand to stroke the beast's back when the tiger seized him by the shoulder and ran down the street with the lad hanging in his jaws.' Efforts to strangle the tiger failed but a few blows with a crowbar made it see reason and it dropped the boy. The tiger was subsequently exhibited as 'The tiger that has swallowed a child' and people paid cheerfully to go and see it.

The pattern of many succeeding stories (as opposed to real-life adventures) was set in the first volume by W. H. G. Kingston's 'From Powder Monkey to Admiral'. Kingston knew his Navy and could tell a brisk story. There was no lack of incident: whatever else the young heroes suffered from it certainly wasn't boredom. If they were not being wrecked, captured, betrayed, shot at, imprisoned or awaiting imminent execution they were discovering treasure or performing deeds of great bravery.

But not all followed precisely the same pattern. R. M. Ballantyne's stories seem curiously slow and hesitant, almost pedantic. But undoubtedly they followed a boy's train of thought. Jules Verne first appears in Volume II with a long short story entitled 'The Boy Captain: A Tale of Adventure by Land and Sea'.

Foreigners were given friendly – even if sometimes patronising – treatment. The French suffered most, for they had so often had the temerity to fight against us. Spaniards never emerged out of their Elizabethan period and were probably not thought of as being the same as the contemporary Spanish.

Germans were well-treated until they made the mistake of opposing us in the First

World War. However, even then their characters were not blackened. Russians received extremely favourable mention until after the Revolution in 1917. After that, whenever there was a sinister plot you would always find a Russian somewhere in it and, as likely as not, a German to boot. It was a sharp contrast to the stories of the 1880s about Russia. The nineteenth-century attitude to Russia is illustrated by David Ker's 'Champions of the Kremlin', and friendly feelings lasted till 'At the Call of the Tsar' in 1917.

One of the most popular authors, as mentioned above, was Captain Charles Gilson. Gilson had been at Dulwich College (as had P. G. Wodehouse in the same period), where he had played good cricket and been selected for the Surrey Amateurs. He also played rugby football for Eastern Counties and was a scratch golfer. He joined the army (Sherwood Foresters) and was badly wounded in the Boer War. He continued to serve, in China, Japan, Canada, Africa and the South Seas, but was eventually invalided out with the rank of Captain. In the First World War he was initially rejected but then managed to join the Naval Division. At the end of the war he was granted the final rank of Major.

In the nineteenth century the great adventure writers had been David Ker, George Manville Fenn, Gordon Stables, A. N. Malan and of course Verne and Ballantyne. In the Edwardian period there emerged a very fine writer named J. Claverdon Wood. His stories, 'Sinclair of the Scouts' and 'Jeffrey of the White Wolf Trail', had tremendous life and variety. He was still writing in 1940. Percy F. Westerman began at the same time and was also writing during the Second World War. The early 1920s seem to have been a peak time for vigorous writers, and Wood, Gilson and Co. were ably supported by G. Godfrey Sellick ('The Secret of Canute's Island') and Raymond Raife ('The Quest for the Arctic Poppy'). Most of the serials were published later in book form by the Religious Tract Society. They were well illustrated but never seemed quite as exciting on their reappearance as they had done originally in the *B.O.P.*

SCHOOL STORIES

There are occasionally very strange happenings in schools but they are seldom suitable subjects for school stories. The task of the writer of schoolboy fiction is to create a possible incident in surroundings and circumstances of stereotyped patterns. There is, of course, fun to be had out of ragging, descriptions of football matches, climbing in and out after lock-up, and the oddities of masters, but you don't need to read about such matters; they are part of your own life. Schoolboy fiction needs an authentic yet interesting character who finds himself in unusual circumstances. If he is not absolutely authentic his charlatanism is detected at once and he is discarded. He is not at all a dramatic figure: quite the reverse. Thus Tom Brown is credible in any age but Eric, of Little by Little, as bogus then as now. The characters must be likeable. In any school a boy has a few regular friends, feels quite well-disposed to a number of other boys, is irritated or bored by others, and detests one or two. He is hardly likely to wish to read about those in the latter categories.

Talbot Baines Reed, whose name became a household word, set the standards for schoolboy fiction and probably exerted influence well beyond anyone's expectations or knowledge. He wrote between 1879 and 1893, and in the latter year died of tuberculosis at the age of 42. He was said to have been neither educated at a public school nor to have been a schoolmaster, but he had a considerable educational background nonetheless. His father was an M.P. and was Chairman of the London School Board. His grandfather had founded the London, Reedham and Infant Orphan Asylums, and the Royal Hospital for Incurables. (More than one of Reed's fictional characters was an orphan.)

Reed's skill in describing school life was so marked that the Editor frequently received letters from boys claiming that their own schools were the originals of Parkhurst, St

Dominic's, Fellsgarth, or whatever name Reed had invented. This was considered all the more remarkable because Hutchison had announced that Reed himself had never attended a public school. In 1866 the Public Schools Calendar listed a mere nine 'Public Schools' (Winchester, Eton, St Paul's, Shrewsbury, Westminster, Merchant Taylor's, Rugby, Harrow and Charterhouse – in that order). There followed a list of 'old endowed grammar schools', which included Sherborne, Oundle, Uppingham and Repton, and a list of 'Schools of Modern Foundation' which included Cheltenham, Marlborough, Radley, Clifton, Wellington and the City of London, which Reed attended. The City of London then had 625 pupils and two boarding houses. Reed was probably a day boy. Before that he had been at the Priory School at Upper Clapton. The Priory was a boarding prep school which had a reputation which extended well beyond London. (My own grandfather was sent there from Warwickshire at a very early age; he was awarded Richard Burton's *First Footsteps in East Africa* as a prize; presumably the headmaster had not read it!) Reed's pictures of school life are therefore based on personal experience which was common to many boys of his time. Equally his experience of city life was based on his knowledge of the life of printing apprentices – he himself had the advantage of being the son of the senior partner of a well-known type foundry. He joined the firm himself and, at his death, was Managing Director.

He was a lively all-round athlete, played all current games, and joined the London Rifle Brigade. Twice he walked the fifty-three miles from London to Cambridge, even though the first time it had rained all night; clearly he enjoyed life. He was also an excellent pianist.

Reed's stories give some idea of why compulsory games were instituted. Left to themselves his characters tended to wander off and associate with evilly disposed publicans, con-men and gamblers. Soon the naïve youngsters were in debt and being blackmailed. Driven by threats of exposure they often stole or befrauded to pay the debt. Needless to say they were caught.

Although the most famous, Reed was only one of the many excellent writers of school fiction who appeared in the *B.O.P.* Harold Avery first appeared in 1897 and was still writing prolifically in the 1920s. Avery had been at Eastbourne College. He managed to serve in the army during the First World War although he was then in his fifties. In 'The Fifth Form Mystery' and 'A Sixth Form Feud' he managed to make a compelling story out of very thin plots.

Kent Carr, who wrote popular boys' school stories in the 1920s, was in fact a woman (Gertrude Kent Oliver). It is difficult to see how she got away with it, for she was distinctly shaky on games. It seems that she relied for detail on two nephews, currently at public schools. One of her characters rowed for Oxford for three successive years in the Boat Race but at the same time managed to obtain blues and international caps at rugger. He also took a first in Classics. Dear lady! She had a neat turn of phrase: 'Educated at Eton where his memory was cherished by everyone except the authorities . . .' Of another she wrote: 'He had the sort of voice which might conceivably stir one to enthusiasm if it hadn't stirred one to resentment first.'

The outstanding writer of the 1920s was Richard Bird (William Barradell-Smith). The smells of chalk, rugger jerseys, swimming baths and ancient chapels drifted through his stories. But even the plots seemed real. 'Bird' had been at Durham School and St John's College, Cambridge, and become a master at Glasgow Academy, where he stayed, apart from service in the First World War. He was an excellent all-round athlete, wrote adult novels as well as school stories, and was co-author of the play *Marriage by Instalments*, which ran in London.

A loftier tone was set by Frank Elias, who did not confine himself to school stories.

Elias's characters seem a little too good – or bad – to be true. He was the fictional counterpart of George A. Wade. Boys probably took Elias with a pinch of salt. Real boys do not stare with misty eyes at old Honours Boards hoping to continue those Great Traditions. Nor do Captains' hands on people's shoulders smite, urging them to play up, play up and play the game. They might smite on a boy's shoulders because he is drinking a glass of lemonade but that's for an entirely different and very satisfactory reason. But even boys can be sentimental – for the right reasons.

Gunby Hadath – it was his real name – knew exactly what the right reasons were. He had been a schoolmaster but later became a barrister. He too was an excellent all-round athlete. Much of his best work was published in the rival magazine *Chums*, but he wrote a number of stories for the *B.O.P.* in the 1930s. According to W. O. G. Lofts and D. J. Adley in their book *The Men behind Boys' Fiction* Hadath's handwriting was completely unreadable except to his wife, and therefore she typed all his manuscripts. Hadath's great skill was his mastery of school dialogue, which he made neither too clever nor too fragmentary. He also wrote books under the name of John Mowbray.

THE *B.O.P.*'s RIVALS

When the *B.O.P.* arrived on the scene in 1879 it was by no means a novelty, for there had been many boys' publications before it; there would be even more after it, but it would survive most of them.

Some of its predecessors, like *The Youth's Magazine* of 1839, contained more piety than adventure; the *Boy's Own Volume*, published in the 1860s, was better but lacked variety. *Every Boy's Annual*, published by Routledge in 1866, was promising; it had stories by R. M. Ballantyne and W. H. G. Kingston and articles on nature study by J. G. Wood, but looked far too much like every parent's idea of a boy's annual to be popular.

There existed, however, far meatier fare to be acquired if you were able to read in secret. Through the nineteenth century there was always available a wide selection of thoroughly unsuitable literature. These were the 'bloods', the 'penny dreadfuls', and the description is no exaggeration. Murder, seduction, robbery, hangings, charnel houses, sewers, ghosts, stabbings were presented in detail and profusion. Their crudity makes them seem more bizarre than terrifying to modern eyes but most of them were pretty nasty by any standards. An alarming aspect of their popularity was that they sedulously, though probably unintentionally, preached that the best and quickest way for a poor boy to become rich was not through piety and industry but through violent uninhibited crime. In the nineteenth century it was realised that production of 'bloods' could not easily be stopped but could at least be offset. Thus when the *B.O.P.* arrived on the scene it too abounded in violence, but this time it was good men who were defeating bad men, the British defeating hostile foreigners and, safest of all, besting the lion, tiger, alligator, cobra, swamp, jungle, mountain, blizzard or drought. The lesson it preached, although unobtrusively, was that if you wished to improve your lot it was better to go to the colonies than to take to the road as a footpad. It should not be overlooked that in the nineteenth century millions of poor people, whether working or not, were near to desperation through hunger or deprivation. Rogues abounded but there were plenty of otherwise honest men who might be driven to resort to theft to feed their families and themselves. The *B.O.P.* was read by some very poor boys; it circulated through Board (primary) schools, barracks, church halls, and so on. Any stories about richer and more privileged boys would have a fascination and influence that to some extent still persists. And when the *Gem* appeared in 1907, soon to be followed by the *Magnet*, the stories were all about fearfully posh public schools, with titled boys, ivied towers, Latin quotations, study feasts, merry 'rags' and the like. These endless stories, in which cads and rotters were always downed and received their just deserts, were rarely read by public schoolboys, but they *were* read by every other sort of boy. Many an errand took longer than it should because Greyfriars was playing St Jim's in the match of the year, or an unpopular chemistry master was being ragged. In that eventful though secure schoolboy world it was abundantly clear what was right and what was wrong; if you knocked over an old lady with your bicycle you did not laugh and pedal on; you stopped, helped her to her feet and said you were sorry – just like Harry Wharton or Bob Cherry would have done. And reasonable people settled arguments with their fists, not with knives or Kung-Fu kicks or anything murderous like that. If you accidentally hurt an opponent in a game you did not give him another kick to make sure he stayed down.

Perhaps the *Magnet* owed something to the Talbot Baines Reed stories in the *B.O.P.*; there were, however, more obvious imitators. One of these was *Chums*, a fine rumbustious paper which ran from 1892 till the Second World War; unlike the *B.O.P.* it was never revived. *Chums* was published by Cassell and had Sir Max Pemberton, author of *The Iron Pirate*, as its first editor, but like the first editor of the *B.O.P.* he stayed but one year. In 1894 the paper published *Treasure Island*. This had already appeared in an unwieldy magazine called *Young Folks* under the title of 'Treasure Island or the Mutiny of the Hispaniola' by Captain George North. On that occasion it had little impact. In *Chums* it did better, perhaps because the author's real name was given. *Chums* shared many of the *B.O.P.* writers – Hadath, Gilson, Hylton Cleaver (how prolific all these writers were) – but had many specially its own. S. Walkey wrote from 1895 till the 1930s. He was a bank inspector who only wrote in the evenings, but *Chums* was worth buying for his stories alone.

The Captain, which appeared from Newnes in 1899, was edited by R. S. Warren-Bell and published the first P. G. Wodehouse stories. Copies – in mint condition – are still available today; it is also possible sometimes to obtain copies of the *B.O.P.* and *Chums* which look as if they had just left the shop – seventy years ago. *The Captain* also took in John Buchan, Alec Waugh, C. B. Fry, G. Ward-Price, as well as Charles Gilson and other *B.O.P.* stalwarts. The great cricketer C. B. Fry edited a magazine himself in 1904 – *C. B. Fry's Magazine*. Its principal interest was sport, but it does not seem to have survived very long. *Young England* began in the same year as the *B.O.P.* and was still flourishing in the early part of this century. I have a copy which was given as a prize at the National School, Woolwich, to E. Jago for 'Progress and Examinations'. It includes a series of articles on 'Life at the Great Public Schools'. The tone tended to be moral. One of its contributors was a future editor of the *B.O.P.* – A. L. Haydon.

Closest of all to the *B.O.P.* was *Boys*, whose address was 60, Old Bailey, London E.C. It had some of the same contributors but also netted H. M. Stanley. In the middle of the 1890s it suddenly disappeared and thenceforth the *B.O.P.* was officially entitled *The Boy's Own Paper, with which are incorporated Boys and Every Boy's Magazine.*

In this book we can hardly touch on the vast range of other boys' literature – let alone girls' literature, in which the *Girl's Own Paper* was a steady performer. (The *Girl's Own Paper* had been founded in 1880 and lasted till the 1940s, when it became *The Heiress*. However *The Heiress* did not survive long.) The classic review of the whole field can be found in E. S. Turner's *Boys Will Be Boys*, which covers not only penny dreadfuls but also Sexton Blake, Nelson Lee and even the *Eagle* and *Rainbow*.

CHAPTER ONE
THE FIRST VOLUME

The first three pages of any first number are probably vital to the future success or failure of the paper. In the *B.O.P.* the honour of writing the bulk of these fell to Talbot Baines Reed, although at this time he was not using his own name but was merely 'An Old Boy'. Half the first page was taken up with a picture of a rugby football match. The game looks a little incongruous to modern eyes. Some of the boys are wearing 'colour' caps to play in, and the ball looks round enough for soccer.

Another quarter of the page was taken up with illustrated background to the title. This showed a cricket bat, rabbits, a dog, a book, and other items of a sporting nature, so that even if a boy was not particularly keen on football there was obviously something in it for him. And the text had just that bit of magic in it which almost every boy knows and hopes to experience – 'to be one of the picked fifteen whose glory it was to fight the battles of their school in the Great Close.' Seeing *your* name on the notice board and trying not to look crazy with excitement. Clearly the editor knew his job from the very first page. It was reported that at some schools boys were lined up and given free copies to read; it was a process unlikely to recommend it to a boy accustomed to be lined up and given Latin grammars, impositions and free – and frequent – issues of corporal punishment.

But turn over the pages. Here is a drawing of the mouth of a viper, a description of an Afghan robber, 'How I swam the Channel' by Captain Webb, a ghost story, a story about the Navy ('From Powder Monkey to Admiral'), 'How I manage my Monkeys' by the famous naturalist Frank Buckland (he was said to have eaten every living creature, insects included, in the course of scientific discovery), an article on skating, and a competition.

All this for a penny. Well, even if it was approved by authority, it still looked well worth it. There was no falling-off as the paper continued. Indeed it seemed to become even better. That half-page illustration at the front never lacked drama.

To those who do not know it the *B.O.P.* is darkly suspected of having encouraged jingoism and military ballyhoo. In fact, it was quite the opposite. If soldiering had to be done it should be done cheerfully and bravely but its hardships and perils were not unremarked. In the third issue:

Sir Charles Napier, the great soldier, gives his estimate of military fame. Nine princes have surrendered their swords to me on the field of battle and their kingdoms have been conquered by me, and attached to my own country. Well, all the glory that can be desired is mine and I care so little for it that the moment I can I shall be resigned to live quietly with my wife and girls; no honour nor riches repays me for absence from them.

A little later, sandwiched between an article on frogs and toads and a clergyman's paraphrase of the story of Esau and Jacob, came 'Death of a Famous Fire Horse'. This was later followed by an article on 'The Sharks of Mauritius' by Nicholas Pike, U.S. Consul at Mauritius.

Smoking was branded as a pernicious habit, causing 'various disorders of the circulation and digestion, palpitations of the heart, and a more or less marked taste for strong drink'. On the same page 'Headers in Swimming' says: 'The header [any form of dive] has caused the death of many a promising boy', but then goes on to describe its pleasures.

Snobbery was knocked firmly on the head in 'Industrial origin of peerages'. Cornwallis, it was said, was a Cheapside merchant, Craven was a tailor. 'The founders of Dartmouth, Radnor, Ducie and Pomfret were respectively a skinner, a silk manufacturer, a merchant tailor and a Calais merchant.'

There was useful advice on how to catch ostriches (by wearing a hood of ostrich feathers) and how to make boats and yachts. There were adventures with grizzlies, alligators, and polar bears; all, of course, were true first-hand experiences. Robert Browning's 'How they Brought the Good News from Ghent to Aix' appeared in the tenth issue linked to a competition for the best drawing and best account of the background events to the ride. By now the *B.O.P.* was also issued as a monthly, after each four weekly parts, with a 'Frontispiece on toned paper'. In this particular month the *B.O.P.* already had an illustration of Browning's poetic ride; it was said that a competitor could copy this but *without tracing*.

The results of the first 'picture wanting words' competition produced an interesting insight into boys' minds. The picture had shown a lad returning home to find it deserted:

Generally the lad was one who had disobeyed his parents and come up to London, or been self-willed and run away to sea, or had got into trouble of some kind or other, and coming home, it may be repentant, after long absence, found that while he might strive to live nobly for the future the bygone years could be neither blotted out nor recalled. Father was, perhaps, dead, broken-hearted and the widowed mother had given up her once happy home.

And so on.

City boys, it was noticed,

described the building as a pretty dwelling or even mansion; country lads set it down as a cottage. Many described the lad as being led astray by bad literature, gambling, bad companions or drunkenness. Some however thought the lad had been wrongly charged with theft and run away. One competitor wrote in Latin.

The boy in 'An Unexpected Call', shown on page 32, was luckier. Cold, hungry and penniless, he thought he was to be arrested wrongly for housebreaking, but all was well — the culprits who had falsely accused him had now confessed, and soon he would get back his job as clerk in an office. One might laugh, but in May 1879 there were 4000 qualified clerks unemployed in London.

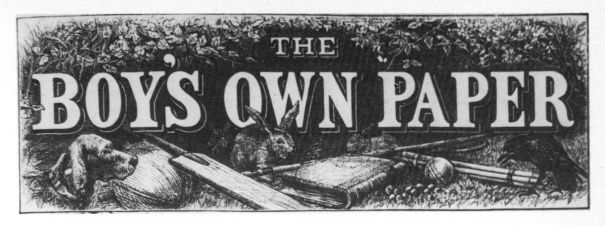

MY FIRST FOOTBALL MATCH

By an Old Boy

Page 1, Number 1, Volume I: Saturday, January 18, 1879 (Price One Penny). Talbot Baines Reed kicks off.

T was a proud moment in my existence when Wright, captain of our football club, came up to me in school one Friday and said, "Adams, your name is down to play in the match against Craven to-morrow."

I could have knighted him on the spot. To be one of the picked "fifteen," whose glory it was to fight the battles of their school in the Great Close, had been the leading ambition of my life—I suppose I ought to be ashamed to confess it—ever since, as a little chap of ten, I entered Parkhurst six years ago. Not a winter Saturday but had seen me either looking on at some big match, or oftener still scrimmaging about with a score or so of other juniors in a scratch game. But for a long time, do what I would, I always seemed as far as ever from the coveted goal, and was half despairing of ever rising to win my "first fifteen cap." Latterly,

however, I had noticed Wright and a few others of our best players more than once lounging about in the Little Close where we juniors used to play, evidently taking observations with an eye to business. Under the awful gaze of these heroes, need I say I exerted myself as I had never done before? What cared I for hacks or bruises, so only that I could distinguish myself in their eyes? And never was music sweeter than the occasional "Bravo, young 'un!" with which some of them would applaud any special feat of skill or daring.

So I knew my time was coming at last, and only hoped it would arrive before the day of the Craven match, the great match of our season,—always looked forward to as *the* event of the Christmas term, when victory was regarded by us boys as the summit of all human glory, and defeat as an overwhelming disgrace.

It will therefore be understood why I was almost beside myself with delight when, the very day before the match, Wright made the announcement I have referred to.

I scarcely slept a wink that night for dreaming of the wonderful exploits which were to signalise my first appearance in the Great Close—how I was to run the ball from one end of the field to the other, overturning, dodging, and distancing every one of the enemy, finishing up with a brilliant and mighty kick over the goal. After which I was to have my broken limbs set by a doctor on the spot, to receive a perfect ovation from friend and foe, to be chaired round the field, to be the "lion" at the supper afterwards, and finally to have a whole column of the "Times" devoted to my exploits! What glorious creatures we are in our dreams!

Well, the eventful day dawned at last. It was a holiday at Parkhurst, and as fine a day as any one could wish.

As I made my appearance, wearing the blue-and-red jersey of a "first fifteen-man" under my jacket, I found myself quite an object of veneration among the juniors who had lately been my compeers, and I accepted their homage with a vast amount of condescension. Nothing was talked of during the forenoon but the coming match. Would the Craven fellows turn up a strong team? Would that fellow Slider, who made the tremendous run last year, play for them again this? Would Wright select the chapel end or the other if we won the choice? How were we off behind the scrimmage?

"Is Adams to be trusted?" I hear one voice ask.

Two or three small boys promptly replied "Yes;" but the seniors said nothing, except Wright, who took the opportunity of giving me a little good advice in private.

"Look here, Adams; you are to play 'half-back,' you know. All you've got to take care of is to keep cool, and never let your eyes go off the ball. You know all the rest."

A lecture half an hour long could not have made more impression. I remembered those two hints,

"Keep cool and watch the ball," as long as I played football, and I would advise every "half-back" to take them to heart in like manner.

At noon the Craven team came down in an omnibus and had lunch in Hall with us, and half an hour later found us all in a straggling procession, making for the scene of conflict in the Great Close. There stood the goals and the boundary-posts, and there was Granger, the ground-keeper, with a bran-new lemon-shaped ball under his arm.

"Look sharp and peel!" cried our captain.

So we hurried to the tent and promptly divested ourselves of our outer garments, turned up the sleeves of our jerseys, and tied an extra knot in our bootlaces. As we emerged, the Craven men were making their appearance on the ground in battle array. I felt so nervous myself that I could not, for the life of me, imagine how some of them could look so unconcerned, whistling, and actually playing leapfrog to keep themselves warm!

An officer in the Crimean War once described his sensation in some of the battles there as precisely similar to those he had experienced when a boy on the football field at Rugby. I can appreciate the comparison, for one. Certainly never soldier went into action with a more solemn do-or-die feeling than that with which I took my place on the field that afternoon.

"They've won the choice of sides," said somebody, "and are going to play with the wind."

"Take your places, Parkhurst!" shouted our captain.

The ball lies in the centre of the ground, and Wright stands ten yards or so behind it, ready for the kick off. Of our fifteen, the ten "forwards" are extended in a line with the ball across the field, ready to charge after it the moment it goes flying. The two best runners of our team are stationed "quarter back," where they can skirmish on the outskirts of the scrimmage. I am posted a little in rear of them at "half back,"—an unusual post for so young a player, but one which was accorded to me by virtue of my light weight and not inconsiderable running powers. Behind me are the two "backs," on whom, when all else fails, the issue of the conflict depends. The Craven players are similarly disposed, and waiting impatiently for our captain's kick.

"Are you ready?" he shouts.

Silence gives consent.

He gives a quick glance round at us, then springs forward, and in an instant the ball is soaring high in the direction of the Cravens' goal amid the shouts of onlooking friend and foe.

Our forwards were after it like lightning, but not before a Craven back had got hold of it and run some distance in the direction of our goal. He did not wait to be attacked, but by a clever drop kick, a knack peculiar to all good "backs," sent it spinning right over the forwards' heads into the hands of one of our quarter-backs. He, tucking it under his arm and crushing his cap on to his head, started to run. Going slowly at first, he steered straight for the forwards of the enemy till within a pace or two of them, when he doubled suddenly, and amid the shouts of our partisans slipped past them and was seen heading straight for the Craven goal. But although he had escaped their forwards, he had yet their rearguard to escape, which was far harder work, for was not one of that rearguard the celebrated Slider himself, who by his prowess had last year carried defeat to our school; and the other, was it not the stalwart Naylor, who only a month ago had played gloriously for his county against 'Gravelshire?

Yet our man was not to be daunted by the prestige of these distinguished adversaries, but held on his way pluckily, and without a swerve. It was a sight to see those two cunningly lay wait for him, like two spiders for a fly. There was nothing for it but to plunge headlong into their web in a desperate effort to break through. Alas! brave man! Naylor has him in his clutches, the Craven forwards come like a deluge on the spot, our forwards pour over the Craven, and in an instant our hero and the ball have vanished from sight under a heap of writhing humanity.

The next thing I was conscious of was that about twenty people had fallen to the ground all of a heap, and that I and the ball were at the bottom.

At last the ball got well away from the scrimmage, and who should secure it but the redoubtable Slider! I felt a passing tremor of deep despair as I saw that hero spring like the wind towards our goal.

"Look out, Adams!" shouted Wright.

Sure enough he was coming in my direction! With the desperation of a doomed man I strode out to meet him. He rushed furiously on,—swerving slightly to avoid my reach, and stretching out his arm to ward off my grasp. I flung myself wildly in his path. There was a heavy thud, and the earth seemed to jump up and strike me. The next moment I was sprawling on my back on the grass. I don't pretend to know how it all happened, but somehow or other I had succeeded in checking the onward career of the victorious Slider; for though I had fallen half stunned before the force of his charge, he had recoiled for an instant from the same shock, and that instant gave time for Wright to get hold of him, and so put an end for the time to his progress.

"Well played!" said some one, as I picked myself up. So I was comforted, and began to think that, after all, football was rather a fine game.

Time would fail me to tell of all the events of that afternoon—how Wright carried the ball within a dozen yards of our opponents' goal; how their forwards passed the ball one to another, and got a "touch-down" behind our line, but missed the kick; how Naylor ran twenty yards with one of our men hanging on his back; how our quarter-back sent the ball nearly over their goal with as neat a drop-kick as ever it has been my lot to witness.

The afternoon was wearing. I heard the timekeeper call out, "Five minutes more!" The partisans of either side were getting frantic with excitement. Unless we could secure an advantage now we should be as good as defeated, for the Craven had scored a "touch-down" to our nothing. Was this desperate fight to end so? Was victory, after all, to escape us? But I had no time for reflection then.

"Now Parkhurst," sang out Wright, "pull yourselves together for once!"

A Craven man is standing to throw the ball out of "touch," and either side stands in confronting rows, impatient for the fray. Wright is at the end of the line, face to face with Naylor, and I am a little behind Wright.

"Keep close!" exclaims the latter to me, as the ball flies towards us.

Wright has it, but in an instant Naylor's long arms are round him, bearing him down.

"Adams!" ejaculates our captain, and in a trice he passes the ball into my hands, and I am off like the wind. So suddenly has it all been done that I have already a yard or two start before my flight is discovered. There is a yelling and a rush behind me; there is a roar from the crowds on either side; there is a clear "Follow up, Parkhurst!" from Wright in the rear; there is a loud "Collar him!" from the Craven captain ahead. I am steering straight for their goal; three men only are between me and it—one, their captain, right back, and Slider and another man in front of him.

I see at a glance that my only hope is to keep as I am going and waste no time in dodging, or assuredly the pursuing host will be upon me. Slider and his companion are closing in right across my path, almost close together. With a bound I dashed between them. Have they got me, or have I escaped them? A shout louder than ever, and a "Bravo!" from Wright tells me I am clear of that danger and have now but their last defence to pass. He is a tall, broad fellow, and a formidable foe to encounter, and waits for me close under their goal. The pace, I feel, is telling on me, the shouting behind sounds nearer, only a few yards divides us now. Shall I double, shall I venture a kick, or shall I charge straight at him?

"Charge at him!" sounds Wright's voice, as if in answer to my thought. I gather up all my remaining force, and charge. There is a flash across my eyes, and a dull shock against my chest. I reel and stagger, and forget where I am. I am being swept along in a torrent; the waters with a roar rush past me and over me. Every moment I get nearer and nearer the fatal edge—I am at it—I hang a moment on the brink, and then—

"Down!" shouts a voice close at my ear, and there is such a noise of cheering and rejoicing that I sit up and rub my eyes like one waking bewildered from a strange dream.

Then I find out what has happened. When I

charged at the Craven captain the shock sent me back staggering into the very arms of Wright and our forwards, who were close at my heels, and who then, in a splendid and irresistible rush, carried me and the ball and half of the other side along with them right behind the enemy's goal line, where we fall *en masse* to the earth—I, with the ball under me, being at the bottom.

Even if I had been hurt—which I was not—there was no time to be wasted on condolences or congratulations. The time-keeper held his watch in his hand, and our goal must be kicked at once, if it was to be kicked at all. So the fifteen paces out were measured, the "nick" for the ball was carefully made, the enemy stood along their goal-line ready to spring the moment the ball should touch the earth. Wright, cool and self-possessed, placed himself in readiness a yard or two behind the ball, which one of our side held an inch off the ground. An anxious moment of expectation followed; then came a sharp "Now!" from our captain. The ball was placed cunningly in the nick, the Craven forwards rushed out on it in a body, but long before they could reach it, Wright's practised foot had sent it flying straight as an arrow over the bar, and my first football match had ended in a glorious victory for the Old School.

BRAVE AND TRUE

WHATEVER you are, be brave, boys!
The liar's a coward and slave, boys!
　　Though clever at ruses,
　　And sharp at excuses,
He's a sneaking and pitiful knave, boys.

Whatever you are, be frank, boys!
'Tis better than money and rank, boys:
　　Still cleave to the right,
　　Be lovers of light,
Be open, above board, and frank, boys.

Whatever you are, be kind, boys!
Be gentle in manners and mind, boys!
　　The man gentle in mien,
　　Words, and temper, I ween,
Is the gentleman truly refined, boys.

But, whatever you are, be true, boys!
Be visible through and through, boys:
　　Leave to others the shamming,
　　The "greening" and "cramming,"
In fun and in earnest, be true, boys!

HENRY DOWNTON.

OUT WITH THE JACK-KNIFE

Rev. J. G. Wood,
M.A., F.L.S.
Author of "Illustrated Natural History," etc.

THE Editor of this Magazine having asked me to show what could be done in Practical Natural History with no other apparatus than a common jack-knife, I have been out with such a weapon, and have had a capital time of it. Perhaps the reader might be tempted to go also, if only he knew what a fund of entertainment there is within his easy reach. Let all who like, then, follow me.

Now, the first thing is to see about our jack-knife. It derives its name from the fact that it is the kind of knife invariably carried by our seamen, or "Jack Tars," and its value is proved by its endurance of the test of long trial.

Should it be possible, and should the reader be still unfurnished with a knife, he cannot do better than purchase a seaman's clasp-knife. It can be obtained at any good cutler's. I am careful in saying that the cutler must be a trustworthy man, or he will put off the purchaser with a showy, cheap, but really useless article.

The material of the handle signifies nothing so long as the blade is of true Sheffield steel, and bears the stamp of a responsible maker.

Only one blade is wanted. Many vendors try to dazzle their customers with complicated pieces of machinery which they are pleased to call universally-useful knives.

There are at least three blades, one large and two small. There is a corkscrew, which invariably doubles up across the fingers when used.

There is an instrument for picking stones out of horses' hoofs. It may be useful enough to those who ride or drive, but as we do not naturalise in a gig or on horseback, it is only in the way.

There is a nutcracker, which might be used during the short time when the nuts are ripe, but is certainly not required for the rest of the year.

There is a saw, which is quite superfluous; and there is a file, which is soon choked and rendered useless. There is a gimlet, a bradawl, and a rymer, and lastly come a pair of tweezers and a gun-picker. In practice, the saw, bradawl, gimlet, corkscrew, and rymer are soon broken, and the gun-picker and tweezers lost.

Nothing is needed in a good, serviceable jack-knife but a single blade. No one wants to make pens when he is on a naturalising expedition, and if he did, the pens could not be used for want of ink.

If possible, the knife should have a ring, so that it can be suspended round the neck, and cannot be lost.

This precaution is, indeed, almost a necessity. There are many cases where some living creature has been brought to light by the knife; both hands must be at liberty, and the knife dropped instantly. . . .

HOW I SWAM THE CHANNEL

Captain Webb

Captain Matthew Webb, at the age of 27, was the first person to swim the Channel — in 1875. It took him 21 hours 45 minutes.

WHEN I did start for my Channel swim I certainly had nothing to complain about in regard to the weather. I originally determined to start about one o'clock in the morning, as I expected to accomplish my journey in about fourteen hours, so that I should finish my task in open daylight. Fortunately for me, several gentlemen, who were special cor-

respondents to London papers, remained at Dover, and we all together took a midnight stroll on the Admiralty Pier, Dover, on the evening of the 23rd. I remember how very disappointed I felt when once again the sea proved too rough for me to start, and the night before I swam the Channel I went to bed feeling that everything was going against me, and

that I should never have a fair chance at all. The gentlemen who were down from London had told me that they could not wait more than another day. You may imagine my delight, therefore, when the next morning I found the sea just what was wanted. I accordingly determined to start at once. Everything was hurriedly prepared. A large hamper of provisions was got ready for those on board the lugger. And at four minutes before one o'clock in the afternoon of August the 24th, having previously rubbed myself all over with porpoise oil, and with nothing on save a small pair of swimming drawers, such as are usually worn in London baths, I dived in off the end of Admiralty Pier, Dover, and struck out in the direction of Cape Grisnez.

Long accounts have been written of my Channel swim; and one of the best, written by an eye-witness, and a far more graphic one than I can possibly write myself, is published in my Book on Swimming. I will, however, try and describe as accurately as I can exactly what happened. In the first place, two umpires had been appointed, one, Mr. A. G. Payne, of the "Standard" newspaper, and another gentleman who was at the time connected with the "Field." One of these was always in the small boat that kept close to me. Besides these two there were several gentlemen on board the lugger connected with London papers, but I will not mention their names without their permission. At any rate I was fortunate enough to have the "Times," the "Daily Telegraph," and the "Daily News" represented, as well as the "Standard," and consequently I knew that whatever I did would be fully corroborated. In addition to the Press, there were the crew, my cousin Mr. Ward, and a young lad seventeen years of age, C. W. Baker by name, who was a very fine swimmer, far faster for a short distance than I am myself, but still better known as a first-rate diver.

I think it will be found as a rule that boys make better divers than men. Now, the only good divers are boys who have been accustomed to play in the tepid water of swimming-baths, and boys who are accustomed to swim where the water is of a high temperature, like the sea at Aden. Young Baker is also a famous cook, and was very useful during the early part of the trip in preparing food on board the lugger, where there was an open stove. He was reminding me the other day of the wonderful diving of the boys at Aden. He had just returned from India, where he had been in the capacity of "chef" on board one of the Peninsular and Oriental Steamship Company's vessels, and had watched these boys at Aden for hours, who would dive into deep water and fetch up a threepenny-piece, probably before it had reached the bottom. Indeed, I have myself often seen Baker dive after a mother-of-pearl shirt button, and catch it long before it reached the bottom of the bath.

It may be thought what use would a lad of seventeen have been in rescuing a heavy man like myself, weighing some fifteen stone.

Fortunately, Baker's services were not required, but there was no harm in taking proper precautions. In my opinion it is wicked for a man, merely for the sake of gain or of notoriety, to risk his life. Of course I might have been seized with cramp, or I might have had a fit and suddenly have gone down. If such had happened Baker would instantly have dived in after me, would have thrown his arms round me, and we both should have been quickly drawn to the surface. Baker had had a belt made to go round his chest with two straps over the shoulders to prevent its slipping, and to this belt was attached a long, thin, but very strong line. Of course, during the early part of my swim, when I felt perfectly strong and well, no precautions were necessary; but during the latter part of the journey, when the sea got rough and I consequently became exhausted, Baker sat by Mr. Payne's side in the little boat, ready stripped, to dive in at a moment's notice, while Mr. Payne had hold of the end of the rope. And thus he sat all through the long night with a rug only over his shoulders, till, on nearing Calais, he swam the best part of the way by my side.

When I started, the tide was running westward. My start was so suddenly determined on, that only a small crowd had collected, but small as it was, its hearty cheer encouraged me, and I struck out with slow strokes across the tide, which gradually drifted me in the direction of Folkestone, though every stroke took me farther from shore, and nearer the French coast, and I knew that when the tide turned that I should drift the other way, and after getting again in a line with Dover pier, that I should find myself off the South Foreland lighthouse, and perhaps as far east as off Deal, only by that time—viz., eight hours—I fully expected to have got half way across.

The day was certainly lovely. A bright blue and cloudless sky, a hot August sun, were just what I wanted, only I found the glare of light very trying to my eyes. The sea was in that perfectly smooth state when it looks as if oil had been poured on the water, and when at night a bright star is reflected on a single spot like a diamond instead of appearing as the usual long bright flickering line.

Occasionally, indeed, at first, the surface of the water was moved, but this was by some large shoals of mackerel, who rushed by owing to their being chased by some porpoises, and I recollect some chaff being addressed to me from the lugger about the porpoises smelling their own grease and taking me for one of themselves. But I took no notice of anything that was said, and only spoke occasionally to my cousin in the little boat, when I wanted any refreshment, which was chiefly beef-tea, hot coffee made on board the lugger, and a little old ale.

Not a breath of wind of course stirred, and the men on board the lugger had to work hard at their long oars to keep with me, and I shall never forget the monotonous sound of their oars as they creaked like heavy pendulums swinging. Smooth water conveys sound for enormous distances, and I recollect while the water was smooth hearing the heavy chain rattle as the anchor was dropped from ships not even in sight, a noise that conveyed to one of my cockney friends with me the idea of "heaving in coals."

Soon after seven o'clock the sun slowly set, and bathed us all in a flood of rosy coloured light, that gradually faded into grey. The stars one by one began to sparkle above me, while the lighthouses, which are always lit at sunset, soon showed clearly what position I had gained. The double light of the South Foreland was behind me; the South Sand Head light a little more to the eastward, while on my right, in front, the bright revolving light of Cape Grisnez flashed at intervals. Ah! how I longed to reach it.

Anxious, however, as I was to reach the goal, I could not help even then being impressed with the beauty of the scene. The sea was what is known as phosphorescent. Every stroke I took threw around me in the water bright rings of fire, while the heavy oars in the lugger, as they slowly splashed from the water, threw what resembled a little shower of diamonds each stroke, that matched in brilliancy the myriads of stars that twinkled above us in the deep blue sky on that glorious August evening.

At nine o'clock I felt a sudden sharp pain, and I knew at once that I had been stung. I had come in contact with one of those nasty yellow starches, or jelly-fish. The white ones are harmless, but the yellow, and especially the blue, give a most painful sting; fortunately it only just touched my shoulder,—had it gone right against my chest, I should probably have been obliged to have given up my attempt. My cousin gave me a little sip of brandy, the first I had taken, and I soon fortunately felt all right again.

At eleven o'clock I could distinctly hear the sound of paddle-wheels in the distance, but it was not till a quarter before midnight that the Calais steamer reached me. She came close up, and on board my lugger we burn a red light, which brightens the scene, and shows by the flapping sails that no wind is stirring at present. The mail boat gives me a hearty cheer and passes by.

Two more hours soon pass, and by two o'clock I get near the point I had hoped to reach, viz., Cape Grisnez. I had been in the water now thirteen hours. The tide that had been setting westward began soon after to turn, and it had not carried me sufficiently westward. I found to my extreme disappointment that I had swam slower than I had expected, and that I ought to have started about two hours earlier. I could see the light high up, though it had got rather hazy, and I calculated that I must have been within about three miles of the shore; but the tide began to turn soon after, and I gradually got farther and farther from land. By five o'clock in the morning the sun had risen, but a heavy haze was over the shore. I felt getting rather weak, but still swam steadily on across the tide, which was drifting me in the direction of Calais.

By half-past six, or about that time, a slight breeze had sprung up, and the sea became very choppy—a bad thing for swimming. The swell gradually increased, till those in the little boats were wet with the water splashing over the side, and by nine o'clock I began to lose all hope. I had now been in the water twenty hours, and the tide seemed to be carrying me away from the shore. I will quote what my feelings were from my lecture on "My Channel Swim," which I have delivered and still continue to give in various schoolrooms in the country.

"Can I do it!" I anxiously asked Toms, the old pilot, who told me if I could struggle for two hours longer I might just reach Calais Pier. I determined to try. I thought of Boyton in his india-rubber dress, and I felt what a proud thing it would be for me, an Englishman, to accomplish the same task with nought save my muscles to help me. I know this thought encouraged me. I took a little beef-tea and a sip of brandy, and by ten o'clock I had drifted nearly in a line with Calais Pier. A large rowing-boat, belonging to the mail-packet service, had put out and got to windward of me, and slightly sheltered me. The tide began to slacken, and I gradually drew nearer shore.

Never shall I forget when the men in the mail-boat struck up the tune of Rule Britannia, which they sang, or rather shouted, in a hoarse roar. I felt a gulping sensation in my throat as the old tune, which I had heard in all parts of the world, once more struck my ears under circumstances so extraordinary. I felt now I should do it, and I did it. Baker, who had been swimming by my side, now swam in and touched, and swam back to me, and slowly but surely I drew in to Calais Sands. The excitement, I am told, at the time was intense; the tears were literally rolling down poor old Toms's face from pent-up emotion. I try to touch, and fail, so I struggle on. I try again, and fall forward, while a shout goes up, and I am instantly seized by two men who have jumped out of the mail-boat, who help me ashore, assist me into a dry cart that somebody had sent, and I am driven off to the Paris Hotel, Calais.

"I GET NO HOLIDAY, SIR"

RETURNING through the Long Walk to Windsor one day lately, a lad carrying a big parcel was coming in the same direction, and we entered into conversation.

He told me that his father had lain in bed for several months; that he did the beadle work for him in the church; had to be up most of Saturday night minding the fires, and engaged all Sunday to keep his father's pay to the family. He was also engaged at seven shillings per week doing odd work for some family in the neighbourhood. But what has stuck to me is the lad's complaint, "I get no holiday, sir. Never a holiday!" This came in several times in our conversation. It bulked large in the poor lad's eye, no holiday; and nothing seemed to sweeten his lot, since what others enjoyed was denied to him.

I tried to comfort him, reminding him how much he had to be thankful for in health, and strength to work; and as to the work being hard and constant, that might not always be so, for there might be "a good time coming." Besides, he was doing his duty in helping his mother and saving the home. Our Heavenly Father would never fail to reward him, for there is a special promise to those who honour their parents, and helping them is the truest way of

honouring them. Giving him a trifle towards the little store, and telling him he need not envy any one in Windsor Palace, if he was doing his duty and pleasing God, we parted, the poor boy looking much more cheery than when we met.

And I felt assured that for his kindness to the family at home, and to his afflicted father, God would open up a way whereby a good long happy holiday would be given to him, even if it were not till all life's work were ended.

If any boys who read this may be similarly situated, let them take heart and not be discouraged. The writer, when an apprentice, used to be taunted by richer ones in the same shop, that he would never get away from his "mother's apron-strings." She was poor and a widow. But he has lived to see many lands, and sail over many seas, and enjoy many holidays, while some of those who taunted him are still working as they were, worn with toil and the victims of early self-will, and of pleasing themselves. Dear boys, take an old man's kindly advice. Seek to please God in your lot, and He will get you a "holiday."

E.Y.

ETON SIXTY YEARS AGO

IN the autobiography of the Venerable Archdeacon Denison, he gives some pleasant recollections of Eton sixty years ago, when under the rule of Dr. Keate. For our younger readers, we preface the Eton notes with some of his recollections of earlier schooldays, first at Ossington, and then at Southwell, Notts.

Of Ossington he says—

At home, as at school, we had our mischievous recreations.

We had one day a narrow escape. We were about eleven and ten years old.

We had a room to ourselves in the north wing of the house. William said to me, "Let's make some gunpowder."

I said, "I don't know how, and am afraid."

"Oh," he said, "I know how very well, and I ain't a bit afraid."

I said, "How long have you known?"

"Always," said he.

So we got the materials and mixed them, a good big heap, in one of the window-seats of the room.

"Now then," said I, "let's try it;" and I took a

broad-bladed kitchen-knife, and taking some of the mixture up, put it into a candle close by. Happily for ourselves, the house, and family, it was not very well made, and did not explode; but out of the candle there came a number of little blue balls of fire hopping all about; one or more hopped into the heap. In a moment the room was full of little blue balls of fire hopping over the carpet, over the beds, under the beds, over us, over everything. We rushed to the water-jugs, and then, making no head against the blue balls, screamed for help. Under a heavy drenching the blue balls vanished as quickly as they had come, leaving their mark in hundreds of black spots.

Another day we did a curious piece of mischief, and very properly suffered for it.

A clergyman of a neighbouring parish, an old friend of my father's, was very often at Ossington, and had a room in the south wing which went by his name, where we often played tricks with his clothes and shoes, left there from time to time. One day he said to us, "Boys, come and see me, and we will catch eels in my brook." Next day we went. He was not at home. "Very odd," we said, "bringing us all this way for nothing; no worms ready, and no message where we are to try for eels;" looked into the dining-room, found nothing to eat. "We won't stay, but we must let him know we have been here."

In the dining-room was a good mahogany table, second-hand, just bought a bargain, as good as new: we took our knives and cut upon it, "William and George Denison." I often think that, though we did not escape a flogging, we came off very much too lightly.

When William went to Eton, I was transferred to a grammar school of much repute at Southwell. Having been driven there in much state, four-in-hand, and deposited with my small hair-trunk and my cake, I made acquaintance with my schoolmaster and schoolfellows.

The schoolmaster was a good, kindly man, and a good scholar; the classes of schoolfellows much mixed. I was taught to sing, so far as such an accomplishment was possible to me, "Jessie of Dumblane," "The Woodpecker tapping," and "Mr. Boney, if you please, let alone the Portuguese," by a son of the butcher at Newark who supplied our family with meat. In our equestrian combats among the gravestones, in the Minister-yard, which was our playground, my best horse was the hatter's son. There was another school in the town, which looked down upon us with much contempt. The boys had to pass through the churchyard on their way to the fields beyond. Then we avenged our honour. Lying in wait behind the gravestones, we sallied out upon them, and punched their heads; occasionally bringing them in gentle contact with a gravestone. Our church was the beautiful old Minster; its choir at that time, as at this, in great repute.

While I was at Southwell I made two attempts to improve the fashion of my outer wardrobe, which had always issued, and continued so to do when I was at Eton, from the primitive shop of the Ossington tailor; as, to the great punishment of our feet, the family boots and shoes issued from the shop of the village shoemaker. When I came to wear top-boots for hunting, I was obliged to rise very early; it took so much time to get them on, and more time in the evening to get them off. I

represented that I needed repair and reinforcement; and, having obtained leave from home, proceeded to order a suit from the Southwell artist. The material throughout, as selected by me, was a bright green pepper-and-salt; the decoration of it, smooth white metal buttons, about the size of a half-crown. I was much mortified, having asked and received permission to go out into the town, to find that my appearance did not excite the general admiration I expected.

My other attempt· was more ambitious. The "Brummel," the original type of the frock coat, was captivating all hearts. It was my first ambition to possess a "Brummel." So I represented again at home that, as the cold weather was coming on, I should be glad of a great-coat; and, upon permission given, did my best to combine a great-coat with a "Brummel," with velvet collar—the correct thing. Going home for the Christmas holidays, I issued from a side-door in my "Brummel," ready for church, before the eyes of the astonished family; and it was with much difficulty that decency of conduct was re-established at the church-door.

I never had but one serious conflict with the Southwell authorities. I forget other particulars, but recall two: one, that I threw a brass candlestick at the usher's head; the other, that, having been upon this sent to bed, I was hauled out of it in my night-shirt, and taken to by the usher with an ash-plant, in the presence of the boys who had witnessed the assault, and who were not displeased to see the little gentleman taken down. ·

It was not till some time after leaving Southwell that I recovered the more polished pronunciation of the English tongue.

"What is it, George," my brothers asked, "that you call your school-feast?"

"We call it 'Potation.'"

"What is Potation?"

"Ploom boon and nagus," said I.

However, I learnt a good deal of Latin and some Greek at the school, and was sorry to leave it, though it was for Eton, in 1817, when I was eleven and a half.

At Eton I witnessed the Marriott rebellion; the scene in the upper school at "Prose;" the eggs thrown at Keate by many hands, but not before his back was turned. Not one of them hit him, though they spattered him plentifully from the wall and the door-frame. His return, with several masters, in a few minutes; his order to seize the first boy that said a word; the expulsion then and there of a good many boys, and the end of the rebellion; as tidy a bit of sound and wholesome discipline as one would desire to see.

I witnessed also the stand made by the upper boys with Chapman, Captain of the school, now Bishop, at their head, on Barnespool bridge, against the bargees. It made a great impression upon me, and more than fifty years after I told Bishop Chapman that I had greatly respected him

Right-hand column 'A Story Needing Words': an early prize essay subject (see page 16).

all that time.

"What for?" he said; and I told him.

The bargees were furious against a particular boy, and came roaring down the street from the river, saying they would have him and throw him over the bridge. I got near enough to hear what passed; but, being a small boy, was disposed towards the rear, if it came to a fight. Chapman stood in the middle of the bridge, at the head of the boys; a short, stout boy, with his fists ready at his side. When the bargees came close, and demanded the boy, swearing they would have him, come what might, the only words that Chapman spoke were, "You'd better not try."

The bargees looked at the boys, and the boys looked at the bargees; the bargees began to waver, the boys stood fast. No rush was made, no blow struck. The enemy fell back slowly by twos and threes, and the boys remained masters of the bridge.

It is reported of the Duke of Wellington that he said, "Waterloo was won in the Eton playing fields." I never hear this repeated without thinking of Bishop Chapman, and the army of his boyhood.

I suffered at Keate's hands three times; twice for playing tricks in my Dame's house, once for bathing at a forbidden hour, or rather, I ought to say, and with shame I say it, for fibbing to Keate when he caught us, just as we turned into his lane on our return.

I was very happy at Eton, in spite of my clothes. There was one boy only, I remember, whose clothes were made by Stultz, and the boys used to follow him up and down with admiring eyes. He had a swallow-tailed bright blue coat, with gilt buttons, and other things conformable. By his side, the contrast with the artistic developments of the Ossington tailor was very humbling. But I was very happy, clothes, boots, and shoes, and made fast friends there, as I had done at Southwell. I have now, at the age of seventy-two, survived them all; as, indeed, I have nearly all my intimate friends made at Oxford.

Upper School boys, when "taking leave" in my time, used to slip a £10 note into Keate's hand. Being in some fright when I found myself alone with him in chambers, just as I was putting out my hand I dropped the note on the floor. My tact, if I had any, deserted me, and I stooped to pick it up and present it. So doing, my hand came in collision with Keate's foot, which had followed the note, and covered and secured it. Since that time, a great deal of what is called "Reform" has taken place in this and other things at Eton. I don't observe that the "Reform" has done Eton any good. There was a good deal of a sort of prudery and false delicacy, I remember, talked about the note-giving practice. It was nine years after, that going from Oxford to Eton, I came upon Keate at the corner of his "lane." Off went my hat.

"Ah, Denison," he said, "very glad to see you." He had a wonderful faculty of recalling faces.

A STORY NEEDING WORDS

CONJURING

By a Professor of the Art

FIRE-EATING

FIRE-EATING is such a time-honoured trick that, though I do not advise any boys to perform it, they should still know how it is done. This, like many of the mysteries of the ancient wonder-workers—who, pretended on the strength of such feats, to have higher powers than were possessed by the multitude—is really very simple, and, if practised with care, quite harmless. A piece of thick string is soaked in a solution of nitre and then dried. About an inch of this is lighted at one end and wrapped in a piece of tow, of a suitable size, to go into the mouth. Any smoke from this may be concealed by having a larger bundle of the tow held above it. When the small piece is placed in the mouth especial care must be taken to draw air through the nostrils only, and to eject it from the open mouth, when the tow will soon be all aglow. Each time the mouth is closed and the tow tightly pressed the fire is extinguished, save that which smoulders in the piece of string.

MY STRUGGLE WITH A TIGER

Charles Jamrach

ST. GEORGE'S-IN-THE-EAST

IT is now a good many years ago, when one morning a van-load of wild beasts, which I had bought the previous day from a captain in the London Docks, who brought them from the East Indies, arrived at my repository in Bett Street, St. George's-in-the-East. I myself superintended the unloading of the animals, and had given directions to my men to place a den containing a very ferocious full-grown Bengal tiger, with its iron-barred front close against the wall.

They were proceeding to take down a den with leopards, when all of a sudden I heard a crash, and to my horror found the big tiger had pushed out the back part of his den with his hind-quarters, and was walking down the yard into the street, which was then full of people watching the arrival of this curious merchandise. The tiger, in putting his forepaws against the iron bars in front of the den, had exerted his full strength to push with his back

against the boards behind, and had thus succeeded in gaining his liberty.

As soon as he got into the street, a boy of about nine years of age put out his hand to stroke the beast's back, when the tiger seized him by the shoulder and run down the street with the lad hanging in his jaws. This was done in less time than it takes me to relate; but when I saw the boy being carried off in this manner, and witnessed the panic that had seized hold of the people, without further thought I dashed after the brute, and got hold of him by the loose skin of the back of his neck. I was then of a more vigorous frame than now, and had plenty of pluck and dash in me.

I tried thus to stop his further progress, but he was too strong for me, and dragged me, too, along with him. I then succeeded in putting my leg under his hind legs, tripping him up, so to say, and he fell in consequence on his knees. I now, with all my

strength and weight, knelt on him, and releasing the loose skin I had hold of, I pushed my thumbs with all my strength behind his ears, trying to strangulate him thus. All this time the beast held fast to the boy.

My men had been seized with the same panic as the bystanders, but now I discovered one lurking round a corner, so I shouted to him to come with a crowbar; he fetched one, and hit the tiger three tremendous blows over the eyes.

It was only now he released the boy. His jaws opened and his tongue protruded about seven inches. I thought the brute was dead or dying, and let go of him, but no sooner had I done so than he jumped up again. In the same moment I seized the crowbar myself, and gave him, with all the strength I had left, a blow over his head. He seemed to be quite cowed, and, turning tail, went back towards the stables, which fortunately were open. I drove him into the yard, and closed the doors at once. Looking round for my tiger, I found he had sneaked into a large empty den that stood open at the bottom of the yard. Two of my men, who had jumped on to an elephant's box, now descended, and pushed down the iron-barred sliding-door of the den; and so my tiger was safe again under lock and key.

The boy was taken to the hospital, but with the exception of a fright and a scratch, was very little hurt. I lost no time in making inquiry about him, and finding where his father was, I offered him £50 as some compensation for the alarm he had sustained. Nevertheless, the father, a tailor, brought an action against me for damages, and I had to pay £300, of which he had the remaining £240. Of two counsel I employed, only one appeared; the other, however, stuck to his fee right enough. At the trial the judge sympathised very much with me, saying that, instead of being made to pay, I ought to have been rewarded for saving the life of the boy, and perhaps that of a lot of other people. He, however, had to administer the law as he found it, and I was responsible for any dangerous consequences brought about in my business. He suggested, however, as there was not much hurt done to the boy, to put down the damages as low as possible. The jury named £50, the sum I had originally offered to the boy's father of my own good will. The costs were four times that amount. I was fortunate, however, to find a purchaser for my tiger a few days after the accident; for Mr. Edmonds, proprietor of Wombwell's Menagerie, having read the report in the papers, came up to town post haste, and paid me £300 for the tiger. He exhibited him as the tiger that swallowed the child, and by all accounts made a small fortune with him.

MY EARLY SCHOOL-DAYS

By an Old Boy

Recollections of another 'Old Boy'— not, this time, Talbot Baines Reed.

AT the time I am writing of England was engaged in a fierce war with the First Napoleon, and Wellington was fighting hard in the Spanish Peninsula. We boys, of course, had a hatred and a horror of Buonaparte, and used to signalise our holidays by burning him in effigy, the effigy consisting of an old cocked-hat, a big bag stuffed with combustibles, and a huge pair of jackboots. I remember the first time I witnessed this *auto-da-fé* was on the night of the 29th of May. We had had a holiday that day in honour of King Charles the Second, in memory of whose escape from his pursuers nearly every house in the town was ornamented with a spreading branch of oak, and everybody who could procure them wore oakapples in their hats.

No shop was opened on that day, and no decent woman dared to go out of doors until sundown, for early in the day Oliver Cromwell was let loose in the guise of a black demon, with liberty to worry and torment all he could lay hold of. The man who played this part was a huge, powerful fellow, supplied with a bag of mingled grease and soot, and he was kept in restraint by two or three other men, who held the end of a long rope fastened round his waist. The mob pelted the hated Oliver with mud and dirt at their will, and those he caught he half smothered with the contents of his bag, or suffered them to escape only when they could afford to bribe him well.

I watched this frightful business from a window over our grocer's shop, saw several of the mob caught and endure the filthy penalty, and saw others who were but too glad to pay roundly to escape from the grasp of the wretch whom the assaults of the crowd had goaded to savageness.

The furious Oliver, however, was not allowed to catch whom he chose, but was pulled violently to the ground if he ran at persons of any note. After sunset a great bonfire was lighted in the open space near the church; a heap of dried faggots, some old tar-barrels, and the green oak boughs made a rare blaze and a smother, into which old Boney—the Grim Scrag of Mutton—together with a representative of old Oliver, was pitched headlong, and speedily vanished, boots, cocked-hat, grease-bags, and all, amidst the explosion of his combustible entrails.

Apropos of Buonaparte was another source of endless interest and amusement. A gentleman of the neighbourhood had raised a band of volunteers ready and eager to go out to Spain and join Wellington in fighting the French. These, to the number of some five hundred, were undergoing drill almost every evening. They went through their several manœuvres surrounded by a mob of ragged patriots and the boys and lads of the town. Three times a week they were exercised in firing in square, in volleys, and in running fire. Tom and I would get as close to them as we could, would watch them bite off the ends of the cartridges, and note where fell the cartridges that slipped out of their fingers, and as many of these as we could find after the men marched off the ground we made prize of.

Some of these volunteers were men of very bad character, of whom, so it was said, the town and neighbourhood were well rid. One of them, a rather wild fellow, had been in my father's employ, and had joined the troop after a violent quarrel with his wife, whom he declared he would never see again. One evening, after the drill was over and the men were marching off one way, while the spectators were returning by a different route to the town, poor Sukie, whom her husband had refused to speak to, wandered off to a pond, and, sitting down on a tree-trunk, looked despairingly at the water and burst into a wailing cry, calling on the name of her husband, who, without heeding her, went off with his companions. In her anguish she declared she would drown herself and her boy, and I verily believe she would have done so had she been left there alone, but my brother, who knew her well (as she had once been a servant in our house), called some people who were passing, and she was led back to her dwelling. That miserable scene made me wretched for days, child as I was, and even after all these years I can scarcely recall it unmoved.

I am glad to be able to state that after the return of this Devonshire squad from the wars, nearly five years later, poor Sukie's husband came back with the reputation of a gallant soldier. He had left a full third of his comrades on the battle-field, but had himself escaped scot-free, had been promoted, and left the service with a small pension. He was very glad to make up matters with Sukie, and made her a tolerably good husband afterwards.

Also *apropos* of Buonaparte was the arrival of a lot of French prisoners-of-war, who were lodged in a sort of quadrangular enclosure fitted up purely for them. They were in cells not unlike the beast cages in the Zoological Gardens, having barred windows, unglazed, looking out on the enclosure. The townspeople were allowed in the yard at certain hours, and could have free communication with the poor fellows through the grating. We often went to see them, and amused ourselves by watching them at their several employments. Some of them made charming little toys and clever carvings of animals; some drew pictures with pen and ink; some mended shoes or garments. All were quite cheerful and even merry, and were glad to do anything they could in return for anything that was given them. A piece of bread or cheese would purchase a little toy, and for a few pence a really clever piece of work in the shape of dog, cat, horse, cow, pig, or fowl, cut from a scrap of wood, might be had; and any odd bits of deal or willow were thankfully received.

The only Englishman in the town who could speak French was the parson of the parish, and sometimes he would come and act as interpreter. The best friends of the poor prisoners, however, were their own officers, who, being at large on their parole, were able to look well after them.

In the autumn of this year took place the funeral of an officer who had received his death-wound at Busaco. So grand a sight I had never conceived. The streets were lined with soldiers, the shops all shut, every window crammed with spectators, minute guns booming, solemn music playing, and a vast crowd assembled from the neighbouring district, marching slowly and in sad silence towards the grave, all following the hearse and the dead warrior's horse laden with his late master's military trappings; and then came the farewell volleys fired over his last resting-place.

DEATH OF A FAMOUS FIRE-HORSE

IT is now some few months since there died a horse which many a Manchester boy had come to look upon as quite a personal friend; and most certainly he merited all the intense admiration lavished upon him. We allude to a well-known "fire-horse,"

whose great speed and dash, and good fortune in often arriving first at the scene of the conflagration, made him an immense favourite, as we have said, with the street boys of the city. His life and death are thus recorded by one who knew and loved him well:—

At the latter part of the spring of 1864 "Our Bruce" was born. He soon began to show signs of a very promising hunter of over sixteen hands, and in due course commenced his training for the chase. At five years old he had grown to a beautiful animal, very docile and tractable—his mottled grey coat the pride of the groom and the admiration of his master. "Our Bruce" in the hunting-field once stumbled, and in consequence lost the confidence of his master, who disposed of him to the Manchester Carriage Company. In the early part of the year 1870 he was sold by the Carriage Company to the Manchester Corporation for the fire-engine department, and commenced his duties on the 24th of March.

His general appearance, and kind, tractable, willing ways, were soon noticed by the firemen, and in less than a month after he joined the brigade he was the favourite of the whole establishment, having pretty well the free run of the yard, in which he caused much diversion by his singular and funny ways. He was always full of innocent mischief, and one of his greatest delights was to chase the men about the yard. It sometimes happened that he was let out for a gambol when the children were playing. On such occasions it was most interesting to notice how careful he was in not going too near them; at other times, when the engines were in the yard, he seemed not to forget his early training as a hunter, and would amuse himself by jumping over the poles. When tired, he would lift the latch of the door and go into his stable, and just as easily after a rest, when the stable-door was closed, he would let himself out again, or knock loudly at the door to attract attention. Near the stable-door there is a

water-tap with a revolving handle. "Our Bruce" would turn the handle with ease, and help himself to a drink. It sometimes happened that a hose-pipe would be attached to the tap: this would not cause him the least inconvenience; in such a case, after turning on the tap, he would lift up the end of the hose-pipe with his teeth, and hold the end in his mouth until he had satisfied his thirst.

Many curious anecdotes could be told about our pet; how, on one occasion, he picked up the end of the hose and wetted one of the firemen who had offended him; how, at a fire, he would stand amidst the greatest noise and excitement, with showers of sparks falling around him and on his beautiful coat, only to be shaken off, and at other times completely enveloped in smoke; but there was no shying or fretting under fire or smoke with "Our Bruce;" he seemed to know that he had brought those who would fight that ruthless tyrant, fire, and he stood proud and confident that before long he would return home with the victors, when, after being refreshed and groomed, he would again be ready (always first) for the next "turn out."

For nearly six years "Our Bruce" never missed going with the first machine, at the end of which time he was, in consequence of his fine appearance and our desire to give him a less active duty in his old age, transferred from the fire-engine to police patrol duty. We did not altogether lose our faithful animal's services, for one of his duties was to attend fires with the mounted police-sergeant (whose name was also Bruce) to keep back the onlookers, which he most effectively did for nearly two years, during which time he was as great a favourite with the policemen, rarely leaving a police-station without an apple, piece of bread, or some mark of affection.

On the 7th of last August "Our Bruce" fell sick; the veterinary surgeon was sent for, who pronounced him suffering from inflammation of the bowels. The usual remedies were applied, and everything was done to relieve his pain and make

him comfortable, but to no avail. For three weeks afterwards he was never left for a moment night nor day, and at the end of the third day he drew his last breath, surrounded by those who loved him well, and who had been taken by him to the scene of many a hard fight. A *post-mortem* examination was held the following morning to ascertain the cause of death. A stone six inches in diameter, weighing 5 lb. 11 oz., was taken from his bowels; this was, no doubt, the principal cause of the disease which led to the death of the well-known and universally-admired fire-horse, "Our Bruce."

THE SHARKS OF MAURITIUS

Nicholas Pike,
U.S. Consul at Mauritius

I HAVE been very successful in procuring specimens of the large fish of this ocean.

A shark, kindly lent me by Mr. Bewsher, has a terrible incident connected with it. The men of the steamship Ermine caught it, and it was exposed for sale in the bazaar. When cut open a clasp-knife and belt, with the bone of a man's arm, were found in it. This, of course, gave rise to the most horrible surmises, especially as it was rumoured that a few days previously a sailor had deserted from a vessel in the harbour, and was supposed to have been attacked by a shark before he could reach the shore. If it was so, the poor fellow had paid a woeful penalty for desertion. This shark is thirteen feet seven inches in length, with a girth at the gills, even when stuffed and shrunk, of four feet six inches.

One reads and hears of horror relating to sharks, but it is only on examining the mouth of one that I think a true idea of their powers of destruction is fully realised. It made me shudder as I contemplated the jaws of this brute, which, after all, is only a very small one, compared with many that are caught ranging from thirty to thirty-five feet....

'An unexpected call': illustration to a moralising tale (see page 16) — the innocent out-of-work boy goes in fear of wrongful arrest, but all will end well.

FROM POWDER MONKEY TO ADMIRAL

Or, the Stirring Days of the British Navy.

W. H. G. Kingston,
Author of "Peter the Whaler," "True Blue," etc.

CHAPTER I.—PREPARING TO START.

NO steamboats ploughed the ocean, nor were railroads thought of, when our young friends Jack, Tom, and Bill lived. They first met each other on board the Foxhound frigate, on the deck of which ship a score of other lads and some fifty or sixty men were mustered, who had just come up the side from the Viper tender; she having been on a cruise to collect such stray hands as could be found, and a curious lot they were to look at.

Among them were long-shore fellows in swallow-tails and round hats, fishermen in jerseys and fur-skin caps, smugglers in big boots and flushing coats; and not a few whose whitey-brown faces, and close-cropped hair, made it no difficult matter to guess that their last residence was within the walls of a gaol. There were seamen also, pressed most of them, just come in from a long voyage, many months or perhaps years having passed since they left their native land; that they did not look especially amiable was not to be wondered at, since they had been prevented from going, as they had intended, to visit their friends, or maybe in the case of the careless ones, from enjoying a long-expected spree on shore. They were all now waiting to be inspected by the first-lieutenant, before their names were entered on the ship's books.

The rest of the crew were going about their various duties. Most of them were old hands, who had served a year or more on board the gallant frigate. During that time she had fought two fierce actions, which, though she had come off victorious, had greatly thinned her ship's company, and the captain was therefore anxious to make up the complement as fast as possible by every means in his power.

The seamen took but little notice of the new hands, though some of them had been much of the same description themselves, but were not very fond of acknowledging this, or of talking of their previous histories; they had, however, got worked into shape by degrees: and the newcomers, even those with the "long togs," by the time they had gone through the same process, would not be distinguished from the older hands, except, maybe, when they came to splice an eye, or turn in a grummet, when their clumsy work would show what they were; few of them either were likely ever to be the outermost on the yardarms when sail had suddenly to be shortened on a dark night, while it was blowing great guns and small arms.

The frigate lay at Spithead. She had been waiting for these hands to put to sea. Lighters were alongside, and whips were never-ceasing hoisting in casks of rum, with bales and cases of all sorts, which it seemed impossible could ever be stowed away. From the first-lieutenant to the youngest midshipman, all were bawling at the top of their voices, issuing and repeating orders; but there were two persons who outroared all the rest, the boatswain and the boatswain's mate. They were proud of those voices of theirs. Let the hardest gale be blowing, with the wind howling and whistling through the rigging, the canvas flapping like claps of thunder, and the seas roaring and dashing against the bows, they could make themselves heard above the loudest sounds of the storm.

At present the boatswain bawled, or rather roared, because he was so accustomed to roar that he could speak in no gentler voice while carrying on duty on deck, and the boatswain's mate imitated him.

The first-lieutenant had a good voice of his own, though it was not so rough as that of his inferiors. He made it come out with a quick, sharp sound, which could be heard from the poop to the forecastle, even with the wind ahead.

Jack, Tom, and Bill looked at each other, wondering what was next going to happen. They were all three of about the same age, and much of a height, and somehow, as I have said, they found themselves standing close together.

They were too much astonished, not to say frightened, to talk just then, though they all three had tongues in their heads, so they listened to the conversation going on around them.

"Why, mate, where do you come from?" asked a long-shore chap of one of the whitey-brown-faced gentlemen.

"Oh, I've jist dropped from the clouds; don't know where else I've come from," was the answer.

"I suppose you got your hair cropped off as you came down?" was the next query.

"Yes! it was the wind did it as I came scuttling down," answered the other, who was evidently never at a loss what to say. "And now, mate, just tell me how did you get on board this craft?" he inquired.

"I swam off, of course, seized with a fit of patriotism, and determined to fight for the honour and glory of Old England," was the answer.

It cannot, however, be said that this is a fair specimen of the conversation; indeed, it would benefit no one were what was said to be repeated.

Jack, Tom, and Bill felt very much as a person might be supposed to do who had dropped from the moon. Everything around them was so strange and bewildering, for not one of them had ever before been on board a ship, and Bill had never even seen one. Having not been much accustomed to the appearance of trees, he had some idea that the masts grew out of the deck, that the yards were branches, and the blocks curious leaves; not that amid the fearful uproar, and what seemed to him the wildest confusion, he could think of anything clearly.

Bill Rayner had certainly not been born with a silver spoon in his mouth. His father he had never known. His mother lived in a garret, and died in a garret, although not before, happily for him, he was able to do something for himself, and, still more happily, not before she had impressed right principles on his mind. As the poor woman lay on her deathbed, taking her boy's hands and looking earnestly into his eyes, she said, "Be honest, Bill, in the sight of God. Never forget that He sees you, and do your best to please Him. No fear about the rest. I am not much of a scholar, but I know that's right. If others try to persuade you to do what's wrong, don't listen to them. Promise me, Bill, that you will do as I tell you."

"I promise, mother, that I will," answered Bill; and, small lad as he was, meant what he said.

Poor as she was, being a woman of some education, his mother had taught him to read and write and cipher—not that he was a great adept at any of those arts, but he possessed the groundwork, which was an important matter, and he did his best to keep up his knowledge by reading signboards, looking into booksellers' windows, and studying any stray leaves he could obtain.

Bill's mother was buried in a rough shell by the parish, and Bill went out into the world to seek his fortune. He took to curious ways; hunting in dustheaps for anything worth having; running of errands when he could get any one to send him; holding horses for gentlemen, but that was not often; doing duty as a link-boy at houses when grand parties were going forward or during foggy weather; for Bill, though he often went supperless to his nest, either under a market-cart, or in a cask by the river-side, or in some other out-of-the-way place, generally managed to have a little capital with which to buy a link, but the said capital did not grow much, for bad times coming swallowed it all up.

Bill, as are many other London boys, was exposed to temptations of all sorts; often when almost starving, without a roof to sleep under, or a friend to whom he could appeal for help, his shoes worn out, his clothing too scanty to keep him warm; but, ever recollecting his mother's last words, he resisted them all. One day, having wandered farther east than he had ever been before, he found himself in the presence of a press-gang, who were carrying off a party of men and boys to the river's edge. One of the man-of-war's men seized upon him, and Bill, thinking that matters could not be much worse with him than they were at present, willingly accompanied the party, though he had very little notion where they were going. Reaching a boat, they were made to tumble in, some resisting and endeavouring to get away, but a gentle prick from the point of a cutlass, or a clout on the head, made them more reasonable, and most of them sat down resigned to their fate. One of them, however, a stout fellow, when the boat had got some distance from the shore, striking out right and left at the men nearest him, sprang overboard, and before the boat could be pulled round, had already got back nearly half way to the landing-place.

One or two of the press-gang, who had muskets, fired, but they were not good shots. The man looking back as he saw them lifting their weapons, by suddenly diving escaped the first volley, and by the time they had again loaded he had gained such a distance that the shot spattered into the water on either side of him. They were afraid of firing again for fear of hitting some of the people on shore, besides which, darkness coming on, the gloom concealed him from view.

They knew, however, that he must have landed in safety, from the cheers which came off from the quay, uttered by the crowd who had followed the press-gang, hooting them as they embarked with their captives.

Bill began to think that he could not be going to a very pleasant place, since, in spite of the risk he ran, the man had been so eager to escape, but being himself unable to swim, he could not follow his example, even had he wished it. He judged it wiser, therefore, to stay still, and see what would next happen. The boat pulled down the river for some way, till she got alongside a large cutter, up the side of which Bill and his companions were made to climb.

From what he heard he found that she was a man-of-war tender, her business being to collect men, by hook or by crook, for the Royal Navy.

As she was now full—indeed, so crowded that no more men could be stowed on board—she got under way with the first of the ebb, and dropped down the stream, bound for Spithead.

As Bill, with most of the pressed men, was kept below during this his first trip to sea, he gained but little nautical experience. He was, however, very sick, while he arrived at the conclusion that the tender's hold, the dark prison in which he found himself, was a most horrible place.

Several of his more heartless companions jeered at him in his misery; and, indeed poor Bill, thin and pale, shoeless and hatless, clad in patched garments, looked a truly miserable object.

As the wind was fair, the voyage did not last long, and glad enough he was when the cutter got alongside the big frigate, and he with the rest being ordered on board, he could breathe the fresh air which blew across her decks.

Tom Fletcher, who stood next to Bill, had considerably the advantage of him in outward appearance. Tom was dressed in somewhat nautical fashion, though any sailor would have seen with half an eye that his costume had been got up by a shore-going tailor.

Tom had a good-natured but not very sensible-looking countenance. He was strongly built, was in good health, and had the making of a sailor in him, though this was the first time that he had even been on board a ship.

He had a short time before come off with a party of men returning on the expiration of their leave. Telling them that he wished to go to sea, he had been allowed to enter the boat. From the questions some of them had put to him, and the answers he gave, they suspected that he was a runaway, and such in fact was the case. Tom was the son of a solicitor in a country town, who had several other boys, he being the fourth, in the family.

He had for some time taken to reading the voyages of Drake, Cavendish, and Dampier, and the adventures of celebrated pirates, such as those of Captains Kidd, Lowther, Davis, Teach, as also the lives of some of England's naval commanders, Sir Cloudesley Shovell, Benbow, and Admirals Hawke, Keppel, Rodney, and others, whose gallant actions he fully intended some day to imitate.

He had made vain endeavours to induce his father to let him go to sea, but Mr. Fletcher, knowing that he was utterly ignorant of a sea life, set his wish down as a mere fancy, which it would be folly to indulge.

Tom, instead of trying to show that he really was in earnest, took French leave one fine morning, and found his way to Portsmouth, without being traced. Had he waited he would probably have been sent to sea as a midshipman, and placed on the quarter-deck. He now entered as a ship-boy before the mast.

Tom, as he had made his bed had to lie on it, as is the case with many other persons. Even now, had he written home, he might have had his position changed, but he thought himself very clever, and had no intention of letting his father know where he had gone. The last of the trio was far more accustomed to salt water than were either of his companions. Jack Peek was the son of a West country fisherman. He had come to sea because he saw that there was little chance of getting bread to put into his mouth if he remained on shore.

Jack's father had lost his boats and nets the previous winter and had shortly afterwards been pressed on board a man-of-war.

Jack had done his best to support himself without being a burden to his mother, who sold fish in the neighbouring town and country round, and could do very well for herself; so when he proposed going on board a man-of-war, she, having mended his shirts, bought him a new pair of shoes, and gave him her blessing. Accordingly, doing up his spare clothes in a bundle, which he carried at the end of a stick, he trudged off with a stout heart, resolved to serve His Majesty and fight the battles of Old England.

Jack went on board the first man-of-war tender picking up hands he could find, and had been transferred that day to the Foxhound.

He told Tom and Bill thus much of his history. The former, however, was not very ready to be communicative as to his; while Bill's patched garments said as much about him as he was just then willing to narrate.

A boy who had spent all his life in the streets of London was not likely to say more to strangers than was necessary.

In the meantime the fresh hands had been called up before the first-lieutenant, Mr. Saltwell, and their names entered by the purser in the ship's books, after the ordinary questions had been put to them to ascertain for what rating they were qualified.

Some few, including the smugglers, were entered as able seamen; others as ordinary seamen; and the larger number, who were unfit to go aloft, or indeed not likely to be of much use in any way for a

An early frontispiece fold-out picture.

long time to come, were rated as landsmen, and would have to do all the dirty work about the ship.

The boys were next called up, and each of them gave an account of himself.

Tom dreaded lest he should be asked any questions which he would be puzzled to answer.

The first-lieutenant glanced at all three, and in spite of his old dress, entered Bill first, Jack next, and Tom, greatly to his surprise, the last. In those days no questions were asked where men or boys came from. At the present time, a boy who should thus appear on board a man-of-war would find himself in the wrong box, and be quickly sent on shore again, and home to his friends. None are allowed to enter the Navy until they have gone through a regular course of instruction in a training ship, and none are received on board her unless they can read and write well, and have a formally signed certificate that they have obtained permission from their parents or guardians.

George Andrew Hutchison, Editor of the B.O.P. *from 1879 to 1912.*

CHAPTER TWO
THE NEXT TWELVE YEARS
1880-1891

The *B.O.P.* gathered strength and confidence as it went into its second volume. R. M. Ballantyne, already famous – *The Young Fur Traders* had been published in 1856 and he had more than fifty other books to his name – contributed 'The Red Man's Revenge'. Ballantyne was a little too prone to piety to be consistently popular, but his best books, like *Coral Island, Martin Rattler* and *The Gorilla Hunters*, made him a lion among writers. In his early years he had worked for the Hudson's Bay Company in Canada. He wrote for the *B.O.P.* throughout the 1880s.

The great acquisition of 1880 was Jules Verne, who began his long connection with the *B.O.P.* with a story called 'The Boy Captain'. Year after year Verne contributed at least one serial a volume. Most of his famous books, such as *The Cryptogram, Barbicane and Co., The Clipper of the Clouds*, first came to the English public via the *B.O.P.* In 'The Master of the World' he produced an excellent example of what might have been an early flying saucer. Verne, naturally, was immensely popular with the *B.O.P.* readers. In December 1882 the Editor stated firmly to a correspondent: 'The tales by Jules Verne which appear in the *Boy's Own Paper* are specially translated for it and are not published in the English language in book or any other form, in this or any other country, until they have been completed in our pages.'

Another well-known writer, W. H. G. Kingston, died in 1880. However, he had contributed 'From Powder Monkey to Admiral' in Volume I and helped launch the *B.O.P.* on its successful way.

There were a number of American contributors to these early volumes, and somehow the Atlantic did not seem so wide then as it does today.

And, of course, there was the immortal W. G. Grace. He was the first of a long line of experts who discussed how to play their particular game. But in the 1880s boys seemed less interested in games than in making things or keeping pets. They were also interested in themselves, and a series of illustrated character sketches of schoolboys proved popular.

Boys tended to be scatter-brained and frivolous but young men were clearly serious. The heroes of the Oxford and Cambridge Boat Race are pleasant but unsmiling.

Dr Gordon Stables made his first appearance in 1880. Year after year the indefatigable doctor, who had once served in the Royal Navy but now toured the country in a caravan, produced stories and advice. His stories had a fine rollicking touch but some of his articles are nauseatingly patronising.

The roll-call of artists is already no less impressive than that of writers. Notable among the former at this stage were R. Caton Woodville, Alfred Pearse, Geo Cruickshank. Most of them had R.A. or R.I. after their names. J. T. Nettleship, Frank Feller, Tom Browne would follow.

Ascot R. Hope, whose real name was R. Hope Moncrieff, was yet another prolific writer who seemed to be able to run serials in several magazines simultaneously. Talbot

Baines Reed's serials began with 'The Adventures of a Three Guinea Watch' in October 1880.

Volume III contained a number of songs set to music. One was 'The Orphan Miner Boy's Song to his Mother'. It was illustrated by a scene at the pithead after a disaster. One verse ran:

> 'My father met his fate, mother
> In yon dark mine below
> Yet though the peril's great, mother
> I shall be safe I know
> For there's one who reigns oer all, mother
> Our cause his own will make
> If on his love we lean, mother
> He never will forsake.'

However the last verse ends with:

> 'And should his [his father's] fate be mine, mother
> Still heaven will comfort thee.'

But – even for a miner – all was not gloom. A few pages later there is an article on 'How a Coal Pit Boy Rose to be a Member of Parliament'.

The fourth volume began with the most famous of Talbot Baines Reed's stories – 'The Fifth Form at St Dominic's'. It was by 'the Author of "The Adventures of a Three Guinea Watch"' – later the mere name of Reed would make readers sit up and take notice. (It appeared at the head of his next serial.) The formula was one which would be used successfully over and over again by school story writers. The 'hero', called Loman, gets himself – and his fag, whom he uses for illegal errands – into debt to an unpleasant publican called Cripps. Loman steals an examination paper in the hope that it will enable him to win a prize and pay off his debts, but, of course, it does not. Eventually he redeems himself in Australia.

Described in outline like this, the story may seem merely priggish. In the telling it was full of real life, amusing schoolboy characters and incidents. The background, in fact, was better than the main plot. Reed knew that schoolboys were only too likely to stray off poaching, drinking, consorting with rogues, gambling and generally making fools of themselves. Compulsory games were instituted as part of the answer to the problem. A boy who has to play football or cricket on a half-day cannot usually stray far enough to get into much mischief. He will probably employ his spare time making explosive spiders or swapping stamps, breeding canaries or playing a violin – all of which he had instructions to do in Volume IV.

In these early days women writers often appeared. Mrs Eiloart, who wrote 'The Ill-used Boy; or Lawrence Hartley's Grievances', seems lucky to have got into the *B.O.P.* team. Lady Broome, who wrote about colonial life, was much better.

In the 1880s, though not snobbish about it, the *B.O.P.* was liable to refer to 'Great Schools'. Its definitions are interesting and show how reputations have risen or fallen with the years. Among the 35 'Great Schools' are Mercer's (now extinct), Wells, Grocers, Stationers, Haberdashers, City of London and Manchester. In 1884 a list of 39 'leading schools' included Newton College, East Retford, The Clergy Orphan School (Canterbury), Chatham House, Oscott, Bruce Castle and Devon County School, plus of course Eton, Harrow, Rugby, Winchester etcetera. In the same year pictures of some of the 'Heads of our Great Schools' were published. None of them looked as if they would stand any nonsense!

Reed covered a very wide variety of schools. In 'My Friend Smith' (1882) his hero was at a small boarding grammar school before going on to a hard life in the city. In 'The Willoughby Captains' (1883) he stuck closely to the conventional boarding school story. In 'Reginald Cruden' in 1883 the hero was suddenly fatherless and penniless. He obtains a clerk's job but unfortunately for him his employer is a swindler who advertises goods, receives payment, but never sends them. Cruden, of course, gets the blame. In a dosshouse he is befriended by an urchin, who soon dies of smallpox (he has of course never been vaccinated). Fortunately for Cruden, at about the same time as he is brought to court as accessory to a swindler his family fortunes are unexpectedly found to be better than formerly supposed. He is reunited with his mother and brother but does not forget his experiences in dire poverty.

Reed's story 'A Dog with a Bad Name' concerned a boy (Jeffreys) who had lost his temper in a rugby football match. The circumstances were these. Charging for the line he was opposed by a smaller boy who had previously cheeked him and whom he made no attempt to avoid. The younger boy was knocked unconscious and seemed unlikely to survive. Jeffreys ran away from school in shame. At home his guardian, an unscrupulous but not unfamiliar type, told him he was in any case penniless. (The guardian had, of course, appropriated his ward's money.) Jeffreys was turned loose, accompanied only by a faithful dog. Needless to say there were plenty of complications and sub-plots before he was restored to his former life and environment.

The next story, 'The Master of the Shell', had the unusual expedient of a master rather than a boy for the hero. It was followed by 'Sir Ludar', an Elizabethan adventure story, but soon Reed was back in school again with 'The Cock House at Fellsgarth'.

At school or at home boys were always trying to keep pets, aided by expert advice. Dr Stradling, C.M.Z.S., advised on 'Snakes and How to Tame Them'. A little later Dr Gordon Stables was writing articles on 'Reptiles and Fishes: How to Stuff and set them up'. There were articles on 'Peculiar Punishments', in which it was stated (among other gory details) that 'It is singular that a Chinaman will prefer to die by crucifixion rather than beheading. He has the greatest horror of appearing in the next world without his head and therefore chooses a slow and lingering death rather than a quick one.'

Stradling outbid Stables in an article on 'How to Skin, Stuff and Mount a Bird in Five Minutes'. More gruesome details occurred in an article entitled 'Trial by Ordeal' by the author of 'Peculiar Punishments'. W. G. Grace was now advising on the choice of a cricket bat, but the saga of punishment was continued by Cuthbert Bede, B.A., in 'Under the Rod: or Swishing Anecdotes'. 'Cuthbert Bede' was the pen name of the Rev. Edward Bradley, a Lincolnshire parson who had written many books including the once-famous *Verdant Green*. Boys regarded punishment as the natural consequence of misdoings if they were caught; it was also likely to catch them somewhat undeservedly on occasion. Nobody thought of such punishment as physical and spiritual degradation; these ideas belong to an age which often laments the absence of former discipline while deploring the methods by which it was instilled. Undoubtedly much harsh and unnecessary punishment was inflicted in Victorian days, but the victims often made a philosophy out of it by exhibiting the marks to each other as a form of honourable war scar.

An unusually qualified writer appeared in 1884. He was 'Professor J. F. Hodgetts, Late Examiner to the University of Moscow, Professor in the Russian Imperial College of Practical Science etc., etc'. One wonders what 'etc., etc.' betokened. Hodgetts wrote stories about Norsemen.

The correspondence columns were clearly enormously popular, although many of the replies were somewhat harsh. One deaf boy is discouraged from going to sea, for 'A deaf steward is hardly likely to prove popular with seasick passengers.' C. Chandler is told: 'Forty-four miles is almost too much for a boy to walk in a day.' 'A Gentleman Commoner' is informed in 1885: 'Ordinary Knighthoods are now given for so many reasons they are no longer a test of ability or merit. No poor man is made a knight, except by mistake.'

'Otto' is cross-examined: 'How do you expect us to name a bumble bee which has first been pressed flat in a letter and then pounded flatter still by some energetic postal authority?'

But, in spite of priggishness, occasional sarcasm, and a trace of pomposity, this was a page which undoubtedly removed many a youthful worry, even if only for the health of a pet.

In 1886 the *B.O.P.* ran a series entitled 'Half Hours with Hard Workers'. These included cabmen, conductors and drivers, firemen, policemen, river workers, railway servants and scavengers. There were also articles on Eton (of which we show accompanying prints), Harrow, Westminster and Winchester, but the New Working Lads Institute in Whitechapel was also described and fully illustrated, as was the Humber Training Ship at Southampton. There were descriptive articles on castles and abbeys in England and Wales and graphic accounts of 'Great Shipwrecks of the World', 'Great Mining Disasters', and 'Great Railway Accidents'.

By 1891 the *B.O.P.* had clearly established the fact that clean robust fun, and advice to the troubled, were a successful market formula. Success was assured, but rivals and competitors were girding their loins for the next decade.

THE BOY'S OWN PAPER

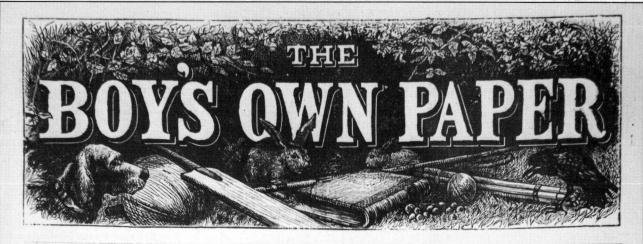

No. 38.—Vol. II. SATURDAY, OCTOBER 4, 1879. Price One Penny.
[ALL RIGHTS RESERVED.]

THE RED MAN'S REVENGE:

A TALE OF THE RED RIVER FLOOD.

By R. M. BALLANTYNE,
Author of "The Lifeboat," "Post Haste," etc.

CHAPTER I.—OPENS THE BALL.

IF there ever was a man who possessed a gem in the form of a daughter of nineteen that man was Samuel Ravenshaw; and if ever there was a girl who owned a bluff, jovial, fiery, hot-tempered, irascible old father, that girl was Elsie Ravenshaw.

Although a gem, Elsie was exceedingly imperfect. Had she been the reverse she would not have been worth writing about.

Old Ravenshaw, as his familiars styled him, was a settler, if we may use such a term in reference to one who was, perhaps,

Victor and Ian on the Red River.

THE BOY'S OWN PAPER

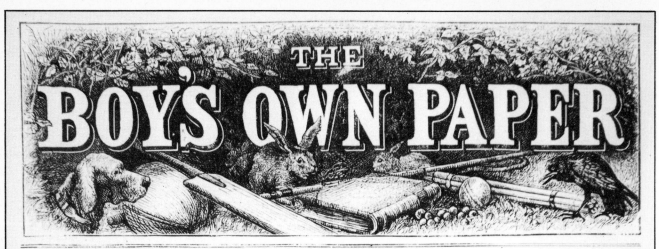

No. 44.—Vol. II.   SATURDAY, NOVEMBER 15, 1879.   Price One Penny.
[ALL RIGHTS RESERVED.]

THE RED MAN'S REVENGE;
A TALE OF THE RED RIVER FLOOD.

By R. M. BALLANTYNE,
Author of "The Lifeboat," "Post Haste," etc.

CHAPTER VII.—SOME OF THE SHADOWS OF A
BUFFALO HUNTER'S LIFE.

IN order to give the women time to prepare some pemmican for them, Victor
Ravenshaw and his companions agreed to
spend another day with the hunters, and
again, as a matter of course, followed
them to the chase.

The same wild pursuit, accompanied by
accidents, serious and serio-comic, took
place, and success again attended the hunt,
but the day did not end so happily, owing
to an event which filled the camp with

"He fell pierced by a shower of arrows."

CRICKET: AND HOW TO EXCEL IN IT

By W. G. Grace

...HOLD the bat firmly, and do not flourish and twirl it about as you see some young people do. Hold it straight and in an easy position. Keep your left shoulder well forward and you are sure to play with a straight bat. Keep upright, and watch well the bowler's hand; you will very soon find out which way he means the ball to twist, and this little bit of information is no slight help when you are batting.

You should not let the ball hit the bat, but rather

LEG HIT

make the bat hit the ball. A great many cricketers of the present day forget that the bat was made for this purpose, and simply hold it to protect the wicket, allowing the ball to play itself. Of course every now and again you have a ball that it is impossible to do anything with but stop, but on the other hand there are hundreds that ought to be punished, and are by indifferent players permitted to escape.

If you make up your mind to hit, hit hard. No

half-and-half style as a rule will pay. And when you block infuse a little power into what you do, and do not be content to stop the ball by simply putting the bat in its way—any one can do that—but try and score off it. Hit with your arms, but use your wrists as much as you can—the wrist-work is the secret of balls that you block flying off far enough to make runs. Hit, then, hard, and get well over the ball, never spoon it up; the ball travels farthest when hit

FORWARD PLAY.

along the ground—a skying hit never goes so far as one that skims across the grass. It may please some people, but it is nearly all show—a high hitter is invariably a low scorer.

Hit at the ball, not at the place where you think the ball ought to be, and watch the ball along the whole of its journey to the bat. Never make up your mind how you will play a ball until the ball is bowled and you ascertain the "manner of its coming." After a time you will instinctively feel, as the ball approaches you, how it should be treated.

Play forward whenever you can.

There is no hard-and-fast rule which will apply to every one as to how to treat the various kinds of balls; each will be met best by different men in a different way.

Long-reached men will smother forward many a ball that shorter-reached players can only play close-back.

Never get too far back, and always beware of the bowler driving you on to your wicket.

Never play across the wicket, or pull balls over,

undeniable leg ball should be hit to leg, but take care that it is a leg ball.

In cutting keep the ball down—pat it, so to speak, and if you shift your right foot, be careful that you take up your old position before the bowler has another try at your wicket.

THE CUT

HITTING.
RIGHT   WRONG
STRAIGHT PLAY.   CROSS PLAY.

Below Cricket in 1740 as played on a Surrey green. Sketch made by Alfred Pearse from an oil painting by Francis Hayman, R.A.

and take care what you are doing if you step in. There is such a tendency among young players to swipe to leg, that unless it is checked they are scarcely able to do anything else, and never attain to even respectable mediocrity in the game. Of course an

Never be in a hurry to get runs. Study the bowler's attack and find out if you can what he thinks is your weak point and is aiming at.

Practise often but not too much at a time, and practise intelligently. Practise playing the ball and

not merely slogging at it. Be as careful at the wickets when the net is behind you as you would be during a match. If you can manage it, get some one who knows the game well to bowl to you, and ask him to point out where your defence is weak and where you make mistakes, and give heed to what he says.

Think what you are doing, and watch the effect of different hits on different balls. Notice the different angles made by different strokes, and try to apply the knowledge thus gained by placing the ball in different directions.

A great deal has been written as to the positions of the legs in making the various hits. I do not attach much importance to this myself, as I think it almost impossible to describe such things lucidly and correctly, certainly not without the aid of two or three diagrams to each subject. The figures given herewith afford a general idea of the best known hits, sufficient at all events to enable you to recognise them in the field.

This has been my object throughout, as I hinted at first. Watch a really good batsman and take your style from him; you cannot help modifying it to suit your own peculiarities, try what you will. Practice intelligently and assiduously until you have obtained a perfect familiarity with the powers of the weapon you wield, play with a straight bat, meet the ball, and hit hard, and you will very possibly soon excel the man you have taken as your model.

BACK-PLAY.

Heroes of the University Boat Race, 1880.

THE UNIVERSITY BOAT RACE.

CAMBRIDGE.

L. R. JONES (Jesus), BOW.　　W. W. BAILLIE (Jesus), STROKE.

OXFORD.

R. J. H. POOLE (Brasenose), BOW.　　L. R. WEST (Ch. Ch.), STROKE.

THE BOY'S OWN PAPER

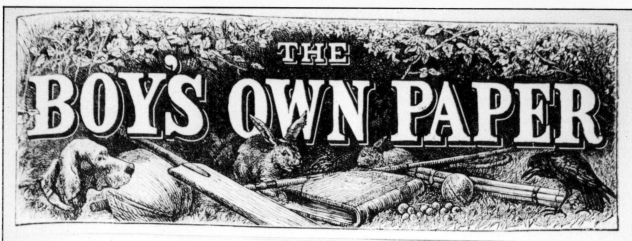

No. 72.—Vol. II.   SATURDAY, MAY 29, 1880.   Price One Penny
[ALL RIGHTS RESERVED.

BEN NORTON:
A FRONTIER STORY.
By S. S. ROBBINS, U.S.A.
CHAPTER III.

THE travellers had hardly gone before Mr. Norton made his appearance, riding leisurely home over the prairies in another direction. As soon as Ben caught sight of him, he ran eagerly out to meet him. Without stopping, his father put out hand and foot, which the boy grasped, then swung himself up easily behind the saddle, and both came galloping to the hostelry.

Mrs. Norton was waiting for them at the door, and the first impression which her husband had of the seriousness of their danger came from her pale

"He had no more fear of the Indians than he expressed."

THE BOY'S OWN PAPER

No. 68.—Vol. II.   SATURDAY, MAY 1, 1880.   Price One Penny. [ALL RIGHTS RESERVED.]

HOW I LOST MY FINGER.

By James Cox, R.N.

Not many years ago I belonged to her Majesty's ship Iris, a smart little gun-vessel stationed on the West Coast of Africa.

We had been cruising off the mouth of the River Congo for several weeks, watching a suspicious-looking merchant barque, named the Dahomé, which had been anchored off Shark's Point (just inside the river) for the past two months.

Now King Peter, a native chief who lived in the vicinity of the point, had hinted to our captain that the master of the barque was only waiting for the Iris to leave the Congo, when a cargo of slaves would be taken on board for the slave-market in Cuba.

In consequence of this information we

"While we were rolling together my faithful coxswain rushed in."

THE BOY'S OWN PAPER

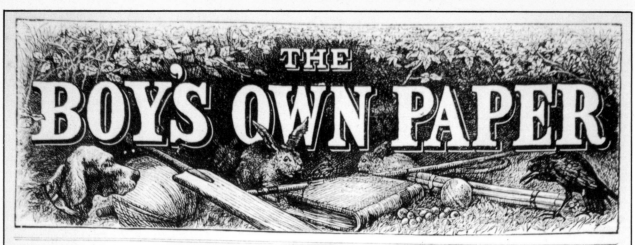

No. 91.—Vol. III.   SATURDAY, OCTOBER 9, 1880.   Price One Penny.
[ALL RIGHTS RESERVED.]

ADVENTURES OF A BOSTON BOY AMONGST SAVAGES.

By Ascott R. Hope,

Author of "The Amateur Dominie," "A Boy's Campaign," etc.

CHAPTER II.

On the following morning, the 22nd March, the Boston being almost ready to put to sea, a number of the Indians came as usual, bringing salmon, and remained idling on board, apparently from no other motive than curiosity. Captain Salter, a sailor all over, frank as well as blunt himself, was slow to suspect malice in others, and having probably forgotten all about the little quarrel of the day before, saw no reason for special precautions.

About noon Maquina, with a good many of his head warriors, came alongside, and, after going through the customary examination to show that they carried no arms, they were admitted into the ship. The chief, who pretended to be very gay and

"He asked me if I would be his slave during my life."

The Editor (4) with some of his contributors:
R. M. Ballantyne (1), J. G. Wood (2), Talbot Baines Reed (3) and
the Rev. T. S. Millington (5).

*By the Author of "My First Football Match,"
"A Boating Adventure at Parkhurst," etc.*

CHAPTER I.—MY INFANCY AND EDUCATION—
HOW I WAS SOLD, AND WHO BOUGHT ME

*Talbot Baines Reed's first
serial. Opening pages of
chapters from his most famous
school story appear on pp.
56–57.*

"THEN you can guarantee it to be a good one to
go?"

"You couldn't have a better, sir."

"And it will stand a little roughish wear, you
think?"

"I'm sure of it, sir; it's an uncommon strong
watch."

"Then I'll take it."

These few sentences determined my destiny, and
from that moment my career may be said to have
begun.

I am old, and run down, and good for nothing
now; but many a time do I find my thoughts
wandering back to this far off day; and
remembering all that has befallen me since that
eventful moment, I humbly hope my life has not
been one to disgrace the good character with which
I went out into the world.

I was young at the time, very young—scarcely a
month old. Watches, however, as every one knows,
are a good deal more precocious in their infancy
than human beings. They generally settle down to
business as soon as they are born, without having to
spend much of their time either in the nursery or
the schoolroom.

Indeed, after my face and hands had once been
well cleaned, and a brand-new shiny coat had been
put on my back, it was years before I found myself
again called upon to submit to that operation which
is such a terror to all mortal children.

As to my education, it lasted just a week; and
although I am bound to say, while it lasted, it was
both carefully and skilfully managed, I did not at all
fancy the discipline I was subjected to in the
process. I used to be handed over to a creature who
took me up and examined me (as if he were a
policeman and a magistrate combined), and according as I answered his questions he exlaimed,
"You're going too fast," or "You're going too
slow," and with that he set himself to "regulate"
me, as he called it. I was ordered to turn round,
take off my coat, and submit my poor shoulders to
his instrument of correction. But why need I
describe this experience to boys? *They* know what
"regulating" means as well as I do!

Well, in due time, I profited by the instructions
received, and one day my tutor, after the usual
examination, grumpily told me, "You're right at
last; you can go." And I did go, and I've been going
ever since.

The troubles of my infancy, however, were not all
over. I discovered at a very early age that the one
thing a watch is never allowed to do is to go to
sleep. They'd as soon think of leaving an infant to
starve as of letting a watch go to sleep.

But to my story. Every since I had left school—or,
in other words, gone through my due course of
regulation—I had remained shut up under a glass
case, lying comfortably upon a bed of purple velvet,
and decorated with a little white label bearing the
mysterious inscription, "Only Three Guineas."
From this stately repose I was only once a day disturbed in order to be kept from sleeping, and had
all the rest of my time to look about me and observe
what went on in the world in which I found myself.

It was not a big world, indeed, but I could see I
was not the only inhabitant. All around me were
watches like myself, some of a golden complexion,
and some—of which I was one—of a silvery. Some

were big, and made an awful noise, and some were tiny, and just whispered what they had to say. Some were very proud, and showed off their jewels and chains in a way which made me blush for the vanity of my fellow-creatures—"dear" watches, the ladies called these—and others were as plain as plain could be.

Every now and then our case would be opened, and one of my neighbours taken out and never put back. Then we knew he had been sold, and we who were left spent our time in gossiping about what had become of him, and speculating whose turn would come next. A gold repeater near me was very confident the turn would be his, and so impressed us with the sense of his "striking" importance and claims, that when the next time our glass house was entered, and a hand came groping in our direction, I at once concluded it was his summons into publicity and honour. Imagine my astonishment, then, when the hand, instead of reaching my gold neighbour, took hold of me and cautiously drew me out of the case! My heart leaped to my mouth—or whatever part of a watch's anatomy corresponds with that organ—and I was ready to faint with excitement. I had always imagined I was to lie in that case for years, but now, when I was barely a month old, here was I going out into the world!

It made me quite bashful to listen to all the flattering things my master said of me. I was worth twice the price he was selling me at, he said; in fact, if trade had been good he would not have parted with me under three times that price. It was a relief

to think the repeater could not overhear this, or he would have sneered in a way to extinguish me altogether. As it was, no other watch was by, so that I was not very much embarrassed.

After turning me over, and feeling my pulse, and listening to the beating of my heart, and taking off my coat and waistcoat to inspect my muscle, my master's customer at last laid me down on the counter and pronounced the sentences with which I have begun my story.

"Then I'll take it," he said, and pulled out his purse. "Stop a bit, though!" exclaimed he; "I'd better have a chain too, my little chap will think more of that than the watch. Let me see some silver chains, will you?"

So my master went and fetched a tray containing a large number of tempting-looking chains.

While he was gone my new owner took me up again in his hand and turned me over and put me to his ear; then as he laid me down again he smiled to himself and murmured,

"Bless his little heart! how proud he'll be!"

I was quite taken aback. Who was this taking upon himself to bless my little heart and prophesy that I should be proud? Then all of a sudden it occurred to me this remark may have been intended to refer not to me, but to the "little chap" the gentleman had just now spoken of. So I recovered my composure, especially when I saw what a kind, gentle face my purchaser had.

He chose a neat, strong silver chain, which was forthwith, in accordance with the barbarous practice of the age, fixed to my poor neck. I could not help sighing as I felt for the first time the burden of bondage.

What had I done to be thus chained like a Roman captive, like a dog, like a parrot? But it was no use being in a rage. I swallowed my indignation as well as I could, and consoled myself with the reflection that every watch, even gold repeaters themselves, are subject to the same hardship.

Ah! I was young then, and my knowledge of the world was small. Many a time since I have blessed the chain that held me, just as the ship, could it speak, would bless the cable that saved it from the rocks. Take the advice of an old ticker, you young watches, and instead of rebelling against your chains, rather hope they may be strong and sound in every link!

"That will be just five pounds, won't it?" said my purchaser. "Here is a bank note. Never mind about doing it up, I'll just slip it into my pocket. Good morning."

And with that I was conscious of being lowered into a dark deep pit, and without time to bid my comrades good-bye, or to take a last look at my old master, I felt myself hurried away, I knew not whither.

This, then, was my first step into the world.

I lay untouched and apparently forgotten for several hours. Gradually getting my eyes accustomed to the darkness, and looking about me as far as I was able, I heard a ticking going on in a pocket not very far from the one I was in, which I at once concluded to proceed from the watch of my new master. Thinking I might be able to gain some information from him, I groped about till I found a small hole in my lodgings through which I was able to peep, and call.

"Tick!" said I, as loud as I could, to secure the attention of my fellow-watch. "Who's that?" at once exclaimed the other.

"I'm a new watch, bought to-day."

"Humph! How much?"

"Three guineas."

"Chain and all?"

"No; five pounds with the chain."

"Humph, I cost thirty guineas. Never mind, you're for the boy."

"What boy?"

"The governor's. I heard him say he was going to get him one. That boy will be spoiled, as sure as I go on springs; he's made such a lot of. Have you been regulated?"

"I should think I have!" exclaimed I, in indignant recollection of my education.

"All right; keep your temper. What time are you?"

"Seven minutes to six."

"Wrong! It's seven and three-quarters!"

"How do you know?"

"Because that's what I make it."

"How do you know you are right?" I asked, wondering at my own impudence in thus questioning an old ticker.

"Look here, young fellow," said the other, in an awful voice; "you don't seem to know you are addressing a gold watch that has neither gained nor lost a minute for five years! There! You may think yourself clever; but you're too fast."

"I'm sure I beg your—"

"That'll do!" said the offended veteran. "I want no more words."

I was completely shut up at this, and retired back to my pocket very crestfallen.

Presently I began to feel drowsy; my nerves seemed to get unstrung, and my circulation flagged. It was long after the time I had generally been in the habit of being wound up; and I began to be afraid I was really going to be left to go to sleep. That, by this time, I knew would be nothing short of a calamity. I therefore gave a sly tug at my chain.

"What's the matter?" it said, looking down.

"I've not been wound up."

"I can't help that," said the chain.

"Can't you let him know somehow?" I gasped, faintly.

"How can I? He's busy packing up books."

"Couldn't you catch yourself in his fingers, or something; I'm in a bad way."

"I'll see," said the chain.

Presently I felt an awful tug at my neck, and I knew the chain had managed to entangle itself somehow with his fingers.

"Hullo!" I heard my master exclaim, "I mustn't smash Charlie's chain before I give it to him. I'd better put it and the watch away in my drawer till the morning. Heigho! it'll be a sad day for me to-morrow!"

As he spoke he drew me from the pocket, and, disengaging the chain from his buttonhole, he laid us both in a drawer and shut it up. I was in despair, and already was nearly swooning from weakness.

He had shut the drawer, and his hand was still on the knob, when all of a sudden he exclaimed,

"By the way, I must wind it up, or it'll stop!"

With what joy and relief I saw the drawer again opened, and felt myself taken out and wound up! Instantly new life seemed to infuse itself through my frame; my circulation revived, my nerves were strung again, and my drooping heart resumed its usual healthy throb. Little did my master think of the difference this winding up made to my health and comfort.

"Now you're happy!" said the chain, as we found ourselves once more in the drawer.

"Yes; I'm all right now, I'm glad to say," said I.

"What's going to happen to us to-morrow?" I asked, presently.

"We're going to be given to the boy, and he's going to school;" so the gold chain told me. "Nice time we shall have of it, I expect."

After that he went to sleep, and I fell to counting the seconds, and wondering what sort of life I was destined to lead.

About an hour after I heard two voices talking in the room.

"Well," said one, and I recognised it at once as my master's, "the packing's all finished at last."

"Ah, Charles," said the other, and it seemed to be a woman's voice speaking amid tears, "I never thought it would be so hard to part with him."

"Tut, tut!" said the first, "you mustn't give way, Mary. You women are so ready to break down. He'll soon be back;" but before my master had got to the end of his sentence he too had broken down.

For a long time they talked about their boy, their fine boy who had never before left his parents' roof, and was now about to step out into the treacherous world. How they trembled for him, yet how proudly and confidently they spoke of his prospects; how lovingly they recalled all their life together, from the days when he could first toddle about, down to the present.

Many tears were mingled with their talk, and many a smothered sob bespoke a desperate effort to subdue their common sorrow. At last they became quieter, then I heard my master say,

"I positively have never shown you the watch I got for him," and with that he opened the drawer and produced me.

"Oh, Charles," cried the mother, "how delighted he will be, and what a capital watch it is!"

And she looked at me affectionately for a long time, for her son's sake, smiling through her tears, and then put me back.

Need I say that as these two knelt together that

night, their only son was not forgotten in their prayers?

So ended the first day of my adventures.

'Oh, take anything but that!'
An episode from the
subsequent adventures of the
Three-Guinea Watch.

UNDER THE ROD;
OR, SWISHING ANECDOTES

Cuthbert Bede, B.A.,
Author of "Verdant Green," etc.

HAS the reader seen the interesting and amusing volume published from the pen of James Brinsley-Richards, entitled "Seven Years at Eton (1857–1864)." It will be read with pleasure, not only by Etonians of the past and present day, but by all schoolboys, as well as by those whose schooldays are a memory and a recollection.

One of its chapters, "Under the Rod," contains several good "swishing anecdotes," as the author

happily terms them, in which Dr. Goodford figures prominently. When he had flogged one Smith in mistake for another, he calmly apologised for his error, and promised that the real delinquent should get off.

"I might tell how he once 'swiped' Sir Frederick Johnstone on the morning of St. Andrew's Day, ten minutes before the baronet came to breakfast with him, in his capacity as a Scotch boy, and how,

CORRESPONDENCE.

Lightheart.—1. Consult Armatage's "Book of the Horse," published by Messrs. F. Warne and Co. 2. Keep the canoe well oiled. 3. Wash your feet morning and evening.

Conquisitor.—You should spell your *nom de plume* with a z instead of an s. We answer one or two of your queries, but we cannot write essays in these columns. The best food for pigeons is not the cheapest—good grey peas, tick beans, maize, barley, rice, etc., and a little hemp. Fan-tails—small (say 12 oz.), long firm beak, head long and narrow and flat and smooth, no beak wattle, and little eye wattle. Lyell says it should look like a pigeon pressed into the shape of a ball. Legs longish, head back on root of tail, which should be long and broad. You need ocular demonstration of the carriage.

C. W. E.—The best way to prevent chilblains is to wash your feet in warm water night and morning.

Brighton.—1. To make your boots waterproof, varnish the soles with copal varnish and dose the uppers with castor oil. 2. Slip an india-rubber ring over each bottle before you put it in the box; this will prevent the glass touching the glass, and so save breakage. It is by far the simplest packing.

E. B. G. (Norwich), "A Girl," and Others.—You are quite eligible as competitors.

W. W. Alger.—Apply for advice to the Government Emigration Office, 31, Broadway, Westminster.

greeting his guest with exquisite *bonhommie*, he said, 'Well, Johnstone, here we are again!'" The familiar explanation of the Christmas clown was never more pleasantly expressed.

Mr. Brinsley-Richards also tells another "swishing anecdote" concerning Mr. Day, one of the assistant-masters, to whom a sixth-form præpostor came to say that a boy named Elwes, in his division, was to "stay," that is, to be flogged. Presently a second præpostor came with a similar message. "It's a pity for you, Elwes," said Mr. Day, "that two affirmatives don't make a negative." This remark reminds me of a grammar-school boy who was put forward as the spokesman of his companions, and asked the master to grant them a half-holiday for cricket, as it was a very fine day. "No, no!" hastily replied the master. The lad promptly said, "Two negatives make an affirmative. We are very much obliged to you, sir, for granting our request." The master was pleased with his ready wit, and gave them the half-holiday.

Many swishing anecdotes might be told of Dr. Busby, who died in 1695, after being headmaster of Winchester School for fifty-five years. His epitaph in Westminster Abbey does not record his persistent love for the birch, nor does it quote the familiar text as to sparing the rod and spoiling the child. According to Dr. Johnson, Busby was wont to call the rod his "sieve," and to remark that "whoever did not pass through it was no boy for him." In a clever design—wrongly attributed to Sir Peter Lely—that was published representing "Dr. Busby's chair," the coat-of-arms on the chair-back showed a hand brandishing a birch-rod, with the motto, "In hoc signo vinces."

One of the best etchings that George Cruikshank executed for Thackeray's story of "Stubbs's Calendar, or the Fatal Boots," published in the "Almanack" for 1839, depicts the scene where the hero was flogged at Dr. Swishtail's Academy. The swishing anecdote concludes thus: "Sam Hopkins, the biggest boy, horsed me, and I was flogged, sir; yes, flogged! Oh, revenge! I, Robert Stubbs, who had done nothing but what was right, was brutally flogged at ten years of age! Though February was the shortest month, I remembered it long." Dr. Swishtail is represented with arm on high, the rod ready to descend; while the face of the sufferer suggests that he might have aptly quoted "Hamlet" relative to a certain custom. Thackeray's school was the Charter House, and he does not appear to have retained very favourable impressions either of his school or of its head-master, Dr. Russell; for, although in "The Newcomes" he called the Charter House "Grey Friars," yet in his earlier works it always appeared as "the Slaughter-house." He also seems to have associated the ideas of a head-master and a flogger; for, in the scene just quoted, the schoolmaster appears as Dr. Swishtail—many of Thackeray's names are like those in a pantomime—and, subsequently he reappeared as "Dr.

Birch," whose "young friends," helped to make up a Christmas book. Similarly, when Thackeray had to coin a name for a schoolmistress it was that of "Miss Tickletoby," whose "Lectures on English History" were his earliest contributions to "Punch" in 1843. This name may have been partly suggested by Ingoldsby's

"Two Misses Tickler, of Clapham Rise,"

to whom the Jane, of "The Babes in the Wood," was to be sent to school. The fight between Biggs and Berry at "Slaughter House" was recorded by Thackeray in those early contributions to "Fraser's Magazine" that he wrote under the title of "Mr. George Fitz-Boodle's Confessions."

Two centuries ago students went from school to college at an earlier age than is now usual; and there were Dr. Busbys and Dr. Swishtails at every college and hall, who ruled with a rod which, though not of iron, was an instrument of punishment; and even when the rod was composed of nine stiff twigs, dedicated to the nine Muses, the poetry of the idea was wholly lost in the very prosaic use to which the nine twigs were placed. John Aubrey, writing in 1678, says that the rod was frequently used at Oxford—and he believed also at Cambridge—by tutors and deans; and that he knew right well that Dr. Potter, of Trinity College, whipped his pupil with his sword by his side, when he came to take his leave of him to go to the Inns of Court. Another President of Trinity College, Oxford, was Dr. Ralph Bathurst, who (according to T. Warton) often carried a whip in his hand, as he "delighted to surprise scholars when walking in the grove at unseasonable hours." In the statutes of that same college, so late as the year 1556, scholars of the foundation could be whipped up to their twentieth year. In the Paston Letters, of the date of Henry the Sixth, a mother writes to the master of a Cambridge college, begging him "to belash" her son, as his last master had done. It was Dr. Thomas Bainbrigge, of Christ's College, who is said to have been the master who flogged Milton over the buttery-hatch, though this humiliation of Milton has been denied by some historians. The future poet was a few months over sixteen years of age when he went up to Cambridge.

The Oxford Statutes ordered that any student, not a graduate, and under the age of eighteen, should be flogged in public for visiting inns, eating-houses, and wine-shops, where wine, and drink, and the Nicotian herb—commonly called tobacco—was sold. Hunting wild animals with dogs, and visiting the exhibitions of rope-dancers, actors, and sword-players, were also to be punished by a visit to the whipping-block. And it was there that Dean Walsh, of Corpus Christi College, Oxford, in 1554, soundly flogged Edward Anne for writing verses that were deemed to be heretical. "Corporal punishment" could be inflicted for numerous trifling offences at both Universities, and the under-graduates of those days must have passed a con-

CORRESPONDENCE.

Military.—1. The regiments taking part in the Light Cavalry charge at Balaclava were the 4th Light Dragoons with 118 men, out of which they lost 79; the 8th Hussars with 104 men, out of which they lost 66; the 11th Hussars with 110 men, out of which they lost 85; the 13th Light Dragoons with 130 men, out of which they lost 69; and the 17th Lancers with 145 men, out of which they lost 110. Total 607 men, of whom 409 were lost. 2. Lord Cardigan died in 1868. 3. No.

B. Arkell.—You could change foreign coins at any money-changer's. If you are in the City try Baum, in Lombard Street.

siderable portion of their academic career "under the rod." Possibly it was one of them, like Cowper's Boadicea, "smarting from the Roman rods," who was guilty of the free translation: "*Arma virumque cano Trojœ qui primus ab oris*—A man with a cane for his arms, and his mouth as prim as a Trojan's." This must have been the same freshman who rendered "*Anteponit tenuem victum copioso*—He places before them a thin man conquered by a stout one;" and "*Coctilibus Muris*—Cocktailed mice."

Flogging children as an aid to memory was an old custom not only in this country, where it played its part in the ceremony of beating the bounds, but also in the Western Highlands of Scotland, at least two centuries ago, where the whipping of children to record the boundaries of land was a custom connected with territorial property. When commenting upon this, in his "Highlands and Western Isles," Macculloch says: "Those who deal in Apollo, Baal, and Anaitis may, if they choose, trace this rite to the Spartans, who flogged their children every Monday morning in the temple of Diana, to prevent them from crying." The peasants of Anjou and Brittany are said to instil mnemonics into their children by the aid of the rod, a custom which may have come down to them through several generations. For, when Gillez de Retz, Marshal of France—who is believed to have been the veritable Blue Beard—was sentenced to be led in chains to the place of execution, and there to be burnt alive at the stake, on the twenty-third day of October, 1440, the date was impressed on the minds of all the children of Anjou and Maine by their parents soundly flogging them.

It has been wickedly suggested that if a schoolmaster who, in his fondness for the rod, resembles Dr. Birch, Dr. Busby, or Dr. Swishtail, and wants stimulus and variety, it would surely be a vast improvement to flog the master once a day, "pour le désennuyer." This might shorten the process of education, and lead to an entirely novel series of swishing anecdotes.

The Rev. William Budworth, Vicar of Brewood, Staffordshire, and master of the Free Grammar School, is mentioned (in "Nichol's Literary Anecdotes") as being subject to fits of melancholy, during which he was mildness itself; but when he had "the convalescent turn, a different change of temper took place, and he would chastise pretty severely." Yet it is also said of him that "he never once in his life sent a boy home with anything like a piece of buckram attached to him, common as it was with those famous tutors, Osbalston and Busby." Mr. Budworth's "morning face" must have been studied by his pupils very much in the same way that the "boding tremblers" watched the smiles and frowns of Goldsmith's village schoolmaster.

Lord Byron's advice was—

"Oh! ye who teach the ingenuous youth of nations,
　　Holland, France, England, Germany, or Spain,
I pray ye flog them upon all occasions,
　　It mends their morals, never mind the pain."

But this was advice that was given, and taken, two generations ago, when it was the fashion to instruct youths "under the rod." The system is now, happily, superseded, and the rarity of the punishment will considerably lessen the occasions for new "swishing anecdotes."

'The Mermaid': how she got herself into the B.O.P. cannot be explained. Whatever fate overtook such a brazen hussy was clearly richly deserved. But this was in 1881.

THE
BOY'S OWN PAPER

No. 147.—Vol. IV.   SATURDAY, NOVEMBER 5, 1881.   Price One Penny.
[ALL RIGHTS RESERVED.]

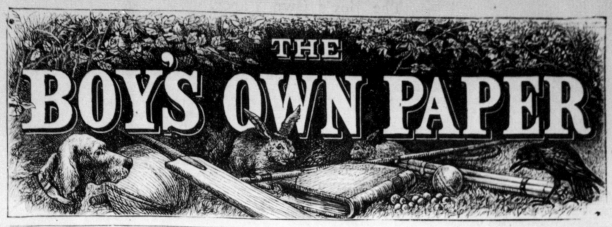

THE FIFTH FORM AT ST. DOMINIC'S:
A PUBLIC SCHOOL STORY.

By the Author of
"The Adventures of a Three Guinea Watch," etc.

CHAPTER VI.—MR. CRIPPS THE YOUNGER.

LOMAN was a comparatively new boy at St. Dominic's. He had entered eighteen months ago, in the Fifth Form, having come direct from another school. He was what many persons would call an agreeable boy, although for some reason or other he was never very popular. What that something was, no one could exactly define. He was clever, and good-tempered, and inoffensive. He rarely quarrelled or interfered with any one, and he had been known to do more than one good-natured act. But whether it was that he was conceited, or selfish, or not quite straight, or a little bit of all three, he never made any very great friends at St. Dominic's, and since he had got into the Sixth and been made a monitor, he had quite lost the favour of his old comrades in the Fifth.

As far as Wraysford and Greenfield were

Stephen and Mr. Cripps.

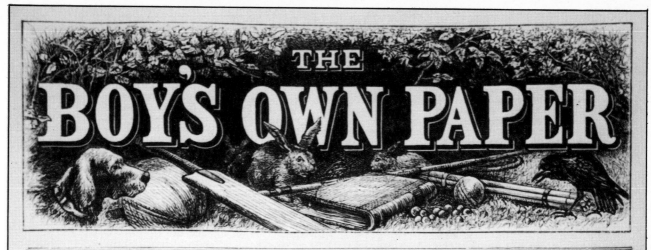

THE
BOY'S OWN PAPER

No. 152.—Vol. IV.   SATURDAY, DECEMBER 10, 1881.   Price One Penny.
[ALL RIGHTS RESERVED.]

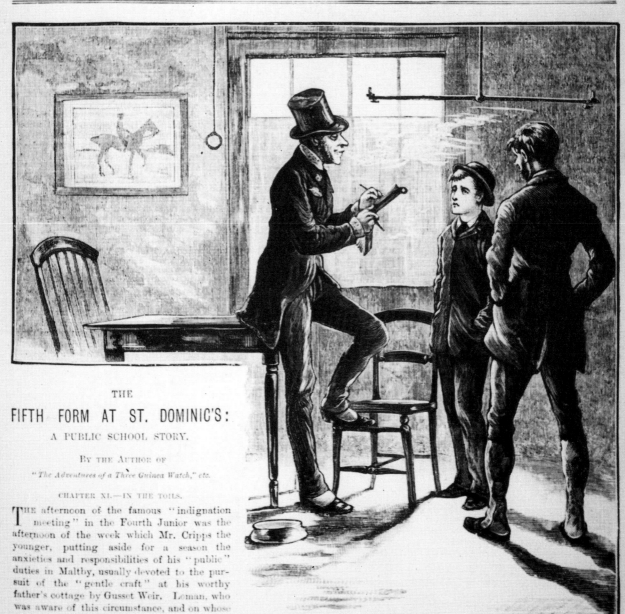

THE
FIFTH FORM AT ST. DOMINIC'S:
A PUBLIC SCHOOL STORY.

BY THE AUTHOR OF
"The Adventures of a Three Guinea Watch," etc.

CHAPTER XL.—IN THE TOILS.

THE afternoon of the famous "indignation meeting" in the Fourth Junior was the afternoon of the week which Mr. Cripps the younger, putting aside for a season the anxieties and responsibilities of his "public" duties in Maltby, usually devoted to the pursuit of the "gentle craft" at his worthy father's cottage by Gusset Weir. Leman, who was aware of this circumstance, and on whose spirit that restless top joint had continued to prey ever since the evening of the misadventure

"How he repented listening to that first temptation to deceive!"

EXPLOSIVE SPIDERS, AND HOW TO MAKE THEM

Dr. Scoffern.

GOOD reader, on announcing that I am going to teach you boys how to make the curiously explosive body, iodide of nitrogen, and when made to perform some amusing experiments with it, doubtless certain theoretical blackboard-chalking "professors" will stand aghast. "Give a dog a bad name, and hang him," says the proverb; and iodide of nitrogen has got a bad name, not because of its own misdeeds, but because of its family alliance with the terrible "chloride of nitrogen." Iodide of nitrogen, indeed, is curiously and captiously explosive, but then—at least in quantities far larger than I shall let you meddle with—its explosion does no harm. It is made by a wet process, and until dry will not explode at all. When dry it cannot be made to explode by contact with flame, or by touch with a red-hot poker; but just touch it with a cool body, or even let it fall upon a surface of water, and off it goes with a bang. Should you touch it when dry with your finger, it explodes, giving the finger a smart blow, but not burning. The finger, however, will be stained red, very much as it would have been had blood been smeared over it.

Before explaining to you how to make this curious body, I will tell you a short and true anecdote about it. Some years ago I occupied a house in the suburbs having a back court-yard, separated from some yet unoccupied building land by a low wall. The building plot was a great sporting ground for roughs, who, not content with using the spot as a playground, occasionally climbed over the wall, and, forgetful of the distinction between *meum* and *teum*, appropriated—more plainly, stole—any portable thing they found handy. Resolving to abate the nuisance, I bethought myself of iodide of nitrogen. Having prepared a sufficient quantity, I smeared it before drying over the wall-top, knowing well that so soon as dry any larcenously-disposed rough touching it would be smartly castigated without bodily harm. It was a hot day. Watching the progress of drying from an invisible outlook, the first incident was that of a big fly which had been imprudent enough to alight on the smeared wall. Crack! off went a dried patch of iodide; a violet-hued cloud ascended, and the fly was demolished. It is a faculty of the iodide to explode in patches. You cannot well explode a train of it, as you could a train of gunpowder; so the bulk of my explosive remained.

Continuing my outlook, rough boys and youths, of varying ages and dimensions, continued to flock in upon the patch of waste ground. Generally one or more favoured me by vaulting over my garden wall and exploring my back premises. But instead of doing so on this occasion they formed into groups and began to settle down to games, such as rounders, cricket, tip-cat, and kite-flying. Whilst debating in my own mind whether I should have any sport that day, my cat Tom suddenly appeared upon the scene and precipitated the issue. The season was autumn, the day was hot, the hour about 4 p.m. My cat Tom boasted a large circle of acquaintances. He was a magnificent fellow, a miniature Bengal tiger to look at, the terror of all neighbouring Toms, the pet of neighbouring tabbies. It would seem that either for purposes of combat or courting, he had an appointment for about 4 p.m. on the day in question. Making his appearance in the garden he yawned, to dissipate effects of sleep, stretched out his tail, put out his claws, then jumped on the garden wall, alighting on a patch of my iodide. A sharp explosion followed, and Thomas sprang into the air, a cloud of mysterious-looking violet-tinted smoke enveloping him, then back he came into the garden and retired moodily to his lair. The noise of explosion was so loud, and the smoke-cloud so conspicuous, that the roughs paused in their games. "He's a shooting of the cat," was the cry they extemporised, and they emphasised their view of the matter by a volley of stones launched against my premises. The volley intended for a back window of mine was badly aimed. Instead of smashing my glass the volley broke a pane for my next door neighbour. So he appears on the scene, raving and gesticulating. The row was by this time considerable. My friends, the roughs, having ceased from their games, collected in groups, finally resolving themselves into deliberative assemblies. It would seem that the result of debate was the resolve that some boy acquainted with my premises should edge on to my

Canada.—Fix one end of the board under a rail, and attach a weight to its other end. Then steam the line of the intended curve, and you will find it will gradually form. Instead of steam you can use hot sand.

T. Clarkson.—The "spirits" used in the glasses that give forth their sounds under the fingers of the street musician are simply water. Any fluid will do, and the instrument will keep in tune for a long time providing you do not play it in a shower of rain.

J. B. L.—The best thing to expand your chest is regular morning practice with Indian clubs. For diagrams, see Nos. 184, 185, 186, in the fourth volume.

I. R. A. M.—The present standard for the Hussar regiments is between 5ft. 6in. and 5ft. 8in., 34in. round chest, and 125lb. in weight.

A Lovely Mist.—To make birdlime, boil mistletoe berries till they begin to break, and then pound them in a mortar. Keep birdlime in a tin under water.

C. C.—All lighthouse appointments are made by the Board of Trinity House on Tower Hill. Lighthouse-keepers are generally yachtsmen or boatmen. It is not often that ordinary sailors take to the work. See an article on "The Lightship Mail" in last August's "Leisure Hour."

H. S. Black.—For a young man with capital there is certainly an opening in any of the Australian colonies; but careful inquiry should be made before investing.

59

garden wall and make a reconnaissance. It was done. Up came a bold urchin to the wall and laid hands on the top of it preparatory to making a spring over. But a shock awaited him.

I have already told you it is a faculty of the nitrogen iodide to explode in patches. Neither the accident which had befallen the blue-bottle-fly nor the subsequent accident to Tom, had exhausted or near exhausted my explosive resources. So bang! Off went another portion under the pair of larcenous hands laid upon it, with the bang, the usual violet smoke, and, I will answer for it, so painful a blow on the boy's two raw palms that our exploring rough had not experienced even under the ferrule of a schoolmaster. He screamed an agonised Oh! then waving his hands aloft I could see they were stained all blood-like; next running away, he, as subsequent events proved, rushed home to take counsel of his mother. Presently that lady put in an appearance, and not a little contributed to the clamour. But the explosion having occurred, it seemed to the assembled roughs there could follow no more. Acting upon this idea, several came up to the wall, laid hands upon it, and were more or less castigated. What began as a row ended in a riot. Policemen appeared on the scene, nobody could make head or tail of it. I thought it best not to appear. Darkness came on and there was quiet; but months and months after the cry arose whenever I chanced to look over my garden wall into the waste playground, "Who shot the cat?"

And now about making this iodide of nitrogen, which again I tell you, all bad character for danger notwithstanding, is perfectly harmless, if not handled in much larger quantities than I shall tell you to make or you would care about making. Take of iodine about sufficient to fill a saltspoon. Put it into a porcelain or glass vessel—nothing better than a tea-cup—and pour upon it about one tablespoonful of strong hartshorn, which I hope I need not tell you is ammoniacal gas dissolved in water. Stir up with a glass rod if you chance to have it, if not, with a bonnet straw or a splint of wood. Allow the hartshorn and the iodine to stand at rest for about half-an-hour, and then pour all upon a filter of white blotting-paper. A ruddy liquid filters through, and upon the filter remains a black pasty matter, which ultimately dries into a light powder. So long as it is wet and pasty, it cannot be made to explode, but once dry it cannot be touched without explosion. The dry iodide will even explode by the mere shock of throwing upon the surface of cold water. So you must have made up your mind what to do with it whilst yet in the pasty condition. For this once you shall distribute it in little patches over a sheet of blotting-paper. The patches may be about two inches distant from each other. Thus distributed, you may, when the iodide is dry, generally succeed in firing off any one of the little patches without affecting the next.

It will be curious to note how the iodide will not

bang off when touched with either actual flame, that of a match, for example, or an incandescent body such as a red-hot wire. This is a faculty which it possesses in common with all its family relatives, such as gun-cotton, chloride of nitrogen, and nitroglycerine. Long after the discovery of gun-cotton, its capricious nature in regard to banging-explosion puzzled chemists, engineers, and artillerists not a little. Some times it would burn quite innocently, noiselessly; at other times it would violently explode. The reason was at length made manifest; all depended on the mode of firing. The greatest explosive effect of these things is now commanded by firing an explosive cap in the midst of them; so it is not the fire of the cap, as one might at first think, but the smart blow given by the firing of the cap, which causes the explosion.

Well, now, having cleared the way, it is time to talk about our spiders. Some of you can make fishing-flies, perhaps, a far more difficult matter than to make artificial spiders. Your necessary materials will be a piece of cork, a sharp penknife, and some stiff black bristles, such as may be found in a blacking-brush. Out of the cork you are to cut the spider's body, and the bristles are for the legs. Catch a spider and study the shape of the thing. Observe, I do not say "the insect;" spiders are no insects, though one not unfrequently hears young ladies—ay, even young ladies who have studied the "ologies" in schools—call them so. Catch your spider, I say; observe her well; count her legs; notice how the antennæ are set upon her pate. Then take your cork and penknife, and carve out a form as much like the spider's as you can. When this is done, hollow out the under part of the body, forming a cavity for holding the charge of iodide of nitrogen. Next dip the body in ink, and dry, so that it may be rusty black. It remains now to attach the legs and feelers, which you can do, making holes with a pin, sticking into each hole thus made the end of a bristle, trimming to the necessary length, and finally giving the necessary sharp bends to imitate what we may call the knees and fetlocks of a spider. The crowning deed now follows, and after our description will be plain. Having your iodide of nitrogen in a wet and pasty state, insert by means of a quill, cut toothpick fashion, or else a splinter of wood, the necessary quantity to fill up the cavities already made in your spiders. *Finis coronat opus!* The deed is done. At present and until drying is accomplished you may handle your spiders with impunity, but once dry, woe betide the incautious individual who dares to prod or step upon them. It is not that their explosion will do any harm, otherwise I would not have told you how to make them; but ordinary spiders meet their death as lambs do—meekly; they don't resent it with a pistol-shot, and that's the fun of the thing.

A word now about likely places whereon to lodge your spiders. They may be set to stand on any horizontal surface; but some of the best fun I have

THE BOY'S OWN PAPER

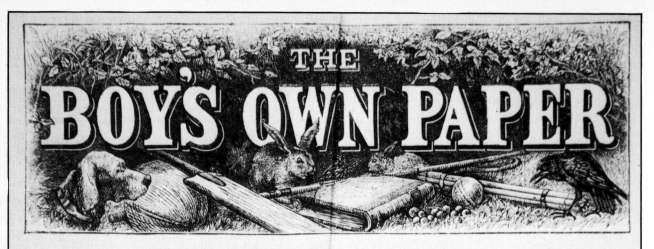

Vol. V.—No. 195.　　SATURDAY, OCTOBER 7, 1882.　　Price One Penny.
[ALL RIGHTS RESERVED.]

CHAPTER I.—HOW I CAME TO BE SENT TO
STONEBRIDGE HOUSE.

"It was perfectly plain, Hudson, the boy
could not be allowed to remain any
longer a disgrace to the neighbourhood,"
said my uncle.

"But, sir," began my poor old nurse.

"That will do, Hudson," said my uncle,
decisively; "the matter is settled—
Frederick is to go to Stonebridge House
on Monday."

And my uncle stood up, and taking a
coat-tail under each arm, established himself upon the hearthrug, with his back to

MY FRIEND SMITH
BY THE AUTHOR OF
THE FIFTH FORM OF St DOMINIC'S

I get into Trouble.

Enoch.—Candidates for appointment as army schoolmasters must, if civilians, apply to the Director-General of Military Education. They must be either pupil teachers who have completed their apprenticeship, or certificated schoolmasters. They have afterwards to pass an entrance examination to the Normal School of the Royal Military Asylum, Chelsea.

G. S. F.—By violent shaking and jerking of the mercury you can expel air-bubbles. Hold the tube slantingly.

Istatimas.—1. The Rorqual is one of the whale family. 2. Elzevir was the name of a firm of Italian printers, whose work has a great reputation for accuracy. 3. Many hundreds.

F. R. S.—We have given so many notices on how to make graphs that we must refer you to back numbers.

had with them has been achieved in another manner—by attaching them to a wall or door panel by the legs with strong gum mucilage. The very first member of female humanity who sees a spider thus wandering is sure to charge the little thing full thrust with a stick or parasol, or, as it may be, a broom. You know with what result, and it is very funny.

ASSOCIATION FOOTBALL, AND HOW TO EXCEL IN IT

C. W. Alcock,
Hon. Sec. Football Association

ONE of the greatest contributories to the general popularity of the football of to-day is its simplicity. One of the chief inducements which attract thousands of spectators—as is the case in some districts of England, more particularly in the north, and in other parts of the United Kingdom—is the readiness with which every detail of the game can be, if not thoroughly understood, at least followed and appreciated by the spectator of the most ordinary attainments.

Its rapid movements, its ever-varying changes, offer an attraction which few other of our English sports present, and it is its advantages in this respect, its exciting situations, and the ease with which they can be grasped, that have conduced to the large gatherings on the occasion of football matches, to the favour it has gained among all classes, and, not the least element towards its success, the enjoyment with which it is witnessed by ladies, who weary over sports of a more complicated nature. And, indeed, nothing can be simpler than the machinery of Association football.

Come with me one Saturday afternoon to the Oval and you will be able to judge for yourself of the Association game. For your own sake, perhaps, it will be best to choose a good match; and if you want to see the perfection of play, it would be advisable to watch for an opportunity when a really first-class Scotch eleven is in the field.

You will see the game at its quickest from the kick-off to the call of time—not a moment wasted, every man working with vigour and confidence, and, what is the most important feature of all, without the slightest thought of self. You will see Association football as it should be played, with every detail carefully mastered, each member studying the welfare of his side rather than of himself. You will note how particular each forward is to pass the ball to a fellow when there is the slightest fear of his being tackled by an opponent—no selfish retention until it is taken from him by an adversary. What an utter absence of flurry when the ball gets near the opposite goal, and the time comes for the shot on which hangs its safety or surrender!

You will observe also how effectively the halfbacks and backs ever carry out the general plan of operations, not content merely with checking that impetuous rush of the opposite forwards, or with getting rid of the ball regardless of its destination. Watch how wary they are even when apparently hampered with the too close attentions of an enemy. There is no hesitation, no precipitancy; the main object is not to repel an assault, but to take advantage of it sufficiently to deliver a counter-attack; and you will see how accurately the ball is passed on to an outlying forward, who is off and away with it before the opposite backs have time to retire on the defence of their lines.

But I am getting, I fear, too soon into the science of the game, before we have quite mastered its rudiments. First let us take a view of the ground and its surroundings.

There is very little in the way of adornment, it will be seen. Four small posts, one at each corner of the field, represent what is known as the corner flag-posts. The first rule of the game provides that the length and breadth shall be marked off with flags, but to the ordinary eye there is no such embellishment, and there is nothing but a bare post symbolical of the law. At each end of the ground are the goals. These are different from those in use at the Rugby game, and merely consist of upright posts, surmounted by a cross-bar. They are embedded in the ground, but still more securely held in their position by guy-ropes on each side. A tape is sometimes used instead of the cross-bar, but the latter is much preferable, as it is firmer, and the tape is so amenable to the wind that it is often very difficult to decide whether the ball has passed over or under. Even with the bar it is not easy always to get wood that will not give considerably in the centre, as the posts are eight yards apart, and indeed there are many clubs whose goals are not strictly within the requirements of the law.

The whole area of the playing-ground is carefully marked off by a continuous line. In some cases it is customary to cut a small trench in the turf to represent the limits of play. This has one advantage, in that it is permanent, and cannot be mistaken even in the worst weather. It is not every owner of a football field, though, that will allow such a practice, and for ordinary purposes it is only necessary to mark off the ground with a white line, easily done with whiting.

A few yards outside the line, all round the groud are ropes, which form the barriers to resist the encroachments of over-zealous spectators. Nothing mars the success of a game more than the interference of the onlookers. So, evidently, think the managers of the ground, for, with a view to impress them with the comfort of their position, the authorities, you will see, with forethought, have placed wooden stands on the ground just outside the ropes—a great boon when the turf is wet, and one evidently appreciated by the spectators, to judge by the way the upper part of the ground, where the stands are two deep, is patronised. . . .

A few of the more eager spirits employ the few minutes that elapse before the last straggler arrives on the field to complete the twenty-two in wasting their superfluous steam on an old football, but the old stagers know better that it will be necessary to husband their powers for the vigorous tussle of the next hour and a half. While huge punts and shots at goal are engaging the thoughts of the more inexperienced, the older players are coolly chatting with foemen as if the last thought in their minds was the desperate struggle in which they are soon to engage . . .

HEADS OF OUR GREAT
SCHOOLS.

(Continued from page 8.)

1. Mr. Jex Blake, Rugby.

2. Dr. Stokoe, King's College School.

3. Dr. Baker, Merchant Taylors.

4. Mr. H. Weston Eve, London
University College School.

(To be continued.)

Left and right *'Schoolboy
life at Eton' – scenes from the
Lower and Upper School.*

Above *'Heads of our great
schools' (1884); 'A
promising outlook'.*

RED-FINGERED CYRIL
or.
The Russian Prince and the
Tartar Boy.
by
DAVID KER

Author of "Drowned Gold,"
"Ilderim the Afghan," etc., etc.

CHAPTER I.
FIGHTING A GIANT

"WHERE is the Russian dog who will dare to look a Tartar warrior in the face? Let him come forth and meet me!"

So spoke a grim giant who stood midway between two armies, which were facing each other on the great plain that stretches along the bank of the Dnieper, in South-Western Russia. The Tartars were making a raid into the Russian country, and the Russians had come out to drive them back.

Could those two armies come back today to their old battle-field, they would find some curious changes there. Along the silent river where their arrows brought down the wild-fowl that rose screaming from the thick reed-beds, steamboats now come puffing and snorting up to a broad landing-place overlooked by a large hotel. Where the wild Tartar horsemen once pitched their camp, steam-cars rattle across the finest railway bridge in Russia half a dozen times a day. The steep hill overhanging the river, which was then crowned only by a few hundred log-huts behind an earthen wall, is now covered with white towers and golden cupolas, and green domes and tall pillars, and terraced gardens and brightly-painted houses, and all the splendour of the great city of Kief.

But all this was still a long way off when the Tartar giant uttered his challenge. In England, Saxon and Dane were still cutting each other's throats. America was not even known to exist. Greeks ruled in Constantinople and what is now Turkey. The Turks were fighting and plundering far away in the heart of Asia. Russia (which had only begun to be heard of about a hundred years before) was peopled with a race of fierce warriors—very much like the Zulus of our own time—fighting with all their neighbours, and worshipping "Peroon, the thunder-god," whose hideous idol looked down upon them that day from the fortress-hill. . . .

SAFETY BICYCLES

Rev. G. Herbert, M.A.,
One of the Chief Consuls of the Cyclists' Touring Club,
Author of "On Cycles and Cycling," etc.

PART I.

DURING the last two seasons the popularity of the various kinds of safety bicycles has increased to such an extent that they seem likely to supplant the ordinary bicycle for road riding; whilst many old bicycle riders, who had taken to the tricycle owing to its greater safety, have returned to the bicycle now that the new type of machine offers them the security they desire.

It seems, therefore, desirable that I should supplement the article I wrote, in the early part of last year, on cycles generally by a special article on the various forms of safety machines.

Broadly, we may divide the safety machines into three classes.

1. The oldest class, driven by levers, and so arranged as to throw the centre of gravity well back.

2. The dwarf machines, in shape and general arrangement resembling the ordinary bicycle,

'The Special Facile' safety bicycle (1887).

driven, however, by two chains, one on each side of the front wheel.

3. A class of machine known as the "Rover" type, from the first of that kind that earned for itself a reputation.

Besides these there are a few with a little wheel in front and a larger driving-wheel behind, looking not unlike a small ordinary bicycle reversed, with a sloping pillar and bicycle handles rising out of the small front wheel. They, however, do not appear to have made much way, and seem hardly deserving of a class to themselves.

In the first class are two machines which have persistently held their own for many years. This fact is a clear proof that they must both of them be possessed of more than ordinary merit.

The first boasts of a somewhat quaint name, which I take it is a slangy adaptation of an adjective descriptive of its peculiar shape. It is called the 'Xtraordinary, and this I imagine is intended as a contracted form of "extraordinary," and certainly the word not inaptly describes the peculiar look of the bicycle and its action. I will try briefly to describe it and to point out its merits. In the first place it is a full-sized bicycle, and does not belong to the class of dwarf machines, though recently, in deference to the prevailing fashion, a smaller size has been made for those who prefer small bicycles.

But instead of the front forks which hold the axle of the front wheel being made vertical, or nearly so, they are made with a very considerable rake backwards. The consequence of this is that the rider has to sit much farther down on the backbone and cannot reach the pedals with his feet. As he cannot get to the pedals, the problem is how to bring the pedals to him. This has been ingeniously effected by a combination of levers, which not only brings the pedals easily within reach of the rider, but gives him much additional power by the judicious arrangement of the levers. The motion of the feet is not rotary but oval, thus more nearly approaching to the verticality of action in walking.

The two great advantages possessed by the 'Xtraordinary over the ordinary are the greater ease of propulsion gained by the action of the levers, and the immunity from what are known as "croppers." This somewhat vulgar piece of cycling phraseology refers to the throwing of the rider forward over the handles of his bicycle. It is an accident to which a bicyclist is very liable in descending hills, and when meeting an obstacle. The cause of it is not far to seek. Any one with a slight knowledge of mechanics is aware that a body will remain firm so long as the vertical line through the centre of gravity falls within the base. The very moment that line falls outside, the body topples over in the direction of the vertical through the centre of gravity. Practical mechanics, therefore, try to make those things which they desire to be stable with as large a base as possible, whilst at the same time they endeavour to throw the centre of gravity as low as possible. These are the two things which have been aimed at in constructing the 'Xtraordinary.

The next machine of this class, known as the "Facile," combines the two characteristics of dwarf and safety. Like the "'Xtraordinary," it is propelled by means of levers, which are, however, somewhat differently arranged from those of the larger machine. In its general build it differs a good deal from the ordinary type of bicycle. These have a very small back wheel very near the front wheel. The Facile has a large back wheel some distance from the front wheel. Thus the wheel base is longer and the stability consequently much greater.

As in the "'Xtraordinary," the rider sits farther back; in addition to this his feet are considerably below the pedals, so that in this case also the problem to be solved is how to bring the pedals to the feet, since the feet cannot reach the pedals. In this case the levers have to be lower, as the feet are so much below the cranks owing to the smallness of the front wheel. This is effected by prolonging the front forks beyond the axle-bearings and curving them well to the front. To the end of each of these prolonged forks a strong lever, nearly horizontal is fixed by a pin, on which it works freely. The other end of this lever is divided, bending upwards; the two divisions are connected by a small bar coated with rubber, which acts as the pedal. As in the case of the "'Xtraordinary," the crank of the front wheel is attached to the lever. Here, however, a small rod intervenes, which is attached at one end to the crank, at the other to the centre of the lever, in such a manner that all can move freely about the points of attachment.

The lever could have been attached directly to the crank, as in the case of the "'Xtraordinary," but the pedal would have then been too high for the feet to reach. The rod interposed brings it to the proper position, and as it is adjustable, it admits of the machine being adapted to riders of different length of leg. It is this which makes his bicycle a very good one for boys, because, as they grow, the pedal can be adjusted to their increased height.

The front wheel being small, it becomes necessary when any speed is required to pedal very fast. This is certainly somewhat of a drawback, but not so great as at first sight would appear, because, unlike an ordinary bicycle, it is not necessary to carry the foot all the way round with the pedal, bending the ankle, but it is quite sufficient just to tap sharply the pedal as it begins to fall. By this means the foot rests between the strokes, and the action is not really much more rapid and is certainly far easier than the action of driving an ordinary pedal all round its circuit.

'Shortening in cable' by Louis Wain: the following year (1888) an article entitled 'Why I am a landlubber' positively discouraged boys from going to sea.
Opposite page In the poem that accompanied this drawing ('Two views of winter') the rich boy gives a penny to the poor boy. When the poor boy dies and is buried in a nameless grave his soul goes to heaven and is 'set from its sorrows free'. In heaven he is asked who has been kind to him. He names the rich boy.

DOG WITH A BAD NAME

Talbot Baines Reed

CHAPTER IV.—GONE AGAIN.

'I draw the line at homicide.'

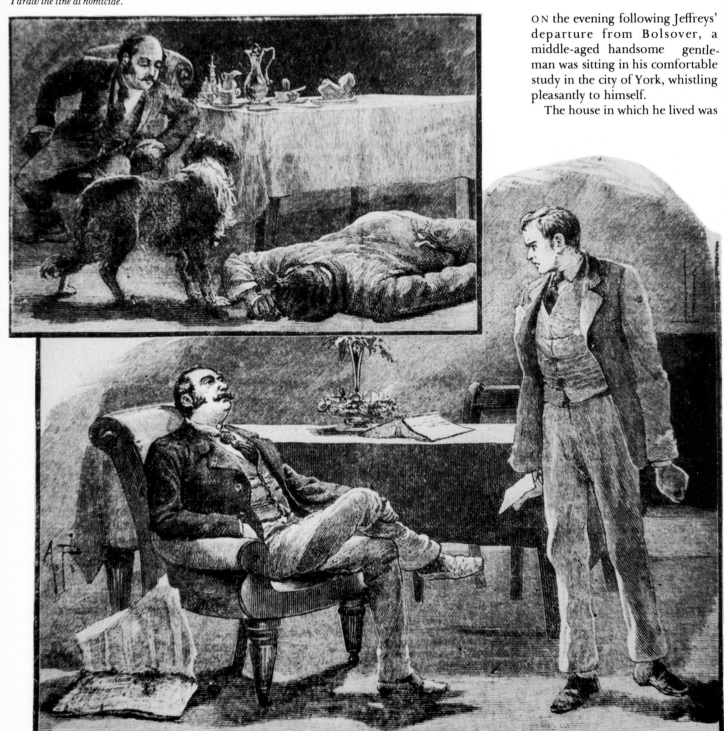

ON the evening following Jeffreys' departure from Bolsover, a middle-aged handsome gentleman was sitting in his comfortable study in the city of York, whistling pleasantly to himself.

The house in which he lived was

a small one; yet roomy enough for an old bachelor. And what it wanted in size it made up for in the elegance and luxury of its furniture and adornments.

Mr. Halgrove was evidently a connoisseur in the art of making himself comfortable. Everything about him was of the best, and bespoke not only a man of taste but a man of means. The books on the shelves—and where can you find any furniture to match a well-filled bookcase?—were well chosen and well bound. The pictures on the walls were all works of art and most tastefully hung. The knickknacks scattered about the room were ornamental as well as useful. Even the collie dog which lay luxuriously on the hearthrug with one eye half open was as beautiful as he was faithful.

Mr. Halgrove whistled pleasantly to himself as he stirred his coffee and glanced down the columns of the London paper.

If you had looked over his shoulder you would have come to the conclusion that Mr. Halgrove's idea of what was interesting in a newspaper and your own by no means coincided. He was in fact reading the money article and running his eye skilfully among the mazes of the stocks and shares there reported.

You could almost tell by the tones of his whistling that his scrutiny was satisfactory. Now and then, in a moment of special abstraction, the music ceased for a second, but went on again as cheerfully as ever. The dog on the hearth began to wish the newspaper at Jericho; for he could never sleep as long as his master whistled, and it bored him to keep an eye open for such a long time together.

Suddenly, however, the whistling did cease; but in an abrupt way which made Julius open both his eyes and prick both his ears. This was something out of the usual course of things. One minute, two, three passed before the music began again; and by that time Mr. Halgrove had swallowed his coffee and tossed the paper into the basket.

Julius hated anything out of the usual course, and he looked up at his master with a little whimper of remonstrance.

"All right, Julius," said Mr. Halgrove, patting the dog's nose with the toe of his slipper; "all right, it's only five thousand gone wrong—nothing!"

Julius wasn't quite satisfied yet, and moved out of reach of the slipper and sulked, with his face to the door.

"Nothing," repeated Mr. Halgrove, whistling a few bars and relapsing again into silence.

Julius was not disposed to argue the point, and gave the least possible inclination of his tail to show that he heard, but was not going to answer.

"If it was our money," continued Mr. Halgrove, still addressing the dog, "it would have been awkward, wouldn't it? But it's not. Accidents will happen: and if we do our best, who's to blame us?"

Julius yawned evasively.

"Whatever induced old Jeffreys to saddle me for

life with that son of his," continued Mr. Halgrove, "and his paltry five thousand pounds? A cheerful legacy, that—and the money's as idiotic as the boy. It's not my fault that it's gone wrong and he's stranded. Old Jeffreys did say something about putting it into consols, certainly, so as to be safe. But how was I to know Terra del Fuegians weren't as safe as consols? and a chance of fifteen per cent? A fellow can't be guardian to an idiot for nothing; and how in the world is the interest on five thousand in the funds to keep him at school and cover me too? Now he's got to live on the interest of nothing at all. Whew!"

The dog looked round to inquire if this last whistle had been intended for him or no one in particular. And satisfying himself it was the latter, he sniffed and dropped off into a doze.

"At all events, Bolsover's cheap and out of the way. Fancy the booby at home here, eating his head off and scaring every one with the sight of his face. Hum! I must be generous, I suppose, and keep him at school in spite of the Terra del Fuegians."

Mr. Halgrove had come to this benevolent conclusion and was proceeding to light a cigar, when Julius started up and gave a most ungentlemanly bark.

"Be quiet, sir, and lie down," said his master.

The dog looked round at the speaker and swung his tail excitedly to and fro.

"What's the matter?" asked Mr. Halgrove.

Julius replied by another bark, short and sharp, and walked to the door.

Now this was a very unusual proceeding on the part of Julius. As a rule he was a most lymphatic dog, and would scarcely have looked round at the Lord Mayor of York himself had he sailed into the room in all his robes of office. Nor did he ever make it his business to bark at beggars or stray members of his own species. Indeed, he would have thought twice before condescending to take notice even of a burglar.

What, then, was putting him so much out of his ordinary aristocratic way tonight?

"Some caller," said Mr. Halgrove, "and I've not a cigar left to offer him!"

There was a ring at the hall door and a man's voice in the hall. Next moment the study door opened, and amid the frantic rejoicings of Julius, John Jeffreys walked into the presence of his guardian.

He was haggard and travel-stained, and Mr. Halgrove, in the midst of his astonishment, noticed that his boots were nearly to pieces. Bolsover was fifty-five miles from York, and the roads were rough and stony.

The guardian, whatever astonishment he felt at this unexpected apparition, gave no sign of it in his face, as he sat back in his chair and took several quiet whiffs of his weed before he addressed his visitor.

"Ah!" said he, "You've broken up early."

"No, sir," said Jeffreys. "Please may I have something to eat?"

"Help yourself to the bread and butter there," said Mr. Halgrove, pointing to the remains of his own tea, "and see if you can squeeze anything out of the coffee-pot. If not, ring for some more hot water. Lie down, Julius."

Jeffreys ate the bread and butter ravenously, and drank what was left in the coffee-pot and milk jug.

Mr. Halgrove went on with his cigar, watching his ward curiously.

"The roads are rough for walking this time of the year," observed he.

"Yes," said Jeffreys; "I've walked all the way."

"Good exercise," said Mr. Halgrove. "How long did it take you?"

"I left Bolsover at half-past four this morning."

Jeffreys dropped heavily into the chair nearest to him, and Julius came up and put his head up between his knees.

"Do you often take country walks of this sort?" said the guardian.

"No, sir; I've run away from Bolsover."

Mr. Halgrove raised his eyebrows.

"Indeed! Was it for the fun of the thing, or for any special reason?" "It was because I have killed a boy," said Jeffreys, hoarsely.

It spoke volumes for Mr. Halgrove's coolness that he took this alarming announcement without any sign of emotion.

"Have you?" said he. "And was that for fun, or for any special reason?"

"I didn't mean it; it was an accident," said Jeffreys.

"Is the story worth repeating?" asked the guardian, knocking the ash off the end of the cigar, and settling himself in his chair.

Jeffreys told the story in a blundering mixed-up way, but quite clearly enough for Mr. Halgrove.

"So you meant to run at him, though you didn't mean to kill him?" said he, when the narrative was ended.

"I did not mean to kill him," repeated the boy, doggedly.

"Of course it would not occur to you that you were twice his size and weight, and that running over him meant—well, manslaughter."

"I never thought it for a moment—not for a moment."

"Was the accident fatal at once, may I ask?"

"No, sir; he was brought to the school insensible, and remained so for more than twelve hours. Then he became conscious, and seemed to be doing well."

"A temporary rally, I suppose?" observed the guardian.

Jeffreys' mouth worked uneasily, and his pale brow became overcast again.

"No, I believe if it hadn't been for me he might have recovered."

"Indeed," said the other, once more raising his eyebrows; "what further attention did you bestow on him—not poison, I hope?"

"No, but I went to his room in the middle of the night and startled him, and gave him a shock."

"Yes; playing bogey is liable to alarm invalids. I have always understood so," said Mr. Halgrove, drily.

"I didn't mean to startle him. I fancied he was asleep, and just wanted to see how he seemed to be getting on. No one would tell me a word about him," said Jeffreys, miserably.

"And that killed him outright?"

"I'm afraid it must have," said Jeffreys. "The doctor had said the least shock would be fatal, and this was a very great shock."

"It would be. You did not, however, wait to see?"

"No; I waited an hour or two, and then I ran away."

"Did you say good-bye to the head master before leaving?"

"No; nobody knew of my going."

"Of course you left your address behind you in case you should be invited to attend the inquest?"

"They know where I live," said Jeffreys.

"Indeed! And may I ask where you live?"

The ward's face fell at the question.

"Here, sir," faltered he.

"Pardon me, I think you are mistaken, John Jeffreys."

Jeffreys looked hard at his guardian, as if to ascertain whether or not he spoke seriously. His one longing at that moment was for food and rest. Since Saturday morning his eyes had never closed, and yet, strange as it may seem, he could take in no more of the future than what lay before him on this one night. The sudden prospect now of being turned out into the street was overwhelming.

"I think you are mistaken," repeated Mr. Halgrove, tossing the end of his cigar into the fireplace, and yawning.

"But, sir," began Jeffreys, raising himself slowly to his feet, for he was stiff and cramped after his long journey, "I've walked—"

"So you said," interrupted Mr. Halgrove, incisively. "You will be used to it."

At that moment Jeffreys decided the question of his night's lodging in a most unlooked-for manner by doing what he had never done before, and what he never did again.

He fainted!

When he next was aware of anything he was lying in his own bed upstairs in broad daylight, and Mr. Halgrove's housekeeper was depositing a tray with some food upon it at his side.

He partook gratefully, and dropped off to sleep again without rousing himself enough to recall the events of the past evening.

When, however, late in the afternoon, he awoke, and went over in his mind the events of the last few days, a dismal feeling of anxiety came over him and dispelled the comfort of his present situation.

He got out of bed, slowly and painfully, for he was very stiff and footsore. He knew not at what moment his guardian might return to the unpleasant topic of last night's conversation, and he resolved to end his own suspense as speedily as possible.

He took a bath and dressed, and then descended resolutely but with sad misgivings to the library.

Mr. Halgrove was sitting where his ward had left him yesterday evening.

"Ah," said he, as the boy entered, "early rising's not your strong point, is it?"

"I only woke half an hour ago."

"And you are anxious, of course, to know whether you have been inquired for by the police?" said the guardian, paring his nails.

Jeffreys' face fell.

"Has some one been?" he asked. "Have you heard anything?"

"No one has been as yet except the postman. He brought me a letter from Bolsover, which will probably interest you more than it does me. It's there on the table."

Jeffreys took up a letter addressed in Mr. Frampton's hand.

"Am I to read it?"

"As you please."

Jeffreys opened the letter and read:

"Bolsover, October 12.

"S. Halgrove, Esq.

"Dear Sir,—I regret to inform you that your ward, John Jeffreys, left Bolsover secretly last night, and has not up to the present moment returned. If he has returned to you, you will probably have learned by this time the circumstances which led him to take the step he has. [Here Mr. Frampton briefly repeated the story of the football accident.] The patient still lingers, although the doctors do not at present hold out much hope of ultimate recovery. I am not inclined to credit the statement current in the school with regard to the sad event, that the injury done to the small boy was not wholly due to accident. Still, under the grave circumstances, which are made all the more serious by your ward's flight, I suggest to you that you should use your authority to induce Jeffreys to return here—at any rate for as long as Forrester's fate remains precarious; or, failing that, that you should undertake, in the event of a legal inquiry being necessary, that he shall be present if required.

"Faithfully yours,

"T. FRAMPTON."

"Pleasant letter, is it not?" said Mr. Halgrove as Jeffreys replaced it in its envelope and laid it again on the table.

"I can't go back to Bolsover," said he.

"No? You think you are not appreciated there?"

Jeffreys winced.

"But I will undertake to go there if—"

"If the coroner invites you? eh?"

"Yes," replied the boy.

"The slight difficulty about that is that it is I, not you, that am asked to make the undertaking."

"But you will, won't you?" asked Jeffreys, eagerly.

"I have the peculiarity of being rather particular about the people I give undertakings for," said Mr. Halgrove, flicking a speck of dust off his sleeve; "it may be ridiculous, but I draw the line at homicide."

"You're a liar," explained the ward, in a burst of fury, which, however, he repented of almost before the words had escaped him.

Mr. Halgrove was not in the slightest degree disturbed by this undutiful outbreak, but replied, coolly.

"In that case, you see, my undertaking would be worth nothing. No. What do you say to replying to Mr. Frampton's suggestion yourself?"

"I will write and tell him I will go whenever he wants me."

"The only objection to that," observed the guardian, "will be the difficulty in giving him any precise address, will it not?"

Jeffreys winced again.

"You mean to turn me adrift?" said he, bluntly.

"Your perception is excellent, my young friend."

"When?"

Mr. Halgrove looked at his watch.

"I believe Mrs. Jessop usually locks up about eleven. It would be a pity to keep her up after that hour."

Jeffreys gulped down something like a sigh and turned to the door.

"Not going, are you?" said his guardian. "It's early yet."

"I am going," replied the ward, quietly.

"By the way," said Mr. Halgrove, as he reached the door, "by the way, John!"

Jeffreys stopped with his hand on the latch.

"I was going to say," said the guardian, rising and looking for his cigar-case, "that the little sum of money which was left by your father, and invested for your benefit, has very unfortunately taken to itself wings, owing to the failure of the undertaking in which it happened to be invested. I have the papers here, and should like to show them to you, if you can spare me five minutes."

Jeffreys knew nothing about money. Hitherto his school fees had been paid and a small regular allowance for pocket money had been sent him quarterly by his guardian. Now his guardian's announcement conveyed little meaning to him beyond the fact that he had no money to count upon. He never expected he would have; so he was not disappointed.

"I don't care to see the papers," he said.

"You are a philosopher, my friend," said his guardian. "But I have sufficient interest in you, despite your financial difficulties, to believe you might find this five-pound note of service on your travels."

"No, thank you," said Jeffreys, putting his hand behind his back.

"Don't mention it," said his guardian, returning it to his pocket. "There is, when I come to think of it," added he, "a sovereign which really belongs to you. It is the balance of your last quarter's allowance, which I had been about to send to you this week. I would advise you to take it."

"Is it really mine?"

"Pray come and look over the accounts. I should like to satisfy you."

"If it is really mine I will take it," said the boy.

"You are sensible," said his guardian, putting it into his hand. "You are perfectly safe in taking it. It is yours. It will enable you to buy a few postage-stamps. I shall be interested to hear of your success. Good-bye."

Jeffreys, ignoring the hand which was held out to him, walked silently from the room.

Mr. Halgrove stood a moment and listened to the retreating footsteps. Then he returned to his chair and rang the bell.

"Mrs. Jessop," said he, "Mr. Jeffreys is going on a journey. Will you kindly see he has a good meal before starting?"

Mrs. Jessop went upstairs and found Jeffreys writing a letter.

"Master says you're going a journey, sir."

"Yes. I shall be starting in half an hour."

"Can't you put it off till to-morrow, sir?"

"No, thanks. But I want to finish this letter."

"Well, sir, there'll be some supper for you in the parlour. It's master's orders."

Jeffreys' letter was to Mr. Frampton.

"Sir," he wrote, "I left Bolsover because I could not bear to be there any longer. I did not mean to injure Forrester so awfully, though I was wicked enough to have a spite against him. I am not a murderer, though I am as bad as one. If I could do anything to help Forrester get better I would come, but I should only make everything worse. My guardian has turned me away and I shall have to find employment. But the house-keeper here, Mrs. Jessop, will always know where I am and send on to me if I am wanted. I should not think of hiding away till I hear that Forrester is better. If he dies I should not care to live, so I should be only too glad to give myself up. I cannot come back to Bolsover now, even if I wanted, as I have only a pound, and my guardian tells me that is all the money I have in the world. Please write and say if Forrester is better. I am too miserable to write more.

"Yours truly,
"JOHN JEFFREYS."

Having finished this dismal letter, he packed up one or two of his things in a small handbag and descended to the parlour.

There he found an ample supper provided for him by the tender-hearted Mrs. Jessop, who had a pretty shrewd guess as to the nature of the "journey" that her master's ward was about to take.

But Jeffreys was not hungry, and the announcement that the meal was there by "the master's order" turned him against it.

"I can't eat anything, thank you," he said to Mrs. Jessop, "you gave me such a good tea only a little while ago."

"But you've a long journey, Master John. Is it a long journey, sir?"

"I don't know yet," he said. "But I want you to promise to send on any letter or message that comes, will you?"

"Where to?"

"To the head post-office, here."

"Here? Then you're not going out of York?"

"Not at first. I'll let you know when I go where to send on the letters."

"Mr. John," said the housekeeper, "the master's turned you away. Isn't that it?"

"Perhaps he's got a reason for it. Good-bye, Mrs. Jessop."

"Oh, but, Mr. John—"

But John interrupted her with a kiss on her motherly cheek, and next moment was gone.

Mr. Halgrove in his study heard the hall door close, and put some coals on the fire. Julius, too, heard it close, and whined, and went up to the study door and sniffed.

"It's all right, Julius. Exit my ward. Convenient ward to be responsible for, on my honour. A fool, a homicide, and the loser of £5,000! Hum! Called me a liar, did he, and wouldn't take my five-pound note? Eccentric youth, and remarkably ugly, very ugly indeed. Lie down, Julius, do you hear, and don't make a fool of yourself. He's got a sovereign in his pocket. A fool and his money, eh? Heigho! where on earth does Mrs. Jessop keep my fusees?"

From 'The Last of the Paladins' (1888) by Charles Deslys. Morgana, the décolletée lady, is trying to hack the leg off a blind assailant (she herself had blinded him). She is also trying to pour out a deadly poison. However, both are then killed by the collapsing tumulus.

A SOLDIER'S STORY

C. M. Archibald

CHAPTER I.—ENTHUSIASM; LOVE AND
WAR.

"DON'T be a soldier, my boy; it's a poor life."

So said my Uncle George, as gallant an officer as ever served the Queen. He was my beau-ideal of a man, and from my earliest childhood it had been my ambition to become "a soldier like Uncle George." I was now sixteen years old, and the question as to what profession I should adopt was being discussed in the family circle. My desire was to be a soldier, and I was anxious to enter the College at Sandhurst. The question was referred to my Uncle George, and he gave his opinion in the words stated. I was much disappointed, for I had hoped for his warm approval.

"But, uncle," I pleaded, "you have no reason to complain. You rose from the ranks, and you're now a major, and you've had a lot of fighting, and you've got medals, and you've never had any serious wounds."

He smiled at my boyish enthusiasm.

"Lots of fighting," he slowly repeated; "medals, no serious wounds—and that's what you call the glory of a soldier's life! Ah, my boy, you don't know what it is. How many of my old comrades are now alive? What did they make of their lives? Hard, bitter, anxious work—for what? for glory? No, for the sake of duty. Led into the army from boyish ignorance, of life, or from foolish enthusiasm, or from the desire of occupation, they realised, too late, the stern reality; but they did their duty nobly, sacrificing all for the sake of their country. And what did the country do for their widows and orphans? or for the maimed and enfeebled survivors? What are the honours some of my brother officers obtained in comparison with what they endured? No, my boy; nothing can compensate a man for hard, active service in the army during the best years of his life. "And yet," he added, "perhaps I should not talk that way; some must be soldiers, and I suppose the service has its bright side too."

A gleam of hope was returning to me, and I sought to interest him.

"But how, uncle," I asked, "did you become a soldier?"

"Did I never tell you?" he inquired.

"No," I replied; "you have told me lots of your Crimean adventures, and stories of the Indian Mutiny, and all the places you have been, but you never told me why you became a soldier."

"Well," he answered, "I suppose I must begin by saying that I had always an ambition to be a soldier. This my father encouraged, and I was educated with the view of qualifying for the army, but when I was seventeen my father died, leaving us in such reduced circumstances that all hope of purchasing a commission had to be abandoned. For some time I was very unsettled, but my mother induced a cousin of hers, the head of an East India house in Glasgow, to give me a situation in his office. I did not take to my new life, but a little bit of romance was thrown into it which sweetened the labour and fired my enthusiasm. I fell in love with one of my cousins, a pretty, warm-hearted girl, but her father looked on with disfavour, and finally I had to discontinue my visits to his house. I chafed a good deal; my relative, the head of the firm, was studiously civil, the chief clerk was sarcastic and cynical, and some of the juniors sought to be funny at my expense, for they got to know the story of my unappreciated affection. In my trouble one thought cheered me, like a sunbeam through a cloud—the country was on the eve of a war with Russia.

"I will enlist," I said, "and win my way to a commission. I will show my haughty relative what stuff the man is made of whose worldly prospects he considers too poor for his daughter to share."

I might not have carried out my resolution had not matters been brought to a crisis. My relative offered me the situation of correspondent in their Calcutta house. I was foolish enough to refuse it, for I thought his object was to get me out of the way, and I did not take the trouble to think of the consequences of my refusal until it was too late. When I told him, next day, that on further consideration I had decided to accept his offer, he replied that he had made arrangements with some one else.

It was one of my fellow-clerks, the son of a Scottish clergyman, who advised me to consider what I had done, and when I told him the appointment had been given to some one else, he said,

"You've made a great mistake, George; the governor is very *dour*; he never forgives a thing, and, depend upon it, he'll take it out of you yet."

His words came true. A few weeks later "the governor" told me he was not satisfied with my behaviour, that I did not seem to take an interest in my work, and, as I had refused an advantageous offer for making a position in life, he was afraid I must accept the usual month's notice, etc.

I was completely crushed, and I felt thoroughly humiliated. Then I worked myself into a state of nervous excitement, and when the hour for closing the office arrived, I had made up my mind I would enlist that very day.

The 77th Regiment was then stationed in Glasgow, under orders for the East, and that morning it had been announced in the newspapers that the regiment was to start the following morning at ten o'clock.

"It's done now," I said, as I left the office, "I'll enlist to-night, and be off tomorrow."

A few minutes later my resolution received a check. In one of the principal streets I met the young lady for whose sake I was enduring so much. She blushed, and hesitated, but I lifted my hat stiffly and passed on.

CHAPTER II.—THE MOTH AND THE CANDLE.

WHEN near the vicinity of the barracks I overtook a sergeant of the 77th, and told him I wished to enlist; but, instead of encouraging me, he did all he could to dissuade me. He depicted the dark side of a soldier's life, and urged me to wait until I had cooled down, and not to throw away my chances for life. I took the honest fellow's advice, and I promised I would wait for a week at any rate. He told me that in any case I could not join the 77th, as their complement was full, and recruiting had for some time been stopped. The regiment, he told me, was to start at seven in the morning, not at ten o'clock, and, as my ardour was keen, I promised to be at the barracks in time to see them march off.

Next morning I was early astir, and at a quarter to seven I was in the middle of a noisy crowd, surging and swaying near the barrack gate. There were numbers of crying women, mothers whose sons were under arms in the barrack yard, of whom, perhaps, they would only get one more brief glance; girls whose sweethearts had enlisted; people of the better class mourning over foolish lads who had been carried away by their enthusiasm; and many of the lower class, whose relatives, one might infer, would be no great credit to the British army. Every one was more or less excited and communicative, and seemed to have some special reason for being there.

For one young woman I was deeply sorry. She had but recently married, and, through hastiness of temper on her part, and obstinacy on her husband's, they had quarrelled, and only the previous night she had learned that he had joined the 77th. Her remorse and her excited cries were touching to hear.

A respectable working man, seeing I was affected, told me *his* story. His wife was dead, his son had been a pain to him, and now he was "off with the sodjers," having thus sunk, the poor man seemed to think, to the lowest depth of misfortune.

A poor widow was there, in the vague hope of seeing a profligate son, of whom she had heard nothing for several days.

Inside the barrack gate all was quietness, but the soldier's movements were duly communicated to the impatient crowd by some energetic young men with a smattering of military training, who got a glimpse through the guard-room wicket.

"They've got their great-coats on."

"The officers are inspecting companies."

"The colonel's mounted his horse."

"They're closing to quarter-distance column."

"The band is marching to the front," etc.

Then we heard the clear, ringing voice of the commanding officer, the band struck up, the gates were opened, and the head of the column was soon pushing its way through the excited crowd, who were shouting, and cheering, and crying, and pressing round their friends in the ranks. I was glad to push ahead to avoid the crush.

All the way to the railway station the troops were cheered enthusiastically, but, as the route was different, and the hour earlier than what had been announced, the crowd was not so dense as it would otherwise have been.

Many of the officers and men were married, and it was touching to see their wives walking beside them, realising for the first time the bitterness that a soldier's wife has sometimes to endure. Sobbing children clinging to their fathers; here and there a grim-faced soldier, with tears in his eyes, carrying a child, whom he held with tightened clasp. Girls, with red, swollen eyes clinging to brothers or sweethearts, who were trying to check or to conceal the feelings that were struggling in their breasts. Jaunty soldiers, who cheerily acknowledged the good wishes of the crowd; while others marched thoughtfully, hardly looking to right or left.

In the regiment there were many volunteers from Scotch corps (the 77th is an English regiment—the East Middlesex), and it was round these, and the recruits in the rear, that the groups were largest and the excitement greatest. I did not soon forget the impressions of that day.

When we drew near the railway station the scene reached its climax. A strong body of police was guarding the gates; the crowd saw they would not be allowed to enter, and there was a rush to say the last farewell, to feel the last pressure of the hand, and to be folded in loving arms for the last time.

Several women became hysterical, and fainted; the crush was tremendous, and once or twice the police seemed to lose their temper, but at last the regiment got in, and the gates were closed. Then a hearty cheer was given by some young fellows in the crowd, and the numbers gradually diminished.

CHAPTER III.—IN THE TOILS

All that day, and for many days after, I was very unsettled; but my mind was made up; I would enlist, and chance a bullet or a commission. I informed my mother of my decision, but she was so much distressed that I began to think I was foolish and selfish, and my resolution wavered. Then my relative became conciliatory, apparently anxious to atone for his former severity. My mother, I afterwards learned, had informed him of my resolution, and she begged him to save me from what she considered to be ruin and certain death. Then the probabilities of war diminished, and though our troops were being sent to the East, it was not expected they would take the field. New prospects seemed to open for me, and "the scarlet fever" subsided.

I was greatly delighted when, one day, I was invited to dine at my relative's, but I was cut to the heart when I learned that his daughter, who was so much to me, had been sent to a school in Prussia. Still, I worked on, resolved that one day I would win her.

Three months later the prospects of war were revived, and our troops, which, with the French, had been lying inactive at Gallipoli, were moved to Varna. The national enthusiasm again broke out, and the people clamoured loudly for war. I could not remain passive; I was destined, I thought, to be a soldier. I could never overcome my antipathy to the drudgery of office work, and why, I reasoned, should I spoil the happiness of life by labouring like a slave for my daily bread? So, resolved that no one would this time interfere with my determination, I asked for a week's holiday, and packing up nearly all my earthly goods, I sent them to my mother, telling her I could not restrain my natural impulse, and that I was resolved to win the commission I was unable to purchase.

Next afternoon I went to the principal recruiting rendezvous, and, after a few words with one of the sergeants, I pocketed the Queen's shilling. The sergeant was a garrulous fellow, but as keen as a razor, and I soon felt as if I were in the hands of a detective. I was not the class of recruit to which he was accustomed, and he seemed to fear that I would change my mind, or that some one would come to buy me off. He was resolved, therefore, to make it as difficult as possible for me, and as profitable as he could for himself. He gave me a glowing description of a soldier's life, and guaranteed me a commission in a few months. He was recruiting for the 20th (East Devonshire) Regiment, then lying in Colchester, and, he said, I might depend on being off to the East in a fortnight.

Then began my experiences of the glories of a soldier's life. He took me down a narrow passage, and, climbing a dirty and well-worn circular staircase, he unlocked a door, and ushered me into a long, dismal room, in which were eight or nine men, all more or less drunk and noisy. These, I found, were my future comrades, gallant recruits like myself.

"Now then, wake up," said the sergeant, "fall in."

"I'm going to have the squad 'tested and examined," he explained to me.

We were marched a short distance through the streets to a large drapery warehouse, and, after being kept waiting for some time, we were brought before a vulgar, pompous little man, who asked some formal questions; we took the oath of allegiance; he gave us what he considered sound practical advice, and then, signing some papers, he handed them to the sergeant.

"Now then, quick march," said the sergeant, and we were hurried away. This time we were marched to a dactor's, but, as he was from home, we were taken to another practitioner's, some distance off.

I was exceedingly annoyed at being thus paraded for the gratification, as it seemed to me, of idlers, who followed us about, and patiently waited for us in the streets. Our little party attracted considerable attention, and I was vexed to find that I was the chief object of attraction. When I looked at my fellow-recruits I did not wonder. They were not, so say the least, men with whom I would naturally have associated, and I was humiliated to think they were now my equals.

When we got back to the miserable den, the sergeant called for more drink, and then he left us, after locking us in. Later on he returned with two disreputable-looking characters, and told us he had ordered our suppers. While we were taking supper (such as it was), two detectives came in and scanned us all narrowly. They were, apparently, on intimate terms with the two latest additions to Her Majesty's army, but they spoke kindly, and gave them good advice. One of them was "wanted," but as it was a petty affair, and he gave some desired information, they said they would let him go, and "give him a chance of rising in the army."

I passed a miserable night. My companions were disposed to be hilarious, and were offended that I would not join their noisy bacchanals, but I purchase exemption by giving them half-a-crown, and I was allowed to lie down on a form. Sleep was impossible. The conviction that I had made a serious mistake was forcing itself upon me, but I resolved not to turn back.

CHAPTER IV.—REGRETS AND RESOLUTIONS

I spent the following day a prisoner in this miserable den, bitterly regretting I had been so hasty; but I found solace in condoling with two of my fellow-recruits, thoughtless, but good-hearted lads, who while slightly under the influence of drink, had been led into the meshes by the wily sergeant.

The sergeant had assured me we would start for Colchester early in the morning, but it was late in the evening when he told us to get ready. We were each provided with an old military great-coat, and, along with some others who had been enlisted that day, we were marched to the railway station. Here we were handed over to a sergeant of the Enrolled Pensioners, a thorough old bulldog, who lost no opportunity of showing us he was on the alert, and that to us his will was law.

We had a tedious, uncomfortable journey. On the way we were joined by some more drafts for the regiment, and when we got to Colchester, late in the afternoon, about fifty of us marched into barracks.

It happened that we were halted opposite the Band-room, and one of the cornet-players was playing "Home, sweet home." He played with much feeling, and I confess that I shed tears when my thoughts reverted to *my* home, and to what my poor mother and sisters would at that moment be suffering on my account. My visions were rudely disturbed by the angry shouting of the old sergeant.

"Can't you keep your ears open there, and do as you're told!" followed by a considerable amount of abuse.

I found I was the individual addressed, and that the adjutant had come to inspect the drafts. We were then ordered off.to be bathed, and to have our hair cropped.

Next morning we were medically examined, and those of us who passed were soon installed in undress uniforms, and set to learn the elements of drill and discipline. I made up my mind to do my best, and to learn everything thoroughly, and this was soon noticed and commended by the drill corporal in whose squad I was placed.

The soldiers were all active and bustling, and the cheerfulness with which they did their work, and their jubilation at going on active service, soon had its influence on me. My spirits revived, and when, three weeks after my enlistment, orders came to hold ourselves in readiness for immediate embarkation, I was as jubilant as any. I had written my mother, and I got her reply two days before we left. Poor soul! she had suffered much in body and in mind, but she was trying to make the best of it. Her cheerfulness, her hopefulness, and her prayerfulness impressed me very deeply.

The townspeople gave us a hearty demonstration as we marched off. It recalled to me the scene I had witnessed in Glasgow five months before, but my emotions were very different. In the interval I seemed to have become *a man*, with sober responsibilities to face. I had proposed to myself an ambitious and a difficult task. Who could tell whether I should ever achieve it? I was a private soldier in a Line regiment, and it remained to be seen whether I should ever be anything else.

UNCLE JEREMY'S HOUSEHOLD

A. Conan Doyle, M.D., C.M.,
Author of "The Fate of the Evangeline,"
"An Exciting Christmas Eve," etc.

CHAPTER I.

MY life has been a somewhat chequered one, and it has fallen to my lot during the course of it to have had several unusual experiences. There is one episode, however, which is so surpassingly strange that whenever I look back to it it reduces the others to insignificance. It looms up out of the mists of the past, gloomy and fantastic, over-shadowing the event- less years which preceded and followed it.

'He waved his whip enthusiastically at the sight of me.'

are hard at work, but as you are not actually taking out classes you can read just as well here as in Baker Street. Pack up your books, like a good fellow, and come along! We have a snug little room, with writing-desk and armchair, which will just do for your study. Let me know when we may expect you.

"When I say that I am lonely I do not mean that there is any lack of people in the house. On the contrary, we form rather a large household. First and foremost, of course, comes my poor Uncle Jeremy, garrulous and imbecile, shuffling about in his list slippers, and composing, as is his wont, innumerable bad verses. I think I told you when last we met of that trait in his character. It has attained such a pitch that he has an amanuensis, whose sole duty it is to copy down and preserve these effusions. This fellow, whose name is Copperthorne, has become as necessary to the old man as his foolscap or as the 'Universal Rhyming Dictionary.' I can't say I care for him myself, but then I have always shared Cæsar's prejudice against lean men—though, by the way, little Julius was rather inclined that way himself if we may believe the medals. Then we have the two children of my Uncle Samuel, who were adopted by Jeremy—there were three of them, but one has gone the way of all flesh—and their governess, a stylish-looking brunette with Indian blood in her veins. Besides all these, there are three maid-servants and the old groom, so you see we have quite a little world of our own in this out-of-the-way corner. For all that, my dear Hugh, I long for a familiar face and for a congenial companion. I am deep in chemistry myself, so I won't interrupt your studies. Write by return to your isolated friend,

"JOHN H. THURSTON."

At the time that I received this letter I was in lodgings in London, and was working hard for the final examination which should make me a qualified medical man. Thurston and I had been close friends at Cambridge before I took to the study of medicine, and I had a great desire to see him again. On the other hand, I was rather afraid that, in spite of his assurances, my studies might suffer by the change. I pictured to myself the childish old man, the lean secretary, the stylish governess, the two children, probably spoiled and noisy, and I came to the conclusion that when we were all cooped together in one country house there would be very little room for quiet reading. At the end of two days' cogitation I had almost made up my mind to refuse the invitation, when I received another letter from Yorkshire even more pressing than the first.

"We expect to hear from you by every post," my friend said, "and there is never a knock that I do not think it is a telegram announcing your train. Your room is all ready, and I think you will find it comfortable. Uncle Jeremy bids me say how very happy he will be to see you. He would have written,

It is not a story which I have often told. A few, but only a few, who know me well have heard the facts from my lips. I have been asked from time to time by these to narrate them to some assemblage of friends, but I have invariably refused, for I have no desire to gain a reputation as an amateur Munchausen. I have yielded to their wishes, however, so far as to draw up this written statement of the facts in connection with my visit to Dunkelthwaite.

Here is John Thurston's first letter to me. It is dated April, 1862. I take it from my desk and copy it as it stands:

"My dear Lawrence,—If you knew my utter loneliness and complete *ennui* I am sure you would have pity upon me and come up to share my solitude. You have often made vague promises of visiting Dunkelthwaite and having a look at the Yorkshire Fells. What time could suit you better than the present? Of course I understand that you but he is absorbed in a great epic poem of five thousand lines or so, and he spends his day trotting about the rooms, while Copperthorne stalks behind him like the monster in Frankenstein, with notebook and pencil, jotting down the words of wisdom as they drop from his lips. By the way, I think I mentioned the brunettish governess to you. I might throw her out as a bait to you if you retain your taste for ethnological studies. She is the child of an Indian chieftain, whose wife was an Englishwoman. He was killed in the mutiny, fighting against us, and, his estates being seized by Government, his daughter, then fifteen, was left almost destitute. Some charitable German merchant in Calcutta adopted her, it seems, and brought her over to Europe with him together with his own daughter. The latter died, and then Miss Warrender— as we call her, after her mother—answered uncle's advertisement; and here she is. Now, my dear boy, stand not upon the order of your coming, but come at once."

There were other things in this second letter which prevent me from quoting it in full.

There was no resisting the importunity of my old friend, so, with many inward grumbles, I hastily packed up my books, and, having telegraphed overnight, started for Yorkshire the first thing in the morning. I well remember that it was a miserable day, and that the journey seemed to be an interminable one as I sat huddled up in a corner of the draughty carriage, revolving in my mind many problems of surgery and of medicine. I had been warned that the little wayside station of Ingleton, some fifteen miles from Carnforth, was the nearest to my destination, and there I alighted just as John Thurston came dashing down the country road in a high dog-cart. He waved his whip enthusiastically at the sight of me, and pulling up his horse with a jerk, sprang out and on to the platform.

"My dear Hugh," he cried, "I'm so delighted to see you! It's so kind of you to come!" He wrung my hand until my arm ached.

"I'm afraid you'll find me very bad company now that I am here," I answered; "I am up to my eyes in work."

"Of course, of course," he said, in his good-humoured way. "I reckoned on this. We'll have time for a crack at the rabbits for all that. It's a longish drive, and you must be bitterly cold, so let's start for home at once."

We rattled off along the dusty road.

"I think you'll like your room," my friend remarked. "You'll soon find yourself at home. You know it is not often that I visit Dunkelthwaite myself, and I am only just beginning to settle down and get my laboratory into working order. I have been here a fortnight. It's an open secret that I occupy a prominent position in old Uncle Jeremy's will, so my father thought it only right that I should come up and do the polite. Under the cir-

cumstances I can hardly do less than put myself out a little now and again."

"Certainly not," I said.

"And besides, he's a very good old fellow. You'll be amused at our ménage. A princess for governess—it sounds well, doesn't it? I think our imperturbable secretary is somewhat gone in that direction. Turn up your coat-collar, for the wind is very sharp."

The road ran over a succession of low bleak hills, which were devoid of all vegetation save a few scattered gorse-bushes and a thin covering of stiff wiry grass, which gave nourishment to a scattered flock of lean, hungry-looking sheep. Alternately we dipped down into a hollow or rose to the summit of an eminence from which we could see the road winding as a thin white track over successive hills beyond. Every here and there the monotony of the landscape was broken by jagged scarps, where the grey granite peeped grimly out, as though nature had been sorely wounded until her gaunt bones protruded through their covering. In the distance lay a range of mountains, with one great peak shooting up from amongst them coquettishly draped in a wreath of clouds which reflected the ruddy light of the setting sun.

"That's Ingleborough," my companion said, indicating the mountain with his whip, "and these are the Yorkshire Fells. You won't find a wilder, bleaker place in all England. They breed a good race of men. The raw militia who beat the Scotch chivalry at the Battle of the Standard came from this part of the country. Just jump down, old fellow and open the gate."

We had pulled up at a place where a long moss-grown wall ran parallel to the road. It was broken by a dilapidated iron gate, flanked by two pillars, on the summit of which were stone devices which appeared to represent some heraldic animal, though wind and rain had reduced them to shapeless blocks. A ruined cottage, which may have served at some time as a lodge, stood on one side. I pushed the gate open and we drove up a long, winding avenue, grass-grown and uneven, but lined by magnificent oaks, which shot their branches so thickly over us that the evening twilight deepened suddenly into darkness.

"I'm afraid our avenue won't impress you much," Thurston said, with a laugh. "It's one of the old man's whims to let nature have her way in everything. Here we are at last at Dunkelthwaite."

As he spoke we swung round a curve in the avenue marked by a patriarchal oak which towered high above the others, and came upon a great square white-washed house with a lawn in front of it. The lower part of the building was all in shadow, but up at the top a row of blood-shot windows glimmered out at the setting sun. At the sound of the wheels an old man in livery ran out and seized the horse's head when we pulled up.

"You can put her up, Elijah," my friend said, as

we jumped down. "Hugh, let me introduce you to my Uncle Jeremy."

"How d'ye do? How d'ye do?" cried a wheezy cracked voice, and looking up I saw a little red-faced man who was standing waiting for us in the porch. He wore a cotton cloth tied round his head after the fashion of Pope and other eighteenth-century celebrities, and was further distinguished by a pair of enormous slippers. These contrasted so strangely with his thin spindle shanks that he appeared to be wearing snow-shoes, a resemblance which was heightened by the fact that when he walked he was compelled to slide his feet along the ground in order to retain his grip of these unwieldy appendages.

"You must be tired, sir. Yes, and cold, sir," he said, in a strange jerky way, as he shook me by the hand. "We must be hospitable to you, we must indeed. Hospitality is one of the old-world virtues which we still retain. Let me see, what are those lines? 'Ready and strong the Yorkshire arm, but oh,

the Yorkshire heart is warm?' Neat and terse, sir. That comes from one of my poems. What poem is it, Copperthorne?"

"The Harrying of Borrodaile," said a voice behind him, and a tall long-visaged man stepped forward into the circle of light which was thrown by the lamp above the porch. John introduced us, and I remember that his hand as I shook it was cold and unpleasantly clammy.

This ceremony over, my friend led the way to my room, passing through many passages and corridors connected by old-fashioned and irregular staircases. I noticed as I passed the thickness of the walls and the strange slants and angles of the ceilings, suggestive of mysterious spaces above. The chamber set apart for me proved, as John had said, to be a cheery little sanctum with a crackling fire and a well-stocked bookcase. I began to think as I pulled on my slippers that I might have done worse, after all than accept this Yorkshire invitation. . . .

JULES VERNE

THE CLIPPER OF THE CLOUDS

Jules Verne,
Author of "Godfrey Morgan," "The Boy Captain,"
etc., etc.

VI.—THE PRESIDENT AND SECRETARY SUSPEND HOSTILITIES.

'It is unbreakable glass!'

A BANDAGE over the eyes, a gag in the mouth, a cord round the wrists, a cord round the ankles, unable to see, to speak, or to move, Uncle Prudent, Phil Evans, and Frycollin were anything but pleased with their position. Knowing not who had seized them, nor in what they had been thrown like parcels in a goods waggon, nor where they were, nor what was reserved for them—it was enough to exasperate even the most patient of the ovine race, and we know that the members of the Weldon Institute were not precisely sheep as far as patience went. With his violence of character we can easily imagine how Uncle Prudent felt.

One thing was evident, that Phil Evans and he would find it difficult to attend the club, next evening.

As to Frycollin, with his eyes shut and his mouth closed, it was impossible for him to think of anything. He was more dead than alive.

For an hour the position of the prisoners remained unchanged. No one came to visit them, or to give them that liberty of movement and speech of which they lay in such need. They were reduced to stifled sighs, to grunts emitted over and under their gags, to everything that betrayed anger kept dumb, and fury imprisoned or rather bound down. Then after many fruitless efforts they remained for some time as though lifeless. Then as the sense of sight was denied them they tried by their sense of hearing to obtain some indication of the nature of this disquieting state of things. But in vain did they seek for any other sound than an interminable and inexplicable f-r-r-r which seemed to envelope them in a quivering atmosphere.

At last something happened. Phil Evans, regaining his coolness, managed to slacken the cord which bound his wrists. Little by little the knot slipped, his fingers slipped over each other, and his hands regained their usual freedom.

A vigorous rubbing restored the circulation. A moment after he had slipped off the bandage which bound his eyes, taken the gag out of his mouth, and cut the cords round his ankles with his knife. An American who has not a bowie-knife in his pocket is no longer an American.

But if Phil Evans had regained the power of moving and speaking, that was all. His eyes were useless to him—at present at any rate. The prison was quite dark, though about six feet above him a feeble gleam of light came in through a kind of loophole.

As may be imagined, Phil Evans did not hesitate to at once set free his rival. A few cuts with the bowie settled the knots which bound him foot and hand.

Immediately Uncle Prudent rose to his knees and snatched away his bandage and his gag.

"Thanks," said he, in stifled voice.

"No!" said the other, "no thanks."

"Phil Evans?"

"Uncle Prudent?"

"Here we are no longer the president and secretary of the Weldon Institute. We are adversaries no more."

"You are right," answered Evans. "We are now only two men agreed to avenge ourselves on a third whose attempt deserves severe reprisals. And this third is—"

"Robur!"

"It is Robur!"

On this point both were absolutely in accord. On this subject there was no fear of dispute.

"And your servant?" said Evans, pointing to Frycollin, who was puffing like a grampus. "We must set him free."

"Not yet," said Uncle Prudent. "He would overwhelm us with his jeremiads, and we have something else to do than abuse each other."

"What is that, Uncle Prudent?"

"To save ourselves if possible."

"And even if it is impossible."

"You are right; even if it is impossible."

There could be no doubt that this kidnapping was due to Robur, for an ordinary thief would have relieved them of their watches, jewellery, and purses, and thrown them into the Schuylkill with a good gash in their throats instead of throwing them to the bottom of— Of what? That was a serious question, which would have to be answered before attempting an with any chance of escape success.

"Phil Evans," began Uncle Prudent, "if, when we came away from our meeting, instead of indulging in amenities to which we need not recur, we had kept our eyes more open, this would not have happened. Had we remained in the streets of Philadelphia there would have been none of this. Evidently Robur foresaw what would happen at the club, and had placed some of his bandits on guard at the door. When we left Walnut Street these fellows must have watched us and followed us, and when we imprudently ventured into Fairmont Park they went in for their little game."

"Agreed," said Evans. "We were wrong not to go straight home."

"It is always wrong not to be right," said Prudent.

Here a long-drawn sigh escaped from the darkest corner of the prison.

"What is that?" asked Evans.

"Nothing! Frycollin is dreaming."

"Between the moment we were seized a few steps out into the clearing and the moment we were thrown in here only two minutes elapsed. It is thus evident that these people did not take us out of Fairmont Park."

"And if they had done so we should have felt we

'And what did they see?'

were being moved."

"Undoubtedly; and consequently we must be in some vehicle, perhaps one of those long prairie waggons, or some show caravan—"

"Evidently! For if we were in a boat moored on the Schuylkill we should have noticed the movement due to the current—"

"That is so; and as we are still in the clearing, I think that now is the time to get away, and we can return later to settle with this Robur—"

"And make him pay for this attempt on the liberty of two citizens of the United States."

"And he shall pay pretty dearly!"

"But who is this man? Where does he come from? Is he English, or German, or French—"

"He is a scoundrel, that is enough!" said Uncle Prudent. "Now to work."

And then the two men, with their hands stretched out and their fingers wide apart, began to feel round the walls to find a joint or crack somewhere.

Nothing. Nothing; not even at the door. It was closely shut and it was impossible to shoot back the lock. All that could be done·was to make a hole, and escape through the hole. It remained to be seen if the knives could cut into the walls.

"But whence comes this never-ending rustling?" asked Evans, who was much impressed at the continuous f-r-r-r.

"The wind, doubtless," said Uncle Prudent.

"The wind! But I thought the night was quite calm."

"So it was. But if it isn't the wind, what can it be?"

Phil Evans got out the best blade of his knife and set to work on the wall near the door. Perhaps he might make a hole which would enable him to open it from the outside should it be only bolted or should the key have been left in the lock.

He worked away for some minutes. The only result was to smash up his knife, to snip off its point, and transform what was left of the blade into a saw.

"Doesn't it cut?" asked Uncle Prudent.

"No."

"Is the wall made of sheet iron?"

"No; it gives no metallic sound when you hit it."

"Is it of ironwood?"

"No; it isn't iron and it isn't wood?"

"What is it, then?"

"Impossible to say. But, anyhow, steel doesn't touch it."

Uncle Prudent, in a sudden outburst of fury, began to rave and stamp on the sonorous planks, while his hands sought to strangle an imaginary Robur.

"Be calm, Prudent, be calm! You have a try."

Uncle Prudent had a try, but the bowie-knife could do nothing against a wall which its best blades could not even scratch. The wall seemed to be made of crystal.

So it became evident that all flight was imprac-

ticable except through the door, and for a time they must resign themselves to their fate—not a very pleasant thing for the Yankee temperament, and very much to the disgust of these eminently practical men. But this conclusion was not arrived at without many objurgations and loud-sounding phrases hurled at this Robur—who, from what had been seen of him at the Weldon Institute, was not the sort of man to trouble himself much about them. . . .

RECOLLECTIONS OF A FRESHMAN'S LIFE AT CAMBRIDGE

By a London Barrister

NOW, having told you all about our domestic arrangements, picture to yourself this humble and somewhat abashed individual sitting down about ten o'clock to tea. My next disturbance came from one of the under-porters bringing in my luggage. A friendly person, but not endowed with a great amount of capacity for duly ordering things or for setting down luggage right side uppermost, with no patronising airs, and no curious looks about the eyes. "Good deal of luggage sir," he remarked, after he had brought in the seventh of eighth package, and stood wiping his brow.

"Most of 'em brings up a goodish bit;" a dark saying which I afterwards interpreted to mean, "Most freshmen think fit to over-tax the energies of Mr. Under-Porter, who ought to be duly compensated." This I discovered, owing to a curious and otherwise meaningless pause which the said under-porter performed on his way out; half-a-crown he considered good compensation for work and labour done, and it made him my friend during the whole of my University career.

Note, dear reader, for reasons which I will presently explain unto you, that it is a very excellent thing to make friends with the mammon of unrighteousness in the shape of porters. The pile of luggage rather startled me; unpacking at that late hour was an impossibility, so I took out a few toilet things and my night-shirt, put out the light, and went to bed. Think of me now, kind reader, after my wearisome and exciting day, sleeping away peacefully the hours of my first night in College, a not quite full-fledged undergraduate. How shall I describe to you my sensations on waking up next morning? When any important change comes in upon one's life we never really feel the true effect of it at once. Its real meaning dawns upon us after the first excitement has worn off during the peaceful hours of a good night's rest.

The first day is a day of transition; we have not yet thrown off the old, we have not yet put on the new. But during the night hours the old departs entirely, leaving us for good or evil at the mercy of the new. Then with waking comes the morning, the new reality bursts upon us, the new life has begun. So it was on this eventful morning, when the memories of yesterday's bustle and commotion were banished by the ringing of the chapel bell. Soon afterwards Mrs. Johnson knocked at my door, bringing the necessary water, hot and cold, for my ablutions. She seemed in a better humour this morning, which I was pleased at.

While I was dressing I heard her busily making the sitting-room tidy and preparing breakfast. Presently she asked me if I was going to order anything for breakfast. Certainly, I thought I should like something hot. My thoughts, however, suggested nothing more exciting than a chop. So I informed her of my wishes in my most easy manner. I thought I was getting on comfortably now; but lo! even in so simple a matter as the ordering of a chop, there was a pitfall ready to swallow up the unwary and simple one.

In a few minutes Mrs. Johnson came to my door and told me that I had better give her an order for the kitchens. Well, there was nothing so very terrible in this, I thought, so I emerged from my bedroom, and taking a sheet of note-paper from my travelling writing-case, I began to compose the necessary order for the kitchens. I began thus: "Trin. Coll."—I knew that was right enough—"Oct. 22, 186–. To the Head Cook,"—I fancied this must show Mrs. Johnson that I knew all about it— "Sir, Be good enough to send me one chop for breakfast at 8.30. Yours faithfully, John B—. P.S.—I like it well done." Leaving this document on the table, I proceeded to complete my toilet. Again my worthy bedmaker resumed her occupations. Almost immediately I heard a giggle, which was at once suppressed; and then there came another knock at the door. "Please, sir, this will never do. I am sure you won't mind my telling you, but the gentlemen don't write orders like this. Just a scrap of paper will do, and 'Chop,' with your name and date, is all the cooks want." I blushed crimson, and wrote again as she directed me, and sent her off with the new order. Verily, I thought to myself, I know absolutely nothing of the ways of College life; there is a pitfall at every step; but I felt thankful to Mrs. Johnson that she had lent me a helping hand out of this one into which I had stumbled in my blindness; and I determined, as soon as might be, to get on good terms with her, confess my green innocence, and trust to her for guidance in the future.

And now, while my chop is cooking, please take a walk with me round the room in which I stayed for the whole of my time at College, and which makes so pleasant a background to the happy scenes with which that time was filled. A square room with a nice comfortable fireplace, a capacious mantel-piece, and over it a handsome glass. Low book-cases round two sides, a convenient sideboard with many cupboards, a goodly table in the middle, and some by no means uncomfortable chairs; the room itself being lofty and about twelve feet square. My bedroom was small, not more than a third of the size of the "keeping-room" (this is the proper name for the sitting-room), but there was just room in it to tub with comfort. Then, Mrs. Johnson being absent, we may pry into the third room, which belongs especially to her, the "gyp-room." It is pantry, scullery, and larder, all rolled into one, with a sink and water-tap, and a goodly-sized wine-bin. Now let us look out of that window into New Court.

Dear old court, you have not very many architectural beauties to recommend you, but I love those tall walls pierced with so many windows and lettered doorways. Ever and anon comes a merry laugh across the court, a hearty welcome as old friends meet again after the separation of the Long Vacation. In the centre a circle of greenest grass, sacred to the feet of fellows, but not to be trodden on by the clumsy-footed undergraduate. The staircases are full of life, at each door the shoeblack is busy surrounded by shoes and boots innumerable; gyps and helps and bedmakers flit hither and thither; white-capped cooks carry boxes on their heads containing matutinal refreshments for the inner man. I see one of them approach Letter L; yes, my breakfast comes. Tap. "Come in." My chop arrives, and is deposited by Mr. Cook by the fire.

Far right *'Death rather than dishonour', depicted by Alfred Pearse in 1889. The boy has been given ten seconds to make up his mind whether to join the pirates who have just captured the merchantman on which he is serving. He refuses – and is killed.*

DUMBBELLS, AND HOW TO USE THEM

IN our August and September parts for 1882 we gave a series of articles on Indian Clubs, which received a very hearty welcome from our readers. To those articles we refer such as are anxious to follow up the exercises given herein. We gave the clubs the preference as they are in growing favour amongst gymnasts, and in regular gymnasia are fast

driving out the ancient dumbbell owing to their wonderful power of quickly opening the chest and squaring the shoulders. We say "ancient dumbbell" advisedly, for it is at least two thousand years old. It was first introduced amongst us after being noticed on the Greek vases. The shape there given differed

afterwards, as shown on the vases, the athletes adopted the form (Fig. A), from which our present bells are derived. Curiously enough, these bells were used in springing and leaping, the power given by the weights being well known to the ancient as well as the modern records. Lawton's standing wide jump of 12 ft. 6½ in. in 1876 was done with

dumbbells in his hand, and Howard's flying jump on Chester Racecourse in 1854, when he cleared 29 ft. 7 in., was done from a block of wood, with a five-pound dumbbell in each of his hands, quite in the old Greek style. However, it is not with the ancient

somewhat from that now in use, but there is no break in the chain. The oldest form was that of a pointed capital D, the curved line being the handle;

but the modern practice that we have here to do. And we have no time to waste on archæology.

In the first place, then, two pounds is quite heavy enough for any dumbbell, and under any circumstances no bell, even for a full-sized man, should exceed five pounds. Heavy bells of fifty or even a hundred pounds have been used, but they

are now obsolete. For merely lifting purposes weight was all very well, but as soon as it was shown that health owed more to suppleness than rigidity, and exercises were designed in accordance with the new theory, heavy bells became simply impossible.

When they were used by the very strong they were found to give onesidedness, and by the weak they could not be worked with at all. Four pounds the pair is heavy enough for any boy, and most boys when they come to try the exercises will often wish that the bells were lighter. A word should be said as to price. Plain bells of cast iron cost from twopence to fourpence per pound; if covered with leather,

and thereby made considerably more comfortable to the hand, the price is from fourpence to sixpence per pound. For two shillings a lad can get a pair of bells that will suit him in every way and last him a lifetime. The shape of the bells does not matter; the heads may be round or octagonal, according to fancy, but the handle should be thick enough to give a

good grip, and it should be half an inch longer than the hand is wide.

Next, let it be clearly understood that dumbbell practice performed in a slovenly way does more harm than good. It is essential that the exercises be

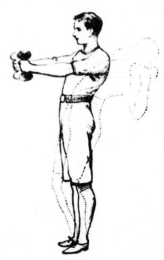

done in strict time, not jerkily, but quickly and accurately as if to the word of command. When the bells are required to be raised together, they should go up together, not one after the other. When they are required to go up alternately, they should go up alternately, at equal speed, the left as fast as the right; when they are to be held out in front together, they should be held out together, and change to the recovery as soon as the weakest arm begins to yield.

This brings us to our third caution. Never over-tire yourself. Ten minutes is quite long enough to practise at a time. Take the exercises in the order in which they are given, advancing gradually from the easy to the difficult, succeeding as you go. Do not practise after much head-work, and do not attempt any of the exercises before or after a heavy meal, no matter how light the bells may be. The best time to practise is immediately after the morning bath, and the best costume to wear is that of the mermaid, or as near an approach to nothing as is consistent with decency. Of course in gymnasia special dresses are worn; but, as absolute freedom is required, the model dress of the gymnast should be easily stowable in a glove-box.

'Our holidays – lunch time':
girls did not make the best of
themselves!

HARRY TREVERTON:

A STORY OF COLONIAL LIFE

Lady Broome.

'Lost in the bush!'

CHAPTER XIII.—LOST!

I HAD been living at Bachelor Hall for about a month, during which period old Dick and I had ground out many a hopper of wheat without any further displays of temper from him. I had worked hard, helping to clear ground and cart in firewood from the bush; my hands had become hard, my face sunburned, and my clothes had taken on the peculiar dirty-white tint peculiar to garments which are subjected to a scrubbing-brush and cold water. Indeed, I quite imagined myself to be the typical healthy young bushman, as I lounged out of the cottage one pleasant Sunday morning, leaving Mr.

Reeves busy inside writing letters, whilst old Dick pottered about as usual among his pigs and poultry.

As I have already mentioned, I had on several occasions accompanied old Dick to the bush, and helped him to cart in loads of firewood for the homestead, so I fancied I knew it well, and on this particular morning I determined to go for a ramble and do a little exploring on my own account in the direction of the firewood clearing. I whistled Rover, our splendid kangaroo dog, to heel, and off we started.

The country about Bachelor Hall was of the usual

hilly character—undulating ground covered with tall trees and rather open scrub. I had not the smallest intention of going more than a very safe distance from home, when suddenly old Rover started off in full chase of a large kangaroo, and I ran after them as hard as I could, to keep in sight of the chase. Fortune favoured me, for just as the dog was about to disappear over the brow of a hill, the kangaroo turned and came bounding along towards me, with old Rover in close pursuit, about ten yards behind him. As the boomer approached I stooped to pick up a stick, when he must have observed me, for again he changed his course, and in a few bounds he and the dog were out of sight.

In less than a minute I heard old Rover barking savagely a good way off, so away I went again after them, and very soon saw the boomer at bay, with his back against a tree, as upright as a man, watching the dog's every move, and ready, on the slightest opportunity, to give him the benefit of his sharp claws and feet. But old Rover was not to be taken advantage of; life a prudent dog he simply "worried round," watching for a chance to attack in the rear. With a view to assist my friend in his strategic movements, I commenced to fling sticks at the enemy, of which he did not take much notice until one of them hit him a good thump on the nose, which liberty he promptly resented, and, to my horror! made a spring at me. Fortunately, old Rover flew at him at the same moment, hoisted him over by the tail, and then, seizing him by the throat, very soon settled him.

Yes, there lay the huge boomer dead at my feet; and I felt not a little proud of my performance as an Australian hunter on that bright, cheery morning. I determined to carry some of my quarry home as evidence of my prowess, so, taking out my knife, I set to work to skin the beast, old Rover looking lazily on, no doubt under the impression that he had already done his full share of work, and might now take things easy.

After a great deal of trouble, I managed to skin the big beast; I then cut, or rather hacked, the body in two, and with great difficulty hoisted it on my back, taking a leg in each hand, which stuck out on each side of my head like huge horns, whilst the long thick tail fell back at an angle of forty-five degrees to the rear. It was a heavy burthen, but the prospect of being able to show it at the homestead encouraged me to my utmost exertions, so on I went, the proud possessor of at least fifty pounds' weight of kangaroo flesh.

After walking for about a mile, it occurred to me that I ought to see the clearing, instead of which, so far as the appearance of the bush was concerned, I seemed to be in exactly the same place from whence I had started. This was by no means a satisfactory state of affairs, for I was becoming very tired of carrying my game, and threw it down to have a spell. Having rested for a short time I made a fresh start, and on I went again until I felt quite tired out,

and still no sign of the clearing. Down went the meat, and once more I seated myself on a fallen tree, wondering how it was that I had not reached home.

Surely I could not have lost myself! It was an unpleasant idea, and I put it from me as quickly as possible. One thing was quite certain, however, that I could not carry the kangaroo any farther, and I resolved to get home as quickly as possible without it, for I felt an imperative need of changing my blood-stained, stiffened clothes, and, above all things, of getting a drink of water. I became suddenly conscious that I was extremely tired, and absolutely parched with thirst, besides which the flies attracted by the kangaroo's blood on my hands and face, worried me almost beyond endurance.

Rover had followed closely on my heels, and was lying panting at my feet, when a bright idea occurred to me. Jumping up, I said, "Go home, Rover; come along, old man! go home!" But Rover did not appear at all inclined to take the hint. Again and again I tried him, but it was of no use, he simply gazed at me and wagged his tail.

"What a stupid brute you are!" I cried, "if you won't go for being told, I'll just see if I can't drive you!" and I lifted a stick in a threatening manner, hoping to see him rush off in a bee-line for the cottage. But no, Rover was not accustomed to being beaten, and did not think I was going to begin now, so he just slunk behind a bush, and lolled his tongue out at me farther than ever.

It was very aggravating; only an hour ago I had looked at the dog with pride and pleasure; now, I felt deeply disgusted and annoyed at his stupidity. However, it was quite evident that I must depend entirely on my own efforts to regain the cottage, and I looked anxiously about, trying to make up my mind in which direction I ought to steer. It was by no means an easy conclusion to arrive at, for the forest was so absolutely uniform and monotonous that one place seemed exactly like another.

I looked up at the sun, and endeavoured to recollect in what direction it rose, having reference to the position of the cottage; but it was well up in the heavens, and I could make nothing of it—in fact, it appeared to be in the wrong place. The more I tried to fix my position the greater became my perplexity. Yet I felt certain I could not be any very great distance from home, even presuming that I had been carrying the kangaroo in the wrong direction, and I determined to try if I could not make myself heard by shouting. I soon found out, however, that to shout lustily with a throat absolutely parched and dry was no easy matter. I had not yet learned how to give forcefully the Australian "coo-e!" and two or three rough, croaking sounds were the only result of my best efforts.

Everything appeared to be in league against me—the position of the sun, the stupidity of the dog, the sameness of the forest, and the torment of the flies, which worried me most dreadfully. My heart failed me as I reflected on the position I was in. If I sat still I *might* be found in a day or two, perhaps sooner, and this is what I ought to have done, but, like many others who have gone through the horrors of being "lost in the bush," I found it impossible to remain inactive. Besides, it seemed so cowardly to sit down without making some effort to save myself, so off I started again, with Rover following at a respectful distance.

The plan of action I had determined on was to make the dead kangaroo my starting-point, and walk about two miles in different directions from that spot, and I hope in this way to come within sight of the clearing. My first attempt, however, proved a distinct failure, for not only did I fail to find the track to the cottage, or any track at all, but in retracing my steps I found I had also lost my starting-point, and felt more confused than ever.

By this time the sun had become terribly hot, my thirst was also increasing to a painful degree, and the hope of being able to obtain a drink urged me to another foolish attempt. I had heard that in travelling through the bush it was a good thing to keep one's shadow in a certain position, but I ought also to have recollected that, unless I knew exactly in what direction to steer, the chances would be ten to one that I should go wrong. However, I determined to try the experiment, arguing with myself that if I kept on a straight course I must surely reach somewhere. So I made another start, this time alone, for the dog had disappeared.

What torture I experienced as I rambled painfully onwards, not knowing whither I was going! The flies worried me nearly to distraction, and at last I tore off my blood-stained garments and threw them away. Fortunately, I had on some underclothing, or the sun would have scorched me to death. As it was, I felt that I could not stand very much more.

After walking for several hours, I found myself in a barren-looking ironstone range—no doubt farther from home than ever, with death staring me fully in the face.

It would have been a great relief could I have had a good cry, like a baby, but even this comfort was denied me, for the fountain of my tears appeared to be literally dried up, and I could only make a moaning, half-idiotic noise, as, in a state of semi-delirium, I called upon God to release me from my sufferings. With swollen tongue, parched and blistered lips, and aching limbs, I threw myself on the ground beneath a shrub. I had done my best and failed, and now nothing remained for me but to die—the sooner the better.

To any English reader it may seem well-nigh impossible that a strong, active lad, in perfect health and training, could be reduced to such terrible straits in a few hours. It must be borne in mind, however, that I had been walking all day, without food or drink, beneath the almost tropical sun of an Australian summer, and that I was absolutely exhausted with fatigue and excitement, to say nothing of a raging thirst and the torment of

Below *'The Balaklava Charge'* – *the veterans of the charge of the Light Brigade:* *'all that was left of them, left of six hundred'. Photograph published in the* B.O.P., *September 1890.*

thousands of flies. There was also the ever-present terror of meeting one of the most awful deaths—a death from slow starvation—which it is possible for a human being to suffer, and my mind was, I confess, quite unhinged and paralysed by the dread of such a fate. Let any one who thinks my sufferings may have been imaginary ask one of his Australian friends how long an English boy of my age would have been likely to exist under the conditions I have attempted to recall and describe.

For hours I lay moaning in my misery, and at last I either slept, or became unconscious. I remember that once during the night I was disturbed by the howls of a pack of dingoes, or native dogs, and that as they came very near me I feebly waved my arms, crying, "Not yet! not yet!" and again I slept, or fainted, I know not which.

When the day broke, and I roused myself up, I found I was considerably revived. A heavy dew had fallen and had moistened my parched lips and fevered body. Again the love of life sprang up in my breast, and again I determined to make an effort to save that life. As I rose to my feet I staggered like a drunken man, and could with difficulty ramble about in an aimless manner, for the renewed strength of mind and body which darkness and rest brought me did not last long under the old conditions of hunger and anxiety. Once more I became thoroughly exhausted, and threw myself again under a tree, moaning hoarsely through my parched lips, "Lost, lost, lost! Come, death; come quickly!" and then I became as unconscious as though the King of Terrors had himself mercifully answered my invocation.

'Suddenly he flung his strong arms right round my body': a later incident from Harry Treverton's story.

CHAPTER THREE
SEEING OUT THE CENTURY: THE 1890s

One of the reasons for the *B.O.P.'s* success was that it never missed a new idea or needlessly discarded an old one. Thus the 1890s saw a number of articles on how to make electrically-driven gadgets, but at the same time the tried and true, the pets, the models and the successful serial writers were kept on (even though new ones were introduced).

One of the best of the known writers was David Ker. He was War Correspondent for the *Daily Telegraph* and permanent correspondent for the *New York Times*. He had campaigned with the Russians and other armies and knew at first-hand the settings of all his stories, whether in Ceylon, Russia, Central Europe, Burma or elsewhere. In his obituary notice in the *B.O.P.* it was said that he wrote all his stories in minute handwriting on small sheets of very thin paper. Ker's stories included 'Champions of the Kremlin' and 'The Tiger Chief of Burmah: or the Adventures of Two Boys on the Upper Irrawaddy'.

The year 1890 produced surely one of the most ponderous titles ever concocted. This was 'George Freeborn: Sailor, Exile and First Parson of Aurora Island'. The author was the Rev. A. Baker, M.A., R.N., but the story was presumably a true one. The perils and hardships of maritime life were never glossed over by the *B.O.P.*, possibly because the paper wished to discourage boys from running away to sea under the impression that this was a quick way to fame and fortune. There were numerous pictures of shipwrecks. In 1891 Brangwyn's Academy painting 'Ashore' was reproduced, and the same volume showed a lifeboat setting out to what was indicated as almost certain destruction. At times the reader was hard put to distinguish truth from fiction. Was 'Pambardi: the Hooded Snake' by the Rev. D'O. Martin fiction? Or 'The Orchid Seekers of Borneo'?

Reginald A. R. Bennet, B. A. Oxon, gave directions for toys which were possibly less popular with parents than boys: 'How to make an electric trumpet', 'How to make an electric drum'. These models usually had the advantage that they could be built of odd pieces of wood, metal and wire; this was infinitely more satisfying than the later, more expensive, kit of specially prepared parts.

Training for athletic sports was for many years mere guesswork. A. Alexander, F.R.G.S., in 1891 said:

Masticate your food well in order to avoid giving too much to your digestive organs and avoid Pork, Pastry and Alcohol. After the afternoon studies a walk is desirable made pleasant by conversation with an intelligent companion. Do not talk about stereotyped subjects or harp upon your everyday work but endeavour to give variety to your topics so that your brain may have some necessary rest.

The same period contained a series of drawings: 'Artistic Studies for Boys of Taste' by Various Representative Artists, and a remarkable article on 'How to boil water in a paper bag'. There was also 'How to make a simple hand camera'.

The cold bath continued to be recommended as a cure not so much for the ills of the body as for those of the mind. In October 1891 'IN TIME (Hopeful)' is answered:

We are glad you have seen the error of your ways in time. Live well. Take lots of exercise and always have something to employ your mind. Cold bath every morning. Hard mattress. Not much bed clothing. Medicine: a simple tonic but not *iron*. Yes, Harness belts are very good.

The cold bath, of course, has much to recommend it, but its efficacy as a restrainer of impure thoughts may well have been over-estimated. Fellows' syrup was also recommended for those troubled with sexual fantasy. The prevalence of letters on this subject showed that the *B.O.P.* had the full confidence of its readers. Teenage marriage today usually requires a good underpinning of social security benefits (i.e. other people's taxes), adolescent sex requires compliant females, easy contraception and abortion, mobility and some privacy. As none of these were readily available in the 1890s most boys, at one time or another, gave masturbation a good trial. The *B.O.P.* view was that to have millions of boys unhappily masturbating was less satisfactory than to have their minds occupied with other matters.

There was an interesting series of 'Letters to Schoolboys' by C. E. Johnstone in 1893, which were full of plain commonsense. Gordon Stables also hammered out his advice on good health and pure thoughts.

Talbot Baines Reed died in November 1893. His last serial in that year was entitled 'Tom, Dick and Harry'. It was, in the opinion of many, his best story. It began with the dramatic sentence: 'A shot! A yell! Silence,' but was a conventional enough school story.

R. M. Ballantyne died a year later, but there was no lack of travelled and experienced authors for the *B.O.P.* J. Stratford Bradish contributed a series on 'Boys I have known'. David Ker was now 'Among Siberian Forests' and there was a series of articles by Lieutenant-General Sir Fred. Middleton on 'The Lord White Elephant and how I missed seeing him'. Gordon Stables was 'In the Land of the Lion and the Ostrich', H. F. Hobden told boys how to make a model gas engine. Jules Verne was with 'Captain Antifer: a story of buried treasure', Reginald Bennet told how to make a stereoscope. J. T. Nettleship was producing a regular series of colour paintings of wild animals.

The pace never slackened. David Ker took his readers out to Siam, Gordon Stables put them in dire peril on 'The Cruise of the Good Ship Boreas'. George Manville Fenn contributed a story with the somewhat confusing title 'Ydoll Gwynn: or the flood beneath the Sea'. It concerned an old Cornish tin mine in which our heroes were trapped underground. The Rev. A. N. Malan wrote a lively school story with the impossible title of 'The Drere of Loanmouth Grange', and G. A. Henty described what it was like to be a war correspondent. He also wrote serials such as 'Among Malay Pirates' in 1897. In 1897 boys were also instructed 'How to take a Photograph of the Moon' and 'How to keep Spiders as Pets'. In advertisements they were told that Mellin's Food when prepared is similar to breast milk – a daring statement. An ex-sergeant M. M. Police contributed three graphic accounts of the Mashona Rising of 1896. W. E. Cule and Harold Avery had both begun writing in the 1890s. The former wrote adventure stories, the latter turned out endless school stories. Both moved easily with the times during the next forty years, as did their artists.

As the century drew to its close the *B.O.P.* gave more attention to real events. There were articles on 'Life in a Cape Mounted Riflemen's Camp' and 'With the Red Cross at Kassala' (which gave a description of the camp after the Dervishes captured it). There was one on 'The Boer Boy', adjoining one on the advantages of a Classical education. Gordon Stables was advising – as he had often done before – on poultry keeping.

A. E. J. Collins, holder of the world-record cricket score of 628, appeared in a photograph in 1899. He was then fourteen. In 1915 it was reported that Lt. A. E. J. Collins, R.E., had been killed in action in France. Other cricketers, distinguished in their different ways, were also featured. One was Prince Christian Victor, another Prince Ranjitsinjhi, whose timing of the ball has never been equalled, let alone surpassed. Jessop, the smiter, was waiting in the wings. His fame as a cricketer was just beginning, but he already had a number of impressive feats to his credit.

Women, of course, existed. They were over-prudent mothers or bullying headmasters' wives. Girls rarely appeared, and those who did scarcely looked alluring.

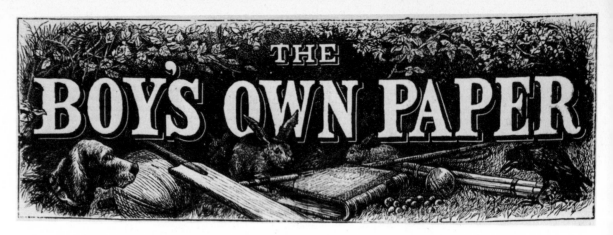

A NEW YEAR'S LETTER TO WORKING LADS

Gordon Stables, M.D., R.N.

"Lives of great men all remind us,
   We can make our lives sublime,
And departing leave behind us
   Footsteps in the sands of time.

"Let us then be up and doing,
   With a heart for any fate,
Still achieving, still pursuing,
   Learn to labour and to wait."
                LONGFELLOW.

I SIT down to write with a considerable amount of venom in me. Nay, never be afraid, my lads. It shan't show through in my article. The story is this: I got the ladder this morning to clear off some leaves from the roof of my caravan, when, whew! I was stung by something which might have been an adder from the far-off forests of Green Caledonia among which I have been roaming all the summer long. I might add, however, that adders don't sting, but bite.

I pulled up another handful, and got stung again. Then the monster appeared, a huge wasp. In my agony of pain that beast looked bigger and broader than one of my cycling shoes. The best thing for a sting of this sort is strong ammonia, or the juice of an onion, but either needs to be applied immediately, and singularly enough nothing nor nobody is ever at hand when wanted, not even a policeman. Never mind, I've been bitten by almost every creature in this world, even by the terrible *Hoc-cacoëthes-scribendi*, and weathered them all. And so shall I weather this.

I knew the case of a captain of the Royal Navy, who had sailed the seas till he was grey, and was finally drowned from a canal boat. When they hooked him out, and pumped him out, he had still

a gasp in him, and he managed to slowly and painfully stammer out "Epitaph—drowned—at—sea."

"Did the bee die after he stung you, papa?" said my smallest boy.

"With remarkable suddenness, my lad," I replied. "In fact, he will never know what hurt him."

"Ah! but I don't mean that. Do bees always die after they sting?"

"No, only hive-bees, because they leave their sting in; the wasps, those cute little chaps in the lawn-tennis suits, can sting fifty times and feel all the happier for it."

Well, boys, wait till I have had another good rub with that sliced onion, and I'll proceed with my discourse. There! How it does "nip," to be sure! For she—that is the bee—after firing my principal pen-finger, walked all along my little one, boring Artesian wells as she went, till she fell off and fainted.

. . . . .

This article, then, is intended for my real working-bees of boys, whose life, I know for a fact, is hard to bear at times. And although I may be accused sometimes of writing only for school "chaps" and young Eton "toffs," I really have all classes, high and low, in my mind while I give advice. And I have a soft side even to mill-hands and miners. While passing through Lancashire, etc., in my "Wanderer," through squalid villages and along dusty roads, which stopped not until I reached Staleybridge, I received no end of favours and courtesy from many a smutty-faced but kind-hearted fellow, who knew me but as a gentleman-gipsy.

Moreover, I was a working boy myself once. Not engaged at factories certainly, but my father, a farmer and landowner, brought my brothers and myself up to work in the fields with the plough or scythe. And in the garden, too. All this time our education was not neglected. In Scotland we have had schools for three hundred years, not the thirty which is all England can date back to. You will do me the credit of believing, I hope, that no man could write *practically* on all subjects concerning country life, as I do, had he not been himself an outdoor worker.

Am I any the worse? I think not; for listen—and our Editor can bear me out in what I say—I could take a month's work to-morrow at farming, gardening, or dykeing (building stone fencing), and trudge happily home in the evening. If I do roll about throughout the length and breadth of Britain in a caravan and pair in summer-time, I labour for it in winter, from five or six in the morning, with my pen and brain, till far into the night.

Now to come closer to the point. Would you be surprised to know, lads, that all the rules of health I try to explain, and all the advice I give in the gentle and gentlemanly "B.O.P.," are suited to every boy in the kingdom?

Now, take the subject of the cold morning tub, first and foremost. Says a courteous correspondent, "How can a lad have his morning tub who starts work at six a.m.? Thousands where I work never know what a bath before breakfast is. This bath they never see. The breakfast they take in a beer can, and there is no time for recreation."

Well, I thought of these words this morning when I awoke at five a.m., my usual hour.

"Now," I said, "I shall time myself, with no unusual hurry."

I got up, lit my lamp and looked at the clock. Remember the "tub" with the big sponge in it was ready and waiting. I stripped off the garments of night, and kneeling down before the sitz bath, soaped and well washed face, arms, and chest. Then in I got, sponged all over, dried with one towel and rough-rubbed with another. Dressed myself in knickerbocker suit, just as a country gentleman should, combed and brushed my hair, brushed my teeth, and stood ready for a long day's work. Now for the time—eleven minutes and a half! Had I had only to throw on a workman's suit I could have done it in ten minutes. I felt as fresh as a daisy, had a draught of water, and then, lantern in hand, set off away down through the grounds to the wigwam where I work, and had to go back for breakfast at eight, after seeing to my great dogs.

Therefore, remembering the enormous advantage to health which the morning tub positively ensures, is there a single working lad in Great Britain who can't afford, say, even ten minutes to bathe and towel?

Recreation.—My correspondent, whom I am glad to say is a life-abstainer, never played a game of cricket or football in his life. Has no time! (*Sic*.) He is therefore an exception. But tens of thousands enjoy their weekly half-holiday in these delightful games. Many work-lads drink a quart of beer a day, one pint with dinner and another at supper time. But lads under twenty are better without stimulants of any kind, and would work more easily if they drank milk, or cold tea and milk. You may start at the words "cold tea." On the road my own tea is made at two o'clock, after dinner, to save lighting the fire again, and when I drink it cold at five o'clock, I feel like a giant refreshed.

Music Halls.—Yes, many of my working lads spend their Saturday evenings at Music Halls. Well, some may be not so bad, but at many the music and songs are vile and the dancing disgusting. Then alas! instead of home sharp afterwards, too often, alas! the gin palace with its vile drink and allurements intervene, and the lad who has been trying to act the part of a full-grown swaggerer the evening before, wakes up with a headache, and wishes he hadn't been there. In this way precious health is lost, and it never, never comes again. Neither physical nor moral strength.

Gambling.—This is a subject I cannot speak on from personal experience, but I do know one thing—endless odds are against the backer of horses, of doing well in the long run. Youths think it very manly to make a grab for the evening paper at a public-house bar, or get hold of the "Little Pink 'Un," and to look as serious as if they had at least a thousand on. What stupidity! And if they do happen to back a winner, oh, dear! they are turfites now, and can give tips and all sorts of things, and are stood "nips" for doing so. Winning on a single horse has proved the ruin of many.

Smoking.—All medical authorities agree that to smoke before one is twenty at least is to weaken every nerve and muscle in the body, including the heart. I do heartily grieve when I see a cigarette or pipe in the mouth of a boy. Mind, I wish you all well, but I do not wish to enforce my opinions on anybody. It is no advantage to me; so smoke away as much as you please, but I am doing my duty in telling you that you are thus drawing drafts on the Bank of Health, and you will remember my words when they are presented for payment.

Food.—Here my young workaday friends have no occasion to envy the richer boys they see on the streets. Most of these not only eat too much, but sleep in too luxurious beds. Hence the unwholesome fat so frequently seen on their cheeks, and hence the pallor of many a face. "He who hath enough may soundly sleep." But I must add another truism to this—if working boys didn't smoke and drink and gamble, they could save money for many a little luxury they do not now enjoy. I'm not your judge nor ruler, lads, but I know many a working chap who has saved enough to buy himself a bicycle, and of all educative exercise this may be made the best, just as it is the healthiest.

Fresh air day and night is as much a necessity of

real life as food is. Without it nerves fail, and you get crabbed, peevish, and not fit for anyone to associate with.

I get so many letters concerning certain debilitating habits, generally learned at school, that I must tell you, as I tell all boys, gently and simply, these lead to trouble that never can be shaken off. After a twenty years' experience of such boys both in Britain and abroad, I ought to know a little about the matter; and I say boldly, for I fear not the face of clay, that not only do those school habits lead to injury, but I've known them lead to semi-imbecility, to the mad-house, and to suicide.

But there is grit and the right sort of sand in many of you factory hands, and I love you for it. And I tell you, or some of you, that sooner than

slave in Britain, I'd get off to Australia or New Zealand, if I had to work my passage out by attending to the skipper's dog, and helping the cook.

Cheer up, lads! Where there is a will there is a way, and better days are, I hope, in store for many of you.

But now 'tis noon, and I confess feeling tired. I'm off to clean out, repair, and re-bed my St. Bernard and Newfoundland kennels. I prefer to do such work myself, and believe me, boys, I'm never ashamed of being seen with my coat off.

Good-bye! I wish my workaday boys a right jolly and happy New Year. And health, not only for the present, but for those years that now seem so far ahead. The foundations of health must be laid in the days of one's youth.

LETTERS TO SCHOOLBOYS

C. E. Johnstone, B.A.

I.—NEW BOYS

"A FOOL—any one whose private opinion happens to differ from your own." This definition is, I believe, to be found originally in a little known but very entertaining book by Horace Smith, called "The Tin Trumpet." But, whatever its source may be, it very aptly illustrates the point of view from which the average public-school boy regards a new-comer. A youth who does not know that Smith ma. is the best bat in the eleven, that Robinson max. can throw the cricket-ball 107 yards, and that chapel is always at half-past-eight on the first night of term, clearly possesses none of the most elementary knowledge that makes life worth living.

The new boy of to-day, however, has in almost every case been to a private school, where he has learnt a good deal about schools and their ways, and is therefore spared the abject misery which generally falls to the lot of a small shy boy, taken straight from home, and chucked into the middle of a public school. This was the kind of boy who, when asked his name, used softly to reply "Algernon," or whatever he happened to be called at home, and then responded to the shouts of derision which his answer elicited, by bursting into tears. Happily this type of new boy is almost extinct as the dodo, and his sufferings nowadays are for the most part far lighter, partly on account of his greater knowledge,

and partly perhaps also because his tormentors are less unfeeling than in the "good old days" of yore. Indeed, it occasionally happens that when the "old hand" sets to work to get a rise out of a new arrival, he encounters an adversary who is quite well able to look after himself.

It was to such a youth that I once heard addressed the time-honoured pleasantry concealed in the question, "Does your mother wash?" As many boys have learnt to their cost, this represents a dilemma, for if the answer "no" is given the repartee is obvious, while, if answered in the affirmative, it enables the tormentor to announce, "He says his mother is a washerwoman." On this occasion however, the boy, who was quite up to date both in his knowledge and his slang, looked his interrogator calmly in the face, and, without giving any direct answer to the question, simply remarked, "Anyhow she doesn't deal in *chestnuts*," whereat the other perceived that he had given himself away.

At the same time it does not by any means always pay for a new boy to be too clever, especially if he is not physically equal to the task of upholding his opinions by force, if necessary, as well as by argument. In fact, what is required here, as in almost everything else, is tact, which in this instance is practically the gift of observing the golden mean

CORRESPONDENCE.

J. Burnside.—Try Biddle's "Corinthian Yachtsman," or Dixon Kemp's "Manual of Yacht and Boat Sailing;" both are good, but the first costs four shillings, and the other five-and-twenty. One is published by Wilson, of 156 Minories; the other, Kemp's, at *The Field* Office, Breams Buildings, E.C.

Brownie.—There was a series of articles on the subject in "The Girl's Own Paper." The matter hardly comes within our scope.

Nemo Nascitur Sapiens.—You are too old for the merchant service, and much too old for the navy in any capacity whatever in the officer line. There are always vacancies for stokers.

between too much "cheek" on the one hand, and too great a tendency to "cushion it" on the other. An excess of meekness is almost as certain to be met with contempt as an excess of "cheek" is to provoke antagonism; and masters are sometimes quite as ready as the boys to take advantage of a new-comer's shyness and timidity.

I remember a case of this kind, where a very small, shy boy, having been at a private school, the head master of which was a sort of father to all his boys, whom they were accustomed to consult in all their little doubts and difficulties, thought that the same state of things prevailed at the public school at which he now found himself. Being in doubt therefore as to whether or not it would be lawful for him to have his bicycle sent to him from home, he waylaid the head-master one day and very timidly put the question, "Please sir, may you ride a bicycle here?" To which the worthy potentate, seeing an opening for a somewhat ponderous pleasantry, replied in the deep throaty voice for which he is well known, "My dear boy, I have not the slightest doubt that I might if I liked; but, curiously enough, I have never felt the slightest inclination to do so." With this brilliant repartee the great man passed on, having no doubt satisfied himself a good deal better than he had satisfied the inquiring mind of the in-judicious infant. Few masters can resist an oppor-tunity of scoring, in spite of Sidgwick's remark that "it is quite easy for them *not* to say clever things."

It not unfrequently falls to the lot of a boy high up in the school to be asked by someone, who is perhaps a friend of his great-aunt's, or has some equally strong claim upon his services, to "look after" a boy coming to the school for the first time. At a school which is situated in the middle of a very beautiful park, of which the boys are all justly proud, a prefect was once taking a new boy round and explaining to him what the different places were, and also what his various duties would be. At the end of it all, the boy remarked in a patronising tone, "Not a bad place on the whole; rather rustic, isn't it?" which so damped the other's ardour that he left him from that time forward to look after himself.

The most self-possessed new boy that ever came under my notice was a very small, but very wiry youth, whose one idea in life was gymnastics. He was also rather deaf—a fact of which I think he made full use whenever he did not wish to hear. When he first arrived at his public-school, he came by himself, and one of the masters, happening to be at the station, and perceiving this youth at rather a loss as to what to do next, went up to him, and said kindly, "I suppose you are a new boy; how d'ye do!"

To this the boy answered in a very harsh voice, which was one of his peculiarities, "Eh? what did you say?"

Rather surprised, the master repeated the ques-tion, and was still further astounded by the boy

saying, all in one breath, "Oh, how d'ye do? How high can you vault?"

This same boy soon made a name for himself on account of his quaint and very cheeky remarks, and also for his deafness, a good deal of which was probably put on. When he had been at the school about a week he was sent one evening with a message to the prefects' study, which he duly delivered, and then stood looking at them as though they were some curious kind of animals.

One of the prefects said sternly, "You can go now."

"Eh? What did you say," he grated out, making an odd face that was intended to mean that he couldn't hear.

The remark was repeated with an appropriate gesture.

"Oh yes! All right! Keep your hair on. Good night. Don't forget your night-cap when you go to bed," and with these words he closed the door just in time to avoid a shower of missiles which were hurled at the speaker for his unheard-of audacity in venturing to beard the prefects in their den.

At many schools they have an excellent practice of giving a boy a fortnight or so to get into the ways of the school, during which time he is not punished by the masters. But this does not save him from having to face the practical jokes and hoaxes of the rest, on which I shall have more to say in my next letter. Also, he finds the responsibilities of life are very much increased for him. He finds that he has to look after his own clothes and his own money, and also to keep a sharp look-out that his books, and at some places his victuals, are not "bagged" by some high-handed marauder.

The best advice which one can give to the new boy himself, is to be civil in answering reasonable questions, and careful in getting out of answering questions which he considers unreasonable. Further, he will find it a good plan to make a "chum" of some other new boy, so that they may unite their knowledge and divide their burdens. Then, if they can find some friendly "old hand" to tell them what to do, and to warn them as to what to avoid, they will not go very far astray. Now that bullying has gone so much out of fashion, there are not, after all, very many perils to be encountered, beyond a little inevitable "greening," and perhaps a little mild teasing. Boys in these days have ceased to find any great pleasure in making one another miserable.

In conclusion let me assure the new boy, for his comfort, that the feeling of loneliness and of "being out of it" is not really half so acute for him when he first arrives at a public-school as it is for the "Fresher" at the beginning of his first term at Oxford or Cambridge; because the latter has most probably come from a school where he was a per-son of the highest importance, and for that reason finds it all the more painful to be in the position of "a man of no account."

THE BOY'S OWN PAPER

No. 656.—Vol. XIII.

SATURDAY, AUGUST 8, 1891.

Price One Penny.
[ALL RIGHTS RESERVED.]

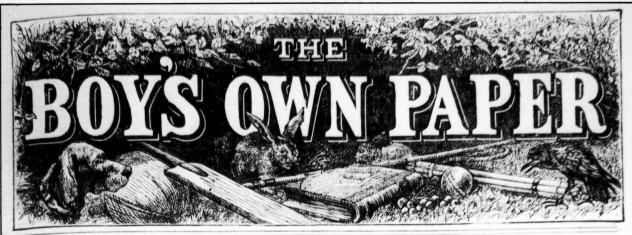

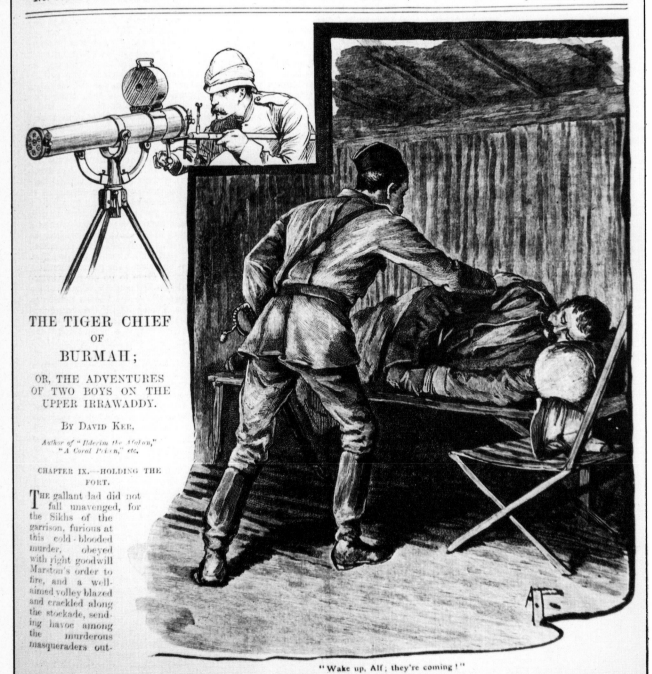

THE TIGER CHIEF OF BURMAH;

OR, THE ADVENTURES OF TWO BOYS ON THE UPPER IRRAWADDY.

By David Ker,

Author of "Ilderim the Afghan," "A Coral Prison," etc.

CHAPTER IX.—HOLDING THE FORT.

THE gallant lad did not fall unavenged, for the Sikhs of the garrison, furious at this cold-blooded murder, obeyed with right goodwill Marston's order to fire, and a well-aimed volley blazed and crackled along the stockade, sending havoc among the murderous masqueraders out-

"Wake up, Alf; they're coming!"

THE
BOY'S OWN PAPER

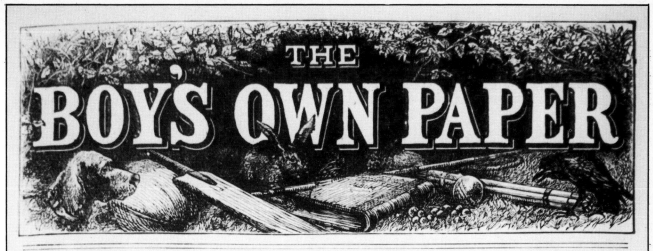

No. 636.—Vol. XIII.   SATURDAY, MARCH 21, 1891.   Price One Penny.
[ALL RIGHTS RESERVED.]

A PUBLIC SCHOOL STORY.

By Talbot Baines Reed,

Author of " My Friend Smith," " Fifth Form at St.-Dominic's," " Sir Ludar," etc.

CHAPTER XI.—FELLSGARTH v. RENDLESHAM.

How it came that Rollitt played, after all, in the Rendlesham match, no one could properly understand.

His name was not down on the original list. Yorke had given up

" Dangle, get off the field."

The Ministry.   The Opposition.   An Obstructionist.

A "Scene" in the House.

The Sergeant-at-Arms removes a disorderly Member.

Mr Speaker espies a Stranger in the House.

THE "BOY'S OWN" PARLIAMENT.

(SHOWING HOW THE BOYS AT HALEHURST EMPLOYED THEMSELVES IMMEDIATELY PRECEDING THE CHRISTMAS "BREAK-UP.")

See page 155.

CHAMPIONS OF THE KREMLIN

A Russian Story

'A strangely downcast look on the bold handsome face.'

David Ker,

Author of "The Tiger Chief of Burmah,"
"Ilderim the Afghan," "A Coral Prison," etc.

CHAPTER III.—
THE BLACK WAR-HORSE.

FOUR years had passed since that parting in the northern woods, and the sunshine of a bright clear morning in May 1612 was streaming over the painted wooden houses, massive ramparts, and broad, dusty streets of the great Russian city of Smolensk, and lighting up the dark towers and battlements of a stately chateau, half castle and half country-house, a few miles beyond it, from one of the high carved windows of which leaned a tall, slender, active lad of sixteen, in the rich dress of a young noble of the period, but with a strangely weary and downcast look on his bold handsome face.

Left B.O.P.'s view of a school debating society.

And well might the poor boy look sad and weary; for he was no other than Yury Nikolaievitch, the son of that Prince Molotkoff who was Ivan Susanin's master, and who (as related by Ivan in the last chapter) had leagued himself, to his eternal shame, with the Polish enemies of his country, and surrendered to them his only son as a hostage for his own fidelity.

Happily the son was more patriotic than the father; and after a four years' separation from his country and people, the young Prince Yury, despite all the gaieties of Cracow and Warsaw, the splendour of the Polish court (at that time one of the most brilliant and luxurious in all Europe) and the notice of King Sigismund himself, was still as staunchly Russian as ever.

He had, indeed, profited by his Polish education to the extent of becoming a skilful rider and a practised swordsman; but although, with a prudence beyond his years, he had appeared to be quite content with his new situation, his one thought day and night was to escape from the gilded bondage in which he was held by his hereditary foes.

But this was easier said than done; and even if he *did* escape, whither was he to go?

Whither, indeed? The power of Russia lay trampled in the dust, and Russia herself seemed to have actually ceased to exist. Palitzin's gloomy prophecy had been terribly fulfilled. The storm foreshadowed in his dream—a storm of Polish invasion—had burst over the whole land, and, from the marshes of Minsk to the banks of the Volga, the soil of "Holy Russia" was in the hands of her enemies.

To the north, a Swedish army was triumphant along the whole border. To the south, bands of robbers were laying waste the entire country, and even exacting tribute from the large towns, no one daring to resist them. Moscow itself had fallen into the hands of the Poles, as it was to fall into those of Napoleon just two centuries later. Their king had solemnly crowned his son, Prince Vladislav, in the Kremlin, proclaiming him King of Russia; and any man who had then ventured to foretell that in the very next century these "subjugated" Russians would crush Sweden, invade Germany, and humble Turkey, and that Poland would be chopped up into detached provinces by Russia herself and her two German neighbours, would have been laughed at as a madman by Pole and Russian alike.

"We've plenty of men ready to fight for Russia, but there's no one to head them," muttered the brave boy, gloomily. "If we had only a leader, I'd escape somehow and join him, if I died for it; but we have neither Czar nor general now."

It was but too true. The great dynasty that had ruled Russia for 700 years had ended with Feodor Ivanovitch, the weak and worthless son of Ivan the Terrible, leaving the vacant throne of Moscow to be scrambled for by various usurpers, bringing civil war, famine, pestilence, and every form of ruin in their train. Russia's best and indeed only general, the gallant Prince Pojarski, was said to be dying of wounds received from the invaders; and many of the chief nobles of Russia, despairing of any other remedy had sworn allegiance to Prince Vladislav and become subjects of Poland.

"A pretty sight, truly," growled the high-spirited lad, frowning at the crowd of soldiers that filled the court-yard below, "to see this rabble herding in my father's house—and half of them *Russians*, too, more shame for them! Ha!"

His sudden start was caused by a few words which he had caught from the talk below, spoken by a tall, hard-featured Polish musketeer with one arm in a sling.

"Say what you please, brothers, a man who could hold a monastery with a handful of soldiers against Pan *Lisovski himself, is not one to laugh at, if he were ten times a Russian and a heretic. I can speak, for I was myself in the last assault on Sergi-Troitza, and warm work it was!"

Prince Yury started again, and bent eagerly forward to listen.

"We were on the top of the wall," pursued the soldier, "shouting that the place was ours; and it seemed so, for the Russian rogues were losing heart, and giving way on all sides—when, all at once, this Father Abraham Palitzin, or whatever you call him, snatched a musket from the hands of a fallen man, beat down my comrade Shalonski with one stroke of the butt-end, and then, shouting in a voice like the thunder of heaven, 'For God and the Fatherland!' he laid about him in such style that he kept us all at bay!"

"And he only an old monk, too!" cried several voices, in tones of involuntary admiration.

"Then," continued the Pole, "back came the Russians like madmen, swept us away as the wind sweeps the dust, hurled down our scaling-ladders, and spoilt the whole business for us just as we were going to win the game! And then a big Russian lay-brother, who had fought like ten, called out to the monk, 'Well done, holy father! you're not named Palitzin for nothing;† you've laid your blessing on the heads of these heretics in true Russian style!' But the old monk looked sadly at him, with tears in those great dark eyes of his (which had been flashing like lightning the moment before), and answered solemnly, 'Speak not so lightly, my son; it is a fearful thing, even in righteous self-defence, to take a life which you cannot give back.'"

A murmur of astonishment ran around the listening circle.

"I was lying at his feet when he said it," went on the veteran, "for luckily I'd fallen off the wall inward instead of outward, or I'd have broken my neck. Even as it was, I broke my arm, and the pain made me so savage that when the old man, seeing I was still alive, bent over me and asked if he could do anything to help me, I growled out, 'Let me die in peace, you old fool! don't you see I'm an enemy?' But he only said, as gently as could be, 'All men

---

* A Polish title of honour, answering to the Spanish "Don."

† A rude play on the Russian word "palitza", which means a club.

alike are the children of God;' and he bound up my wound as tenderly as if he had been my mother, and then had me carried into the monastery to be taken care of."

"Then Sergi-Troitza is not taken, after all, thank God," murmured the young Prince Molotkoff, who, leaning from above, had drunk in every word of the story. "Well done, Father Abraham; there's nobody like *him*! If I can once give these Polish rascals the slip, I'll be off to join him as fast as I can ride. Hullo! who's that gay-feathered fellow yonder?"

A single horseman, in the laced jacket, gilt helmet, and polished steel breastplate of a Polish trooper of the time, had just ridden into the courtyard on a fine grey horse, and was exchanging greetings with the soldiers assembled there, upon whom his first few words seemed to produce a great effect, for they flocked round him with the utmost eagerness, and gave him a boisterous welcome.

"That's the voice of my old playmate Vaska Susanin, if ever I heard it yet," said Yury, trying to catch a glimpse of the stranger's face; "but what's he dressed up like that for? Surely he can't have turned Pole, like those sneaking fellows down in the yard there! It would break good old Vanya's heart to think of a son of *his* turning traitor. But no—*that* can't be; he must have heard that I'm here, and has come in disguise to try and help me to escape! Hurrah!"

It was indeed old Ivan's soldier son, Vaska Susanin, who, having served three campaigns against the Turks in the ranks of a motley army of Poles, Cossacks, Russians, Germans, and Hungarians, had hurried home as soon as the troops were disbanded, to aid his country in her trouble.

This, however, was not his sole motive. The surrender of Prince Molotkoff's only son to the Poles as a hostage was too important an event not to be widely talked of, and young Susanin had heard more than enough of it from his Polish fellow-soldiers; but, though every one spoke of the young Prince* as being quite content with his lot, and completely transformed into a Polish cavalier, Vaska could not believe that the brave, high-spirited boy with whom he had played in his childhood could ever forget Russia, or league himself with her enemies; and (as Yury had rightly guessed) his errand here was to rescue his old master's son, if mortal man could do it.

Vaska's quick eye had recognised at the upper window, the moment he entered the courtyard, the face of the boy whom he sought; but he warily avoided giving any sign of recognition, and mingled with the soldiers, in whose eyes his service against the far-off Turks gave him the same kind of consequence which a man would acquire nowadays

from a perilous Arctic voyage or a Central African exploration.

He was instantly surrounded by an eager crowd, who listened with wondering delight to his account of all the marvels of those strange southern lands which seemed to them so wonderful and so remote, till at length Vaska let slip the startling admission that "in those countries there is *no winter*."

"No winter!" echoed three or four voices at once, in tones of incredulous horror.

"That is, indeed, Heaven's judgment upon those unbelieving heathens—they don't deserve to have a winter!" cried a young Russian soldier, in whose eyes such an explanation was the only possible way of accounting for this appalling fact.

"Ah, Phomka" (Tom), whispered an older man, "don't you see he's making fun of us? As if there *could* be a country without a winter! How would the people manage to live, you know?"

Just then two grooms led out of the stable a splendid black horse, at sight of which Vaska Susanin started visibly.

"Aha! Whirlwind, my lad! are you here?" cried he, patting the smooth, shining neck of the gallant beast, which, evidently recognising him as an old friend, rubbed its nose caressingly against his shoulder, and neighed joyfully.

"Why the beast seems to know you, comrade," cried one of the grooms.

"Know me? I should think he did! Many's the time I've groomed him before a battle on the Turkish border, when I served under his Excellency the great Pan Lisovski, whom Heaven preserve! But why has his Excellency not taken the brave beast to the war with him?"

"Hey! you cavalry fellows think a man can go anywhere on horseback," said the other groom, with a broad grin. "Would you have his Excellency leap his horse over the walls of Sergi-Troitza, like that fellow in the story on 'Konek-Gorboonok?'" (a flying horse of Slavonian legend).

"That's true," rejoined young Susanin; "but if *I* owned such a horse, I would not let him out of my sight for a minute. He's the swiftest beast I ever saw, and any young fellow who was chasing his enemies, *or flying from them*, couldn't wish for a better."

The slight emphasis laid on the last words, and the meaning glance with which Vaska pointed them, were not lost upon the quick-witted young Prince, who began to guess his ally's project, and replied by a look of intelligence.

Then Vaska, pretending to remark for the first time the young noble's presence at the window, made him a low bow, and said fawningly:

"Will the noble Pan (whose handsome face may Heaven bless!) give a poor soldier a few *kopecks* (half-pence) to help him on his way home?"

"*You* won't need much help, my glib-tongued friend," retorted Yury, feigning to be offended; "if you run short of money, it strikes me you're just the man to help yourself."

---

* In Russia all the sons of a Prince rank as Princes themselves.

"Don't make fun of a poor fellow, honoured sir," rejoined Vaska, making a great show of joining heartily in the general laughter that greeted this jest. "If I sing you a good song, will your nobleness let me taste your bounty?"

"I will, if it is a good one," said the Prince; "and that I may the better judge of that, I'll come down into the courtyard, and listen to you."

For more than a year past, Yury Nikolaievitch's Polish guardians had greatly relaxed the vigilance of their watch over him, being convinced that he was now (as he skilfully pretended to be) completely a Pole at heart; and in the house of his own father, whose devotion to the Polish cause was well known, he was naturally left more at liberty than ever. Hence, his coming down into the courtyard to hear the stranger's song aroused no suspicion whatever.

Vaska, with a marked show of officious respect, placed a bench for the Prince to sit down on, and standing humbly before him, struck up, in a deep and mellow voice, a song which he had probably learned from a wandering minstrel in the south:

"Men fret and fume, and pinch and pare,
  For gold they snatch and scramble,
While I, without a grief or care,
  Where'er I please can ramble.
'Neath cloudless sun or clouded moon,
  By market-cross or ferry,
I chant my song, I play my tune,
  And all who hear are merry.

"Let Autumn blight the bonnie flowers,
  And turn the leaves to yellow,
I still am gay 'mid all its showers
  As when the Spring was mellow.
Let Winter shake his icy dart,
  And whirl his snows together;
I carry sunshine in my heart,
  And laugh at storm and weather.

"When Summer's sun unclouded shines,
  And mountain shadows linger,
Our maidens dance among the vines,
  As quicker moves my finger.
And so they sport till day is o'er,
  And black-robed night advances,
And where the maidens tripped before,
  The lonely moonbeam dances.

"When Winter comes with snow and storm,
  When hills and woods are hoary,
They gather round the fireside warm
  To hear my song and story.
I touch the chords, I chant the lay,
  The firelight glimmers o'er us,
And wind and hail, in stormy play,
  Chime in with lusty chorus.

"'Mid rustling leaves, 'neath open sky,
  I live like lark or swallow,
There's not a bird more free to fly
  Than I am free to follow;

And when grim Death his bow shall bend,
  My mortal course suspending,
O, may my life, howe'er it close,
  Have music in its ending."

The song ended amid general applause, and Prince Molotkoff, with a few words of careless approval, tossed to the singer a small silver coin. The Russian bent forward as if bowing in acknowledgment of the gift, and contrived as he did so to whisper a few words, to which the boy-Prince replied with an almost imperceptible nod.

The soldiers now recollected that they had forgotten to offer any food to this man who had amused them so well; and they hastened to load Vaska with eatables of all kinds—black bread, lumps of cheese, scraps of cold mutton and bacon, *piroshki* (small meat-pies), and thick, greasy sausages. The young Russian seemed to eat very heartily; but in reality he contrived to slip unperceived, or else placed with ostentatious care, a large portion of the food into the leathern haversack that hung over his shoulder.

"Thanks, brothers!" said he, when he had finished; "I see you don't let a comrade want bread and salt. And now, lads, shall we not show this noble young Pan some sport, for the honour of the Polish army and our illustrious Hetman (general)? I will try a leaping-match with any of you, and stake this chain of mine against five gold ducats."

The proposal was received with general applause, for Vaska's chain (a trophy of the Turkish war) had already attracted the notice of the Poles by its rich and curious make, and gold ducats were plentiful enough among them since the recent plundering of Smolensk. Half-a-dozen stout fellows stepped forward at once to accept the challenge, while the young Prince looked with a beating heart from them to the black war-horse (which the two grooms were now leading slowly up and down the courtyard), feeling sure that the time was now at hand, and that a few minutes more would see him either free as air or more hopelessly imprisoned than ever.

A space was cleared down the centre of the court, at the farther side of which two soldiers planted themselves, holding a strong cord between them; and then the contest began.

For the first few leaps all seven did equally well; but, as the rope was gradually lifted higher and higher, the competitors fell away one by one, till at length, by the time the cord had been raised to shoulder-height, the match lay between young Susanin and a tall, muscular, sharp-faced Lithuanian, who was renowned as the best leaper of his regiment.

"Now, brother," cried the Russian, "let's have everything fairly settled before we begin; an agreement's better than money, you know" (a Russian proverb). "Those two fellows yonder are your comrades, and I'm a stranger; and I don't see what's to hinder them from lowering the rope an inch or two as you go over it, and then vowing that you cleared it properly. If you want to win my chain, try a leap with me over *that*, unless you're afraid of getting hurt."

So saying, he dragged out and planted in the open space a tall screen of canvas stretched tight between two poles—fully as high as an ordinary man's head—which had formed part of an awning.

"Aha! you want to frighten me off the match, and so to save yourself being beaten!" cried his adversary, stung by the taunt. "You've got hold of the wrong man, my clever fellow. Come along—we'll soon see *who* is afraid!"

"Very good," said Vaska, coolly; "come on. If your feet are as nimble as your *tongue*, I won't have much chance. Stand clear, brothers, and let us see what this *Bogateer* (mighty hero) can do!"

The shrewd Russian had already learned from the looks and words of the bystanders that this swaggering Lithuanian was no favourite, and had seen at once how to turn this feeling to good account. In planting the screen over which they were to leap, he had contrived to place it right in front of a large and pretty deep horse-trough nearly full of water, in such a way that the soldier, when he made his spring, must inevitably jump right into it.

Having satisfied himself that the trough was completely hidden behind the canvas, Susanin gave a sly wink to the lookers-on (who grinned with delight at the thought of what was in store for their bullying comrade), and drew back to make way for the Lithuanian, whispering as he passed Prince Molotkoff:

"Be ready, Yury Nikolaievitch, and, the moment you hear me call out 'Beregiss!' (take care), "up with you!"

The Lithuanian darted forward like a hunted deer, and, with one mighty bound, cleared the canvas screen, and went splash into the trough beyond it with such force that the water was dashed up in a huge jet high into the air, and the luckless athlete rolled over and over in his impromptu bath like a wallowing hippopotamus.

"You shall pay for this, you rascal!" howled he, maddened by the roar of laughter that greeted his mishap; "I'll teach you to play your fool's tricks upon a Polish soldier!"

And he rushed toward the spot where he had laid down his sabre, dripping like a water-cart as he went.

In a moment all was confusion. Some of the soldiers sided with the enraged Lithuanian, but the greater number opposed him—as Vaska had foreseen—loudly declaring that they would not see the stranger maltreated.

Among these wild spirits hard words were always apt to breed hard blows, and the dispute which the wily Russian had so cleverly kindled soon flamed up into a regular brawl. Fisticuffs were freely exchanged, and, while some of the men grappled fiercely with each other, not a few actually drew their swords or daggers, and confronted one another with looks that boded mischief.

Meanwhile Lisovski's fiery war-horse, excited by the sudden tumult and uproar, began to prance and rear so violently that both the grooms together could scarcely hold him.

"Mischief take him—he's always mad for fighting, the silly beast!" panted one of the struggling men; "a man can't blow his nose but what the brute picks up his ears as if he heard a trumpet!"

"Let me handle him, lad," said Vaska Susanin, coming hastily up to them as soon as he saw that the soldiers were fully occupied with their quarrel. "I'll soon quiet him—he knows me."

Taking hold of the bridle, he spoke soothingly to the excited animal, stroked its neck, passed his hand over its sleek muzzle—and then, as it began to grow quieter, suddenly vaulted upon its back!

"*Take care!*" he shouted; and as the men leaped back on every side, thinking that the horse was going to kick out, the daring boy (who had been impatiently awaiting the signal) sprang up behind his friend, and in an instant the fiery horse had shot through the open gate with its two riders, and was speeding like an arrow over the great plain beyond.

There was a moment's pause of blank bewilderment, and then the whole truth flashed upon the thunderstruck soldiers.

A wild clamour broke forth, and a number of the Poles rushed frantically to their horses; but it was too late. The noble charger, urged by Vaska to its utmost speed, flew onward like the whirlwind whose name it bore, and ere the pursuers had time to mount, the two fugitives were already out of sight.

ACTIVE AND PASSIVE COURAGE

Rev. E. J. Hardy,
Chaplain to H.M. Forces.

THE courage that dares and the courage that bears are really one and the same; I never saw or felt the truth of this so much as in the conduct of a delicate nervous lad of 13, on two occasions. The first one was last winter, when he and I were walking together up a steep hill in Devonshire to ease a young favourite mare we were driving in a dog-cart, and we gave the reins to the boy's mother to guide the animal, as we had no groom with us. We happened to look back, and there, at mad top speed from behind us, up the hill came dashing a runaway horse, his rider being flung some way behind. In front of us a carriage and pair was rapidly approaching. The road was narrow, just wide enough for it and the dog-cart to pass each other. Already the spirited young mare the lady was driving was beginning to start the plunge at the noise of the galloping horse behind. Nearer and nearer it came. I confess, strong man though I was, I stood still not knowing what to do, when the boy, the nervous delicate boy, rushed across the road in front of the horses and caught the mare's bridle and drew her to one side just in time to save his mother's life, for the runaway horse grazed him as it shot past. What the mare would have done had not the boy so nobly caught her, I know not. But she knew him, and his touch and voice quieted her like a spell.

Again I saw that boy only two months later, on his deathbed, a victim of hereditary consumption, developed rapidly and suddenly, but his beautiful pure mind clear and brave as ever. His mother, the mother he adored, his faithful nurse; and it was then in those four weeks of death's rapid approach that I saw the courage to bear as I had never seen it before. He was his mother's only and darling child, and he knew how she loved him, and through the long days and nights of fever and pain no murmur of impatience or anguish was allowed to trouble those beloved ears. But always to the very last, the bright smile in the wistful eyes, on the pale lips. Always the glad cry of welcome, the fond anxiety, "Mother, don't tire yourself;" food and medicine were swallowed "to please mother," until the effort could no longer be made.

Alone, but for the Father of mercies, the dying boy and the poor mother met the dread messenger, the boy's courage and patience never giving way until he gently entered his rest and lay still at last, looking like the grand young warrior he was.

A TRICYCLE CATAMARAN

IN one of our old volumes, long since out of print, we described a water tricycle that had been practically tested and found to be satisfactory. A short time afterwards we described another aquatic contrivance, which seemed quite as likely to succeed, but which had not passed its tests under as favourable conditions as the other. That any of our readers took the trouble of building these awkward-looking things we never heard; but it is a remarkable circumstance that both of them are being daily used at the Water Show at West Brompton, and one of them was conspicuous in the aquatic parade from Chelsea to Westminster with which that show was opened.

Such things are at present mere curiosities. They may do their work, but they are evidently not so good as they will be; for there is no reason for doubting but that the treadle will eventually be as powerful on the water as on the land. And while we are waiting for a definite course to be struck, the more patterns we try the better.

Here is one of the latest, a tricycle catamaran, invented by Mr. T. J. Olsen of Chicago, who claims that on it he can run down a sloping bank, and out on to the water, without dismounting or slackening speed. It consists, as is clear from the cut, of two twin boats and an ordinary front-steering tricycle. The boats are made of waterproof canvas, stretched on to wood frames as if they were ordinary canvas. These are hung on to frame of the tricycle, the driving wheels of which are fitted with floats on alternate spokes, while the steering wheel is filled in with light wood panels in order to be used as a rudder.

On the land the wheels hold up the boats; on the water the boats hold up the wheels. The speed of the contrivance is not given, but it cannot be great. We can quite understand that it is equally fast on both elements, for with such small floats the progress would be moderate on the water, and with such big boats it could not amount to much on land. And in

a high wind on either land or water the rider would have his work cut out for him.

At the same time the idea is different from that of the other machines we have given, and the apparatus would seem to be as safe, providing that the centre of gravity is kept low. Velocipede boats are never very fast; even those on Virginia Water belonging to the Prince of Wales have no speed in them, and they are only suited for use in smooth waters. But as no one is likely to try them in a breeze, the objection is, perhaps, to a certain extent, uncalled for. Such curiosities of locomotion are always worth noting, for in them may lie the germ of what the world would profit by.

TOM, DICK, AND HARRY

Talbot Baines Reed

Author of "The Cock House at Fellsgarth," "My Friend Smith," "Fifth Form at St. Dominic's," etc.

CHAPTER VII.—COMING DOWN A PEG OR TWO.

I HAD half hoped Tempest would be down at the station to meet me. But he was not; and I had to consider on the spur of the moment how to make

'What do you mean, sir, by behaving like this?'

my entry into Low Heath.

Either I might walk, as I noticed a good many of the fellows who got out of the train did, or I might charter a private fly, as a few of the swells did, or I might go up in one of the school omnibuses, which was evidently the popular mode of transportation. I was so earnestly desirous to do the correct thing, that I was nearly doing nothing at all, and finally found myself standing almost alone on the platform with the last omnibus ready to start.

Surely they might make some arrangement, thought I, for meeting exhibitioners and taking them up. How did I know this omnibus was not a town boys' vehicle, or one dedicated to the service of the inferior boys? Perhaps it would be better—

"Right away, Jimmy; off you go!" called one of the youths on the knifeboard, whom I recognised as my late travelling companion.

At this point I decided I would risk it, and go up by omnibus after all.

"Wait!" I called. "I'm coming too."

"Fire away, Jimmy. Cut along!" shouted the youth. They could not have heard me surely. The omnibus was actually moving!

"Hi!" called I, beginning to follow, bag in hand; "wait for me."

"Lamm it on Jimmy," was the delighted cry from the knifeboard, as a score of heads craned over to witness the chase. The spectacle of an ordinary youth giving chase to an omnibus crowded the roystering schoolboys is probably amusing enough; but when that youth has his white collar outside the collar of his great-coat, and wears brilliant tan boots and a flat-topped billy-cock, it appears, at least so it seemed to me, to be exceedingly funny for the people on the omnibus.

"Put it on," called one or two, encouragingly; "you're gaining."

"Forge ahead, Jimmy; here comes the bogey man!" cried another.

"Whip behind!" suggested a third.

"Anybody got a copper for the poor beggar?" asked a fourth.

By a desperate effort, at last I succeeded in coming up with the runaway omnibus, when to my disgust I discovered that it was one of those forbidding vehicles of which the step disappears when the door is closed. So that I had nothing to hold on to, still less to climb on to; and to continue to run with my nose at the door, like a well-trained carriage dog, suited neither my wind nor my dignity.

So I gave up the chase and dropped behind, covered with dust and perspiration, amid frantic cheers from the knifeboard and broad grins from the passengers on the pavement.

In such manner, I, an exhibitioner and a living exponent of the latest "form," entered Low Heath! I was almost more grieved for the school than for myself. Those fellows on the omnibus evidently didn't know who I was. To-morrow, when they found out, and saw me arm in arm with Tempest, they would be sorry for what they had done.

I confess that, as I walked up the steep street, and caught sight at last of the chimneys of the school peeping up over the trees, I half wished myself back at home with my mother. I hadn't expected to feel so lonely. I had indeed looked forward to a little pardonable triumph in being recognised at once as the fellow who had taken the entrance exhibition, and who evidently knew what was what. Of course it was foolish, I told myself, to expect such a thing. Fellows could hardly be expected to know who I was until they were told. Still it was a little—just a little—disappointing, and I could not help feeling hurt.

I tramped on, till presently I came to the bridge, and loitered for a moment to rest and watch the boats flitting about below. There went a four, smartly manned by youngsters no older than myself. There lolled a big fellow in a canoe. There swished by a senior in a skiff, calling on the four-oar to get out of the way as he passed. There, too, stood a master in flannels, with the Oxford Blue on his straw, talking to a group of boys, I wish I could have overhead what they were saying. Perhaps they were discussing the merits of some of the new boys.

I strolled on, passing on the way inquisitive stragglers who stared hard at me, till I came to where the road skirts the cricket field. Here, at a broken paling, I stood a moment and glanced in. Fellows were bowling and batting at the nets, others were strolling arm in arm up and down, hailing new arrivals; others were enjoying a little horse-play; others were critically examining the last season's pitch; others, impatient of the seasons, were punting about a brand-new football.

How out of it I was; and yet how sure I felt that if some of those fellows only guessed who was on the other side of the palings, they would feel interested.

I strolled on further, and began now to pass the outbuildings. There was a lecture room, empty at present. Should I be there to-morrow, I wondered, answering to my name and seeing fellows open their eyes as they heard it?

There was the gymnasium, I supposed—the place presided over by the drill master whom Tempest so much detested. I meant to back Tempest up in that feud.

Ah, there was the Lion gate, standing open to receive me. Little I had expected, when once before I entered it on my way to examination, that I should so soon be coming back, so to speak, in triumph like this.

It took some little self-persuasion, I must confess, to feel that it really was a triumph. I did think Tempest might have been on the look-out for me. I did not know where to go, or of whom to inquire my way. The boys I met either took no notice of me at all, or else stared so rudely at my hat and boots that I could not bring myself to accost them. At length I was beginning to think I had better march boldly to the first master's house I came to, when, as luck would have it, I stumbled up against my old travelling companion, who having safely arrived a quarter of an hour before, was now prowling about on the look-out for old acquaintances.

"Please," said I, "would you mind telling me the way to Mr. Sharpe's house?"

"Are you a Sharper then?" he inquired. "My word! what are we coming to? Why didn't you come up by the 'bus?"

"I tried to," said I; "you wouldn't stop."

"Jim's horses were a bit shy," said he, with a grin. "They can't be held in when they see a moke. You should have got in without their spotting you."

I didn't like this fellow. He appeared to me to think he was funny when he was not.

"Do you know if Tempest has come?" said I, hoping to impress him a little.

"Who?"

"Tempest—Harry Tempest. He's at Sharpe's too."

"What sort of looking chap is he?" demanded the youth, who, I suspected, could have told me without any detailed description.

"He's one of the seniors," said I; "he was in the reserve for the Eleven last term."

"Oh, that lout? I hope you aren't a pal of his. That would about finish you up. If you want him, you'd better go and look for him. I don't know whether every snob in the place has come up or not."

And he departed in chase of a friend whom he had just sighted.

This was depressing. Not that I believed what he said about Tempest. But I had hoped that my acquaintance with my old schoolmate would redound to my own dignity, whereas it seemed to do nothing of the kind.

Presently I encountered a very small boy, of chirpy aspect, whom I thought I might safely accost.

"I say," said I, "which is Mr. Sharpe's house?"

"Over there," said he, pointing to an ivy-covered house at some little distance higher up the street. Then regarding me attentively, he added, "I say, you'll get in a jolly row if he sees you in that get-up."

"Oh," said I, feeling that the youngster was entitled to an explanation, "I'm an exhibitioner."

"A who? All I know is he's down on chaps playing the fool. You'd better cut in on the quiet before they bowl you out in that thing," said he, pointing to my hat.

That thing! True, I had not observed many hats like it so far at Low Heath; but that was probably because I had not encountered any other fellow-exhibitioner. Tempest knew more about the form than this kid.

"Thanks," said I. "Mr. Sharpe will know who I am."

"Oh, all right," said he; "don't say I didn't tell you, that's all."

"I say," said I, feeling that enough had been said

on a matter on which we evidently misunderstood each other, "do you know Tempest?"

"Rather. He's in our house. You'll get it pretty hot from him if you cheek him."

"Oh, I know him well; he's an old chum."

The boy laughed incredulously.

"He'd thank you if he heard you say so. Oh my, fancy Tempest—— Hullo, I say, there he is. Cut away, kid, before he sees you." And the youth set me a prompt example.

I was sorry he had not remained to witness the fact that I was not quite the outsider he took me for.

Tempest was strolling across the road, arm in arm with a friend. He certainly was not got up in the "form" which he had prescribed for me. He wore a straw hat on the back of his head, and boots of unmistakable blackness. But then, though an exhibitioner himself once, he had now attained to dignity of a senior, and was probably exempt from the laws binding on new boys.

As he approached I crossed the road to meet him, full of joy at the prospect of encountering at least one friend, and marching under his protection into my new quarters. But I was doomed to a slight disappointment. For though for a moment, when he looked up, I fancied he recognised me, he did not discontinue his conversation with his friend, but drew him out into the middle of the road. They seemed to be enjoying a joke between them. His companion looked round once or twice at me, but Tempest, who was looking quite flushed, apparently did not take me in, and walked on, looking the other way.

It was a little shock to me, or would have been had I not remembered his friendly warning about the etiquette of a junior not accosting a senior till the senior accosted him. I wished he had spoken to me, for just then his help would have been particularly patronising. As it was, I was tantalised by seeing him pass by close to me, and yet being unable, without "shirking form" in a reprehensible way, to bring myself to his notice.

In due time I reached Mr. Sharpe's house. To my dismay the door stood wide open, and the hall was crowded with fellows claiming their luggage as it was being deposited by the railway van. As I arrived there was an ominous silence, in the midst of which I stood on the step, and carefully rung the bell marked, not "servants," but "visitors." No one came, so after a due interval, and amid the smiles of the onlookers, I mustered up resolution to ring again, rather louder. This time I had not to wait long. A person dressed as a sort of butler, very red in the face, emerged from a green baize door at the end of the passage and advanced wrathfully.

"Which of you young gents keeps ringing the bell?" demanded he. "He's to be made an example of this time. Oh, it was you, was it?" said he, catching sight of me.

"Yes," said I. "Is Mr. Sharpe at home?"

"At home!" demanded the official, redder in the

face than ever. "You seem to be pretty much at home." Then, apparently struck by my appearance, he pulled himself up and honoured me with a long stare in which all the assembled boys joined.

"Who is it?"

"One of the porters from the station, I should say, from the looks of him," suggested a boy.

"Whoever it is, don't you ring that visitors' bell—do you hear?" said the man-servant. "If you want anything, go round to the side door, and don't interfere with the young gentleman."

"But I'm a new boy," said I. "I'm—I'm an exhibitioner;" at which there was a great roar of laughter, which even my self-satisfaction could hardly construe into jubilation.

I began to have a horrible suspicion that I had committed some great *faux pas* by ringing the visitors' bell, and blushed consciously, to the increased amusement of my fellow "Sharpers."

"Can I see Mr. Sharpe?" I inquired, thinking it best to take the bull by the horns.

"Can't you wait?" said the servant. "Do you suppose the master has nothing to do but run out and see—wild Indians?" Here followed another laugh at my expense. "He'll see you quite soon enough."

Here a shove from behind precipitated me into the bosom of the speaker, who returned me with thanks, and before I could apologise, into the hands of the sender. Thence I found myself passed on by a side impetus to a knot of juveniles, who, not requiring my presence, passed me on to a senior standing by, who shot me back to a friend, who sent me forward among the boxes into the arms of the matron, who indignantly hustled me up the passage, where finally I pulled up short in the grasp of a gentleman who at that moment emerged from the green baize door.

In the confusion I had lost both my hat and my presence of mind. I was far too confused to observe who the newcomer was, and far too indignant to care. All that I called to my mind as I reeled into his clutches was Tempest's directions about kicking back, which accordingly I proceeded to do, with all the vigour of which my new tan boots were capable.

Mr. Sharpe suffered this assault meekly for a second or two, then he held me out stiffly at arm's length like a puppy in a fit, and demanded:

"What do you mean, sir, by behaving like this?"

I was bound to admit that it was a natural inquiry from a person whose shins had been considerably barked by my new boots. I felt as if I owed Mr. Sharpe an apology.

"Please," said I, "I didn't mean to do it. The boys shoved me, and I didn't know where I was going, really, sir."

Mr. Sharpe seemed inclined to believe me. He was a florid-looking, spectacled young man with sandy whiskers, and a grip—oh that grip!— that could have lifted me easily over the Lion gate.

"Boys," said he, "let us have none of this nonsense, or I must set a house theme. Is Mrs. Smiley here?"

Mrs. Smiley, looking anything but the "moral" of her name, appeared in due course.

"Mrs. Smiley, will you please take charge of this new boy and keep him out of trouble. Run away with Mrs. Smiley, my little man; and you boys, as soon as you have claimed your boxes, clear out till register bell."

What! did my ears deceive me? Was I, an exhibitioner, a scholar who had come up to Low Heath in all the *éclat* of the latest "form," the friend of Tempest, the fellow who had made things too hot for himself at Dangerfield—was I, I say, to be handed over to a sort of washer-womanly person to be kept out of mischief, and called "my little man" in the presence of the whole house? Was this my triumphant entry then?

No sooner had Mr. Sharpe retired, than greetings of "My little man," "Spiteful Sarah," "Run along with his Smiley, then," beset me on all sides. I would fain have explained and corrected any wrong impression, but they only laughed when I tried; finally, when Mrs. Smiley grabbed at my hand and walked me off the scene like a baby, my humiliation was complete.

Mrs. Smiley, who was far too busy with the young gentlemen's luggage to relish the extra duty put upon her by Mr. Sharpe, had a very summary way of dealing with cases of my kind.

"Sit down there, and don't move till you're told," said she, pointing to a little three-legged stool in a corner in the box-room.

"But," began I.

"Hold your tongue; how dare you speak to me?" she retorted.

"I only——"

"Stand in the corner, with your hands behind you, for disobedience," said she.

This was getting serious. The little three-legged stool would not have been exactly luxurious; but to be stood in the corner with my hands behind me by a person of the feminine gender called Smiley was really too bad. The worst of it was that if I made any further protest I might be smacked in addition, and that possibility I hardly dared risk.

So, rather to my own surprise, I found myself standing in the corner, with my hands at my back, scrutinising a blue and pink rose on the wall paper, and wondering whether it would not be worth my while to write to the "Times" about the whole business. I could not help thinking that Mrs. Smiley did not hurry herself on my account. I was conscious of box after box being dragged to the front, emptied of its contents and put back, to be removed presently by a porter, who probably looked at me every time he came in, but, I am bound to say, received very little encouragement from my studiously averted head.

After nearly an hour I began to get tired, and the blood of the Jones's began to rise within me. I was seriously meditating mutiny, or at least a definite explanation with Mrs. Smiley, when at last she broke silence.

"Now, young gentleman, this way, please."

And she led me to a small comfortable-looking apartment, which I surmised to be her particular sanctum.

"What's your name?"

"Jones," said I.

"Ah—you're the boy who's brought down a rubbishy speckled waistcoat and loud striped shirts—eh?"

"Well, yes," said I.

"Did your mother buy them for you, or did you buy them?"

"I did."

"I can see your mother's a lady by the way she has everything else done. You'll find your own trash just where you put it, in the bottom of your trunk. You will not be allowed to wear it. We expect our boys to dress like young gentlemen, whether they

'Late for school: a friendly lift' (1894).

are such or not. What's that in your hand, Jones?"

"My hat," said I, hoping I was coming in for a little credit at last.

"Hat!" Here she was rude enough to laugh. "What made you bring a thing like that here for a hat?"

"But," said I, "I'm an exhibitioner."

"All the more shame on you not dressing like a gentleman. Look at those boots; I am sure your mother did not buy them for you. Take them off at once, sir—and put on your proper ones."

"Aren't they—isn't it the thing, the form you know, for——"

"Form! Fiddlesticks. The thing at Low Heath is to behave and dress like gentlemen, not like vulgar, public-house potmen," said she, with an access of indignation which surprised me. "To think that you, with a nice mother like yours, should come up here a fright like that! There, put the shoes and hat in the trunk with the speckled waistcoat and shirts, and get yourself up decently, and then I'll speak to you."

I was under the impression she *had* spoken to me—pretty strongly too. This, then, was the end of my elaborately prepared toilet.

A horrid suspicion began to come over me at last, not only that Tempest had been having a little joke at my expense, but that I had lent myself to it with an alacrity and eagerness which had almost—nay, very nearly wholly—been ridiculous.

What does the reader think?

My further conversation with good Mrs. Smiley, after I had, to use her own expression, made myself decent, only tended to confirm the painful impression. I even went to the length of adding, of my own accord, my six-button lavender gloves to the pile of sacrificed finery which strewed the bottom of my trunk. And when in due time a bell rang and Mrs. Smiley said, "There now, go down to call over, and don't be a silly any more," I obeyed with a meekness and diffidence of which I could hardly have believed myself capable, had I not been quite sure of the fact.

CORRESPONDENCE.

Vigilantibus (Rockhampton).—The fact of your being of the same name as a peer is no proof that you are of the same family. The Heralds' College will grant arms to anyone, providing he pays the necessary fees. You should use the armorial bearing of your father, and then there would be no difficulty.

T. M.—1 and 2. 1. Let the brush stand in raw linseed-oil for a day or two, and then wash the oil out with soap and water, till the froth is colourless. 2. Holland will serve as a substitute for canvas if properly primed, but as a rule it is neither rough enough nor strong enough for lasting work.

BOYS I HAVE KNOWN

J. Stratford Bradish.

THE BAD BOY—*"Puer malus vel pravus"*

THE Bad Boy, like the Fat Boy, is a very ancient and time-honoured institution, and will probably continue to flourish so long as mischief remains to be done, or until that dread instrument the cane is relegated to a museum of ancient curiosities.

With the departure of the cane the Bad Boy, deprived at once of his chief incentive to wickedness, and of what may be called his "staff of sustenance," must eventually become an extinct species. This may appear a somewhat rash statement at first sight; but I think you will all agree that the proof is amazingly simple, as thus:—*No Bad Boy—no cane.* Hence it follows that: *No cane—no Bad Boy.* Q.E.D.

The Bad Boy is at once the pride and the bane of his maiden aunt's existence; a perfect thorn in the flesh to his elder brother (who is developing high collars and an incipient moustache); whilst his gouty old uncle, albeit he goes in terror of his life when Master Tommy is around, is wont to brag of this *enfant terrible* to his cronies after dinner as "a fine young dog, sir, a chip off the old block. Make his mark some day, if he don't get hanged in the meantime." And the old gentleman laughs so heartily at his own quip that his premature decease appears inevitable, until the butler comes and incontinently wheels him off for his post-prandial snooze.

It seems a pity that the authorities omitted to make a speciality of the Bad Boy at the last census taking. The results might have proved highly interesting to statisticians, and would, I feel confident, have utterly refuted Jones's somewhat peculiar views on this subject. Jones is a bachelor of uncertain age and a certain rotundity of figure, who, in his capacity of second master at Birchemall Academy, claims to speak with some authority on all questions relating to the *genus puer*.

Well, when I told Jones what the subject of this

article was to be, his face unconsciously assumed that magisterial sternness which he usually reserves for the class room, as he observed:

"The Bad Boy, is it? But why put it in the singular? *My* experience goes to prove that *all* boys

Old-Style Scholar

are naturally bad; it is merely a question of degree. I don't deny that there may be some rare exceptions; in fact, I myself, as a boy"—here he tenderly stroked the half-dozen hairs that still remain to adorn his cranium—"I was considered a striking example of youthful merit—" "and insufferable conceit," I mentally ejaculated; but Jones went on: "Now how much better to write about the Good Boy; *there's* a subject upon which you might discourse with so much benefit to your readers and——"

"Jones," I interposed, as I rose to my full height—5 ft. 4 in.—"my *dear* Jones, I have too much regard for my own health; I fear I should break down under the strain. Let me confess to you that I don't know this paragon of yours; I've seen him at a safe distance, I admit, but never yet have I had the courage to make his nearer acquaintance; and—let me whisper the awful revelation in your ear, Jones—what's more, *I don't want to!*"

Up to a certain point, however, Jones was right, only his deductions were wrong. To describe a

single type of the Bad Boy which should embrace all the eccentricities of which the *genus* is capable, would be a task beyond the pen of a Dickens, or even a Mark Twain. Perhaps the latter bears away the palm for a masterly description of the life and possibilities of a bad boy in the person of Huckleberry Finn. You must all be familiar with the career of that unfortunate young savage, who defies all Aunt Polly's well-meant efforts at civilisation; and finally, after a manful struggle to become respectable, relapses into his original state of savagery and bliss in the wilderness. But to return. I was going to say that there are several distinct types of the Bad Boy: though, like the circles in a certain proposition of Euclid, they may all be said to intersect one another at various points. I shall only attempt here to describe four varieties; and as we are in for a square meal (no connection with the circles aforesaid), I will leave the most agreeable specimen—representing the pudding—to the last.

Our first type then will be the loafer, whom we will call *Puer iners*. Of course we all know *him*, and, presumably, we all regard him with mingled pity and contempt. Look at him as he slouches across the quadrangle; his cap—such a rag too—pasted on the back of his head, as though it had grown there and meant to stay; his "Etons" in such a fearful state of dilapidation that a much-enduring matron has declared them beyond *her* powers of rejuvenation; his fists thrust deeply into his pockets, with an accompanying hunch of the shoulders that all too plainly bespeaks his disposition.

The *Puer iners* bears a strong resemblance to our old friend *Puer lymphaticus*. Like the latter he is usually harmless if left to his own devices, and his sins are rather those of omission than of commission. He is rarely to be seen on the field, more rarely does he take any active part in games. He may, occasionally, driven thereto by the stern fiat of his house captain, don the jersey and knickers, and allow himself to be carried along in the "rushes," or lean listlessly against the rearmost man in the scrums. He has even been known, as much to his own surprise as to that of everyone else, to fall, accidentally, on the ball just over the touch line, and to gain thereby the winning try for his side; but such occurrences are about as rare as December primroses. In the cricket season, under the influence of clean flannels and a cloudless sky, he may warm into a sort of temporary activity, and, provided there is a tuck-shop within easy reach, he may even exhibit a languid interest in a house match. This interest—you can hardly call it enthusiasm—usually consists in securing a soft and quiet spot, beyond the reach of possible leg hits, where, having disposed of his stock of eatables, he gradually subsides into a state of somnolence, induced by Bath buns and a scorching sun. And here, with his hat tilted forward over his freckled nose, and his mouth invitingly agape for all and sundry flies, let us leave him, nor seek to disturb a well-earned rest with noisy and ungenerous criticism on the beauty of his recumbent carcase. *Somniat in pace!*

But, after all, the loafing boy is only "indifferent bad," and that is more than can be said of our next type, yclept the "Sneak," who is, perhaps, *facile*

Old-Style Schoolmaster

princeps among this noble brotherhood of bad boys. To seek for a Latin word, however long, which should express the exact meaning conveyed by our own monosyllable, would be a hopeless task, and an insult, moreover, to the warrior race that dwelt of yore by the banks of the Tiber.

What epithet, in boy parlance, could possibly express more utter scorn and disgust than this word—"sneak!" And what boy is there—let his real nature be what it may—who would not run any risk, or cheerfully accept the severest thrashing, rather than incur the shame and opprobrium implied by that epithet? None, indeed, I should think.

But really, the sneak is such a *rara avis* nowadays, and such an unpleasant personage to wit, that it were a waste of good ink to describe him at any length, so I will content myself with relating a little incident which came within my own school experience, as an instance of how we rid ourselves of the sneak at Switchington.

Williams was Pecksniffian sort of fellow, for whom most of us entertained a tacit dislike, amounting in my own case almost to repulsion. He affected the manner of *bon camarade*, and did his level best to get on good terms with every one worth knowing in the house; but in spite of this showy plating of assumed good-fellowship, the hall-mark was wanting, and there were indications that the metal beneath was merely an amalgam of hypocrisy and deceit. At length the test came which conclusively proved the nature of that metal; and behold it was base!

It all happened thus wise. A certain farmer had made himself obnoxious by objecting to paper-chases over his fields—a favourite line of country with us in those days. Accordingly half a dozen turbulent spirits—chiefly fourth and fifth form boys—made a descent upon his orchards, and did a considerable amount of damage to his fruit—far more, indeed, than they ever meant to do. There was an awful row, of course, but they had kept their secret very well, the only outsider who knew who the culprits were being Williams, who professed a great friendship for one of them, Mansell by name; consequently they all hoped to remain unidentified and to escape justice.

But they had reckoned without their sneak! It appears that Williams had quarrelled with Mansell, and, having got considerably the worst of the dispute, the former hied him to the head-master with vengeance in his heart, and informed him, with much apparent reluctance, that Mansell had been concerned in the raid upon Farmer Brown's fruit-trees. He also assured the Head, with the candour he knew so well how to assume, that he only did this thing from a strong sense of duty, and he hoped that his name might not appear in connection with the matter. Mansell and the others, who, to do them justice, had given in their names immediately after, were publicly flogged, and one poor fellow who was in the Eleven had his colours taken away from him.

The fact of Williams having betrayed his friend got about somehow, and although most of the fellows blamed Mansell & Co. for their unwarrantable conduct, this feeling was entirely eclipsed by the universal disgust felt towards Williams. We held a solemn "court-martial" in the day-room at Frere's one evening: witnesses were examined, and "counsel" for and against the prisoner addressed the court. The verdict was a unanimous one of "guilty"; and the sentence "that the prisoner be sent into absolute Coventry for the remainder of term." Well, that sentence was carried out so completely, that Williams must have led a dog's life for the month that remained of the term; and he did not turn up again the following one, which was a bit rough on him perhaps, but a great relief to the House.

Our third specimen of the *Puer Malus*, though he undoubtedly exists, yet we believe to be rapidly becoming extinct; and therefore he merits but a

CORRESPONDENCE.

Tattooing (E. P. Beare).—Only by operation.

Bandy Legs (T. R. German).—The legs may get bandy or bowed long after you are 15, but the cure must commence the very day you see the first deviation, and you must consult a surgeon. Growing does not cease till you are about 20 or 21.

Self-caused Nervousness (J. H. and many others).—Your letter, John, is too long. We never could work through all our correspondence were all letters even half the length. If there be no inherited blood disease, and if with God's help you can lead a pure and holy life, and obey the laws of health, you will, we have no doubt, get strong. The bath will help you much. Freeman's syrup is an excellent tonic. Take it for a fortnight, omit a week, and use it again and again. The cream of malt with hypophosphites is now much used. And if you are pale a little iron will help you. Iron must be used, however, most sparingly, and for many weeks. Get the bi-palatinoids. The dose is one, thrice a day, after food, but don't take more than one twice a day. You thus get a more gentle and certain action, and can take them a long time. Nature doesn't like being rushed. They are simply composed each of one grain of Ferri sulph. exsicc. and Sodii carb. exsicc., but so encased that they do not form chemical union till swallowed. But we repeat, no earthly good can accrue till you conquer self.

short notice at our hands. His little "peculiarity" is cruelty—sheer, wanton, unreasoning cruelty, usually practised upon dumb animals; this type then we will designate *Puer sævus et immisericors*. One of his mildest eccentricities is robbing birds' nests wholesale, and, more often than not, destroying the nests as well; a vile practice that, when one thinks of what it means to the parent birds, all right-minded boys should put down with a strong hand.

But this in many instances is mere thoughtlessness, and is nothing compared to what our friend *can* do when he sets his mind to it. His ingenuity in this respect is often worthy of a better cause, and, provided he be not found out, it becomes a perfect mania with him. But, fortunately, it is usually a temporary disease, especially if it receives "prompt treatment," as the doctors say. Here is a prescription which I can recommend as an almost certain cure for this unpleasant malady. It was originally used by Professor Schmackhardt of Bonn, and given by him to Dr. MacBirch, who assured me he had found it most efficacious:—

R

Baculorum 1
Vergil. linearum 500
Fiat mistura.

Sig. To be taken every other day until the patient improves.

Our last variety of the Bad Boy is one for whom I must confess a sneaking regard: indeed I should scarcely have included him as one of the species on my own responsibility, had it not been for Jones, who thought fit to reproach me for my "depravity" in wishing to omit "the Scamp" from this list. Moreover, Jones wouldn't deign to search the classics for a Latin name to fit the subject, so perhaps some of my readers will come to my aid. Any way, I shall call him simply "the Scamp"—one of those mischievous little chaps (they are always in the Lower School) who are never happy unless they have their fingers in some forbidden pie, so to speak.

Not that they purloin the contents of the pie—oh no! they merely upset all its internal arrangements; so that the cook, who has left it—a very masterpiece of cookery—to cool upon a shelf, comes back and finds it useless as an article of diet, and thereupon vows vengeance on "that young warmint, Master Tommy," whenever she is fortunate enough to "ketch 'im." And Tommy takes precious good care that the good lady does *not* "ketch" him; or if she does, you may be sure the young rogue will manage to get round her with his cherubic face and his blarney. Ah! Tommy, it's yourself knows how to find the soft spot in a lady's heart!

Paddy MacGuire was a scamp of the first water; his *forte* lay in concocting "booby-traps"—of which he possessed a large and varied assortment. You never knew where or when to expect them, and the best of it was that you could never catch the young

rogue in the act. If you did, Paddy's perfect assumption of innocence would make you roar with laughter at your own discomfiture; or else, should you happen to have barked your shins or spoiled the bridge of your nose in the process, his sincere and warmly-expressed sorrow was usually sufficient to smooth your ruffled plumes, till you almost felt that you yourself had been the aggressor. .

The Scamp, then, as I take him, is generally impulsive, thoughtless, and headstrong, but will do half a dozen generous actions for one piece of mischief; and in the long run you are far more likely to remember his goodness of heart, than any little "inconvenience" he may have caused you by his thoughtlessness. Still, this very want of thought may sometimes involve him in serious trouble, and bring a very hornet's nest about his ears.

Our friend Paddy MacGuire, for example, managed in this way to get himself into very hot water, and drew down upon him the displeasure, not only of many of his warmest admirers, but of several of the masters, including Mr. Frere. After he had got over the shock of poor Bly's death, he started on a course of reckless disregard of school rules, which well-nigh landed him in expulsion. But as this is not a record of that hero's adventures, I need say no more about him at present, though I hope, before long, to meet you all again in these pages.

So now, to Good Boys and Bad Boys alike, I will only say "Au revoir!"

CARAVAN LIFE

Dr. Gordon Stables, R.N.

THERE is no more delightful or ideal way of spending a summer, and seeing all the beauties of this lovely land, than travelling in the Gentleman Gipsy Caravan, of which I am the inventor. The expense is great, however, and no one should think of hiring an ordinary gipsy's van. That is *never* clean.

I will describe "The Wanderer," my own "land yacht." She was built by the Bristol Waggon Company, and I have been ten years on the road. My experience cannot be small, therefore.

I should advise no one, however, to have a caravan so large as the Wanderer. She is fully nineteen feet from stem to stern, seven feet four inches outside breadth of beam, six feet wide inside, eleven feet high from ground to top of sky-light, and

Dr Gordon Stables 'on the road'.

requires two strong horses to drag her. She weighs two tons. But my horses don't walk. I have a splendid coachman, and he just does what I tell him, for I sit by his side or lie among rugs in the verandah beside my beautiful caravan dog, the champion-bred St. Bernard "Lassie." I said my horses do not walk; I mean constantly. You see, one must be most careful with one's moving power. Mine are stabled every night knee-deep in straw, at some small road-side inn, because it is imperative to lay the caravan in a green meadow, or no sleep can be obtained, and sleep is essential on the road.

But as to driving. On level roads I do an easy six to seven miles an hour, but I have done four miles in twenty-four minutes. I would as soon have a good give-and-take road as a long monotonous level. . . . Long hills I walk the horses slowly up, short pitches we rush at a fearful gallop, and everthing has to clear out of the way, even dog-carts. If they don't, it is their risk, and Heaven help the dog-cart! In a rolling country we let the horses have their heads when half-way down one hill, and encourage them with a "Gee hoop!" The impetus takes them half-way up the other. This is Scotch and Russian style, and most humane; when we reach the top they have a rest and a mouthful of cool green grass. I have travelled 1,300 miles in one season, and crossed the Grampian Mountains down into Inverness, and my horses have never been sick or sorry. In 1895 I zigzagged from Berkshire across England and Scotland to Aberdeen and Balmoral, and on to wild Brae Mar (1,020 miles record), and my horses were better and harder at the end of this journey than when I started.

But you must not think of hiring from stage to

stage. The nags must be well chosen! One of the best I ever had was from the plough; he was willing, kind, would eat any amount, and pulled—why, he seemed strong enough to pull down a steeple. But there was just a little blood in him. A great clod-hopping beast, with no mouth, would be no use for a caravan. He would break one's coachman's heart.

TURNING OVER NEW LEAVES

Gordon Stables, M.D., C.M., R.N.

"Confess yourself to Heaven."

Repent what's past; avoid what is to come."
                                    SHAKESPEARE.

URNING over new leaves! Yes, lads, and there isn't a man, woman, girl, or boy in this dear land of ours that might not benefit by the advice given by Shakespeare in the two lines that head this paper. We ought to turn over new leaves, not only as regards our minds or souls, but as regards our habits of life, our physical well-being.

"Mens sana in corpore sano!"
"A pure mind in a healthy body!"

Ah! That is just it, and that is what we should aim at. And surely no better time than this for reviewing the past, and making vows to live healthier lives for the future; and as health means happiness, blessed are they who do so. It seems to me, anyhow, that in the snow time, when the wintry winds are sighing through the leafless trees, when the world is robed in its white cocoon, and little robin trills his sweet, sad song upon the gate, God is really nearer to those who seek Him.

"Some say that ever against this season comes,
  Wherein our Saviour's birth is celebrated,
  The bird of dawning singeth all night long,
  And then they say no spirit dare stir abroad.
  The nights are wholesome, then no planets strike,
  No fairy takes, nor witch hath power to charm,
  So hallowed and so gracious is the time."

Yes, there is a good deal of mere sentiment, perhaps, in these lines, but much truth, too, if you can read them in the right spirit.

That among my great army of boy-readers I have a few naughty ones I know, for many who have erred write to seek my advice, and their secrets are ever safe in my keeping.

I want to say a word or two to these first, in this Health Sermon of mine. Ah! what would not some of those poor lads do to get back into the straight and flowery paths of health and purity! But there is a demon that seems for ever dragging them back, and trying more and more every week to force them into the pit of despair.

The worst of it is that they themselves know that they alone have raised that demon. Ill-health and nervousness are bad enough, but ill-health coupled with remorse is too dreadful to contemplate.

"Oh, now, for ever
Farewell the tranquil mind! Farewell content!"

The longer things go on the worse matters become. I have no desire to frighten any boy, even the most erring, but a little holding up of the mirror to Nature, a few solemn warnings, even if they frighten at the time, do good in the end. That is, if advice be taken in time. Many medical men pooh-pooh things, and drive poor lads into the insatiable maw of the murderous, though plausible, advertising quack. Then, indeed, all may be lost.

Well, to talk more cheerfully, our erring boy must fight the demon he has raised with all his strength and mind, morally and physically. He has no wish, I am sure, to grow up a poor, shaking, white-faced, unhappy creature, without nerve enough to look a tom-cat straight in the face. He has no wish to turn into a confirmed invalid, and perhaps end his miserable life in an asylum. So fight he *must!*

He *must* turn over a new leaf, before it is too late. He *must*, to begin with, give up all bad habits, and then set himself to observe and obey the laws of health with regularity. The cold tub in the morning before breakfast, dumb-bells, too, and a run out of doors. Then a healthy, wholesome breakfast. Then to work—work is a cure almost in itself—in a well-ventilated room, if possible. His thoughts need guarding; so, too, his eyes. Exercise and pleasant recreation. No cycling—it only makes a delicate lad weaker in every way. Sleep, but not over-much. Not much bedclothes; a hard mattress. Now and then a warm bath, but constipation to be guarded against. No smoking; and, of course, no stimulants. I have saved hundreds by getting them to adhere to these simple rules. Remember, this, also, you must pray to God earnestly to—as David says—cleanse you from secret faults.

And now a few words to the wise—to my comparatively good boys.

Of course, they may fancy themselves in very good health, but there may be many wee bits of evil habits they should drop by turning over a new leaf.

Smoking.—I am often queried about this. Is it injurious? Most certainly in a boy, and it does not even tend to increase a man's health. If, then, you have already acquired the habit, throw away those half-cabbage-leaf cigarettes. Oh, I don't want to force my advice on anyone. I do but give it.

Smoke away as long as you please, then, if you think it looks brave; or if you desire to grow up a miserable, palpitating mite of a monkey, instead of a hardy man beneath whose tread the ground shall ring. Tobacco attacks the nerve-centres; the lungs and every organ of the body are rendered weak, the heart pale and flabby; and being thus unable to discharge sufficient blood to nourish the body properly, growth is stopped. So much for smoking.

Cycling.—There is no greater lover of this charming exercise than I, who have ridden for five-and-twenty years; and many is the book I have written on the subject. But I am dead against two things: 1. Bending too far over the bar, which renders a boy in time round-shouldered, and often contracts the intestinal canal. 2. *Scorching.*—Past my wigwam every fine Saturday rush hundreds of poor little chaps that I positively pity. Perched they are upon their bits of bikes, like cats on a garden wall, and probably smoking because it looks manly. Making records, they think they are. When they get home at last in a lather they boast about their mighty deeds (oh my!) before their mothers or sisters. Poor things! Ah, well, they help to keep down the population, for a scorcher never did nor could live long.

'What would the first inhabitant say?': the sort of situation in which the B.O.P. hero — and reader — was likely to find himself.

THE
BOYS OWN PAPER

No. 947.—Vol. XIX.
[NO. 25 OF NEW VOL.]

SATURDAY, MARCH 6, 1897.

Price One Penny.
[ALL RIGHTS RESERVED]

The Triple Alliance,
its Trials & Triumphs.
By Harold Avery

Author of "The School's Honour," "An Old Boy's Yarns," etc. etc.

(Illustrated by Alfred Pearse.)

"Please, sir, . . . it's a ghost!"

"The bear and man, still united, rolled over the brink."

PRINCE CHRISTIAN VICTOR AT SCHOOL

A Chat about his Cricket Days

THERE are few more respected men among cricketers than Mr. Tom Hearne, the ground man at Lord's, and he had the good fortune to be at Wellington College when Prince Christian Victor was there, in the years 1883–4–5. The other day the writer called in and asked him about those distant times.

He expressed great personal sorrow at the loss of one who was a gallant soldier and good sportsman, and who in the school was a great favourite.

"He came to the school, a thorough gentleman, at the age of fourteen, and I was one day talking to another lad when he said casually. 'Let me introduce you to Prince Christian Victor'—and the Prince came up, cordially greeted me and chatted about cricket—a game at which he was always good and, if he had not had other claims on his time and attention, would have become first class. He was very genial and was a member of the Blucher Dormitory. At the College there are several boarding houses, and His Royal Highness lived in one of these.

"His first year in the Eleven was in 1884, and in the following season he became captain, an honour that he greatly appreciated. The important position involved the trying of a good many men before they got their colours, and there is always great competition in this way. There is also naturally a strong desire to win the Inter-School contests—these are with Haileybury and Charterhouse. In one of these contests Mr. Markham was playing, and the Prince got twenty-two. Markham was a genius at the game, and was to have been tried for his county, Derbyshire, when he got a chill and died very suddenly.

"The Prince took a great interest in the most trivial details of the game, and at the commencement of the May Term had the boys practising on asphalte when the weather was not favourable."

"On the Bat's back I do fly"

Addresses of Doctors (E. P. T.).—Cannot do it. Even the doctors whose addresses we gave would not like it. It would be a breach of etiquette. Look in the "London Directory."

Spots on Forehead (W. J. L.).—Your blood is impure. Read our reply to J. H. on Self-caused **Ner**vousness. Do you **study** to keep pure in thought by day? This will help you very much. Don't despair.

Palpitation of Heart (Palpitation).—Yes, your food is somewhat at fault. Live on plain food, and avoid the stout. One glass of stout may be the thin end of the wedge. 2. You must give up the deal of exercise you take, especially swimming, bells, and clubs. Walking exercise is best for you for a year at least. Take plenty of that, but do not spurt. 3. No, we don't think you want iron and quinine. You say you are naturally hot-blooded. Well, iron is exciting, you know.

Cat Scalded (Harry).— No; we think it probable that the roots have been destroyed.

Cross-eyed (Afflicted). —We advise you to seek advice, next time you are in London, at some of the large hospitals. We could not advise you without examination, and this is impossible.

Six Feet Two in his Socks (Nitram).—It is unfortunate your being so thin. Good living, regular exercise, and an occasional tonic are the only things to fill you out.

Left *A tribute to W. G. Grace.*
Below left *A. E. J. Collins, who made the record score of 628 not out at Clifton College in 1899.*
Below *Prince Ranjitsinghi makes his famous leg glide.*

124

A SNAKE STORY

By Lieut.-General Sir Fred. Middleton,
K.C.M.G., C.B.,

Author of "A Monkey Yarn," etc.

"NOW, Fardy," exclaimed my boy Willie, as we were sitting on the lawn, "tell us some more stories, snake stories this time, and if I like them you can send them to the 'B.O.P.' as you did the monkey yarn."

The cheek of the boy—"if he likes them!" Well, it was at his suggestion that I sent my last story to the Editor, so I complied with his request as follows:—

When I first went to India, alas! now many years ago, I was a little imbued with the popular idea that one would be constantly meeting and tumbling over tigers, snakes, and scorpions, the two latter being frequent tenants of your boots, slippers, and bed.

A few days after I had joined my regiment in Cawnpore I was dressing for morning parade—more like night parade, it seemed to me, being about 3 a.m. and pitch dark. I was sitting on the side of my "charpoy"—or bed—half awake, drawing on my Wellington boots, when, as one of my feet was gliding into its place, I felt something move under it. Of course, it instantaneously flashed upon me that it was a snake, and as I had heard or read somewhere of the proper thing to do in such a case. I rammed my foot well home in the boot and began to dance and stamp about the room on one leg, to the evident alarm and astonishment of my bearer, or native valet, who began to think his master—"pagal ho gaya"—had gone crazy. At last, feeling that I must have succeeded in flattening out the intrusive reptile, I proceeded, with the bearer's assistance, to draw off the boot; and, turning it upside down, with the help of a stick extracted a flattened, bleeding mass, which, after close inspection, my bearer, with a grin, declared to be "mendak"—a frog! Alas, it was too true, and all my heroism and presence of mind had been called into play to squelch a poor harmless froggy!

"Oh, I say!" exclaimed my boy, with an air of disappointment, "that is not a story about a snake!"

"No, my boy," I replied; "but at the time it occurred I thought it was!"

Well, now for a real snake story. I was staying at an up-country station in India with a married friend in the Bengal Civil Service. In the forenoon of a piping hot day, my host having gone to his "cutcherry"—Office—I was sitting alone behind a "Kasjas tattie"—a sort of screen made of odorous grass and kept wet for coolness—reading, when all at once I heard a series of screams mingled with cries of "Ayah, ayah, idher ao jaldi!"—Servant, servant, come here quickly!

I rushed out into the verandah and found the screams came from a "ghusl-khanah"—bathroom—which was at the end of, and opening on to, the verandah. I ran to the door, and knocking, asked what was the matter. A voice, which I recognised as that of my hostess, replied pathetically, "Oh! there is a dreadful snake in the bath-room, and I do not know what to do."

"Go back into your bedroom," replied I, "and I will go in and demolish the intruder."

She replied, "Oh! but I cannot, because the snake is between me and the bedroom door. Oh! what shall I do?"

I began to get alarmed, and found myself in a dilemma. Something must be done, and that quickly; but evidently I could neither ask the lady to come out on the verandah, nor could I rush into the bathroom myself, and the "ayah"—native lady's-maid—who had by this time appeared on the scene, was weeping, but altogether declined to go in and face the terrible "samp"—snake.

The unfortunate lady began to scream again, and in a fit of desperation I shouted out:

"Unlock the door opening on to the verandah, get into the corner farthest from the snake, cover yourself with your towels, and I will go in and kill the beast."

"Oh no, you can't come in here," was her answer; "where, oh where is the ayah?" I told her that she was with me, but declined to face the snake.

I then imperatively reiterated my former directions, telling her to let me know when she was ready.

I heard the door unlocked, and a few seconds later a smothered voice said something, upon which I opened the door and cautiously entered the bathroom. The room appeared quite dark to one entering suddenly from the glaring sunlight. I could not see at first, and so tripped over something and fell upon my face. From the smothered exclamation which came from the towels in the corner, I concluded that the something was my hostess's legs. I hastily scrambled up, congratulating myself that I had not tumbled on to the snake.

In a short time my eyes got accustomed to the subdued light, and I advanced, looking anxiously for the "samp". "The towels" again spoke, and I gathered that the terrible snake was somewhere among the "chatthies"—or water-jars— and so advanced cautiously in their direction. I had been picturing to myself a huge cobra balanced on his coiled body with hood expanded, eyes all aflame, and forked tongue vibrating, guarding the bedroom door. What I now saw, rather to my relief I confess, was a small thin snake, its head peeping out from between two "chatthies" on the ground, its body being coiled round one of them, for coolness most probably, the jars being porous. When I drew near its little beady eyes flashed, and it hissed for all it was worth.

Knowing that some of the smaller snakes were extremely venomous, and having nothing in my hand to strike it with, I made a kick at it, breaking the jar, and rather damaging my foot, but effectual-ly breaking the back of my young ophidian. I seized it by the tail, and, telling "the towels" that it was all right, rushed out in triumph into the verandah, to the infinite relief of my hostess, who told me afterwards that she would have been smothered had her stay under the towels been prolonged another instant.

The native servants, who by this time had crowded into the verandah, received me with loud praise and cries of "Shabash!" as if I had slain a dragon. Of course they all declared that the slaughtered snake was "burra krab"—very bad. Whether it was venomous or not I cannot say, as my kick had been so vigorous that its head was smashed, and I could not see whether it had fangs or not; but it is probable that it was venomous. . . .

OUR NOTE BOOK.

The Fat Boy of Kent.

[Charles Watts, of Woodchurch, Ashford, Kent, who is only fourteen years of age, stands 6 feet high, and turns the scale at 23 stone ! What do you think of that for size and weight !]

OUR PRIZE COMPETITION AWARDS

Writing Competition

(Age 18.)
Prize—10s. 6d.
WILLIAM JOHN ALLAN, 29 Chapel Place, Erskine Street, Liverpool.

CERTIFICATES.
[*Names stand in order of merit.*]
Thomas Oliver, 2 Albert Terrace, South Shields; Stanley W. Gully, 263 Gillas Street, Adelaide, South Australia; Henry Francis Taylor, Padstow Villa, Weston-super-Mare; Maude M. A. Blair, Bridge of Allan, N.B.; Bernard Francis Northcote Till, 8 Melville Road, Edgbaston, Birmingham; Archibald William MacCallum, 17 North Park Street, Glasgow; Richard James Delf, 101 City Road, Lakenham, Norwich; John Percy Cox, 46 Elm Street, Cardiff; Charles Albert Walker, St. Philip's School, 92 Smyth Street, Georgetown, British Guiana; James E. Dennison, Warwickshire Reformatory, Weston, Leamington; Lily Hamilton, St. Rumon's, Tavistock; D. Hebenton, Grahamsland Estate, Badulla, Ceylon; Henry A. Townsend, 20 London Road, Clapton, N.E.; John Eden Ball, Station Road, Poulton-le-Fylde, Lancashire; Albert Hastings, 8 Humberstone Road, Leicester; Evan Thomas, 26 Morris Lane, St. Thomas, Swansea; Robert Horton Best, 44 High Street, Rotherham; Herbert J. K. Field, "Ingle-neuk," 5 Piermont Road, East Dulwich, S.E.; William S. Lea, 4 St. John's Hill, Tenby, South Wales; William I. Godwin, The Rosarium, Ashbourne; Ernest Wright, Warwickshire Reformatory, Weston, Leamington; Alfred James Morris, 13 Great Brickkiln Street, Wolverhampton.

(Age 19.)
Prize—10s. 6d.
GEORGE HERBERT HAYWOOD, Albany, West Australia.

CERTIFICATES.
Ethel Harston, 12 Monks Road, Lincoln; Kate Gertrude Johns, 13 Tredegar Road, Bow; David Pearson Robinson, 35 Wood Street, Maryport; John Cushing Eales White, 47 Lancaster Park, Richmond, Surrey; Philip Maclagan Henderson, 15 Castlegate, Berwick-on-Tweed; Henry Welch, Helsby, near Warrington; Joan Johnson, Devonshire House, Youghal, co. Cork, Ireland; Henry S. Black, Nassau N. P. Bahamas, West Indies.

(Age 20.)
Prize—10s. 6d.
GEORGE JAMES ENDACOTT, 22 Parr Street, Newtown, Exeter.

CERTIFICATES.
W. A. Carter, 13 Henwood Road, Rotherhithe, S.E.; Richard Harrison Walker, 43 Russell Street, Hull; Ralph Thomas, Wyck Rissington, Stow-on-the-Wold; William Brookes, 55 Waterloo Street, Tipton, Staffs; Samuel W. H. Humm, 37 Mall Chambers, Kensington, W.; Leonard Smith, The Oaks, Rosebank, near Cape Town, C.C.; M. Annie Laurie, Nat. School, Swalecliffe, Canterbury; Wilton Alford Williams, Great Record Mineral Water Springs, Queen's Road, Clarendon Park, Leicester.

Right *The list of prize-winners shows the age range (18–57) and variety of B.O.P. readers (two came from a reformatory school and many from overseas).* Below *'Signs of the season'.*

(*Age* 21–24.)

Prize—10s. 6d.

CATHERINE A. VERNON, "Holmleigh,"
Dunstable, Beds.

CERTIFICATES.

John Robert Johnson, 31 Osborne Avenue,
South Shields; Florence Elizabeth Williams,
"Glenwood," Queen's Road, Clarendon Park,
Leicester; E. Jessie Vincent, c/o Mrs. Hutchinson,
Ivy Bank, Leytonstone; George Charles Hull, 42
Linhope Street, Dorset Square, London, N.W.;
William Hatch Harding, 32 Ince Green Lane,
Higher Ince, Wigan; Amy C. J. Pine, 35 College
Street, Chelsea, s.w.; William T. W. Tatnell, 47
Bampton Road, St. Anne's Road, South
Tottenham; John B. Wheatcroft, c/o Y.M.C.A.
Sheffield; Arthur W. Coulson, 5 Algernon Road,
Rotton Park; William Norman Wilson, 17 Silver-
dale, Sydenham, S.E.; Fleming William Goddard, 76
Brookdale Road, Hoe Street, Walthamstow.

(*Over age.*)

Prize—10s. 6d.

JAMES DAWSON HALEY (age 57), 4 Raeberry
Street, Glasgow.

CERTIFICATES.

Wilfrid James Lewis, 52 Oakthorpe Road,
Oxford; Nelly Bruford Side, 2 Maismore Terrace,
Peckham Park Road, S.E.; G. A. M. Wilson, Rose
Cottage, Culcabock, Inverness; George Pontin,
Church House, Yapton, Arundel; Thomas Green, 9
Crackenedge Terrace, Dewsbury, Yorks; William
John Hall, 14 Pier Terrace, South Shields; Mary
Gillespie Godby, 28 Regent Street, Shirley,
Southampton.

A FACT FROM THE BOARD SCHOOLS

HE never missed a single day
At school—he never stopped away
For sickness or for truant-play.

"Good boy!" exclaimed th' approving Board;
"Good boy indeed, with learning stored!"—
And gave a medal as reward.

But how, they queried, could it be—
Such wondrous regularity?—
Had he no childish malady?—

No chicken-pox or ailment small
That to the boyish lot befall?
"Yes," said the boy, "he'd had them all."

Oh boy deserving of all praise!—
Not to encroach on learning's ways—
He'd "had them *in the holidays.*"

Oh virtuous lad!—when other boys
Distressed their friends with strife and noise—
He nursed the measles' homely joys.

Or when the lads went forth in flocks
In cricket shirt or football socks,
He took the mumps or chicken-pox.

Oh noble lad, oh prodigy!
I marvel, when I think of thee,
What will thy future record be?

A. LESLIE.

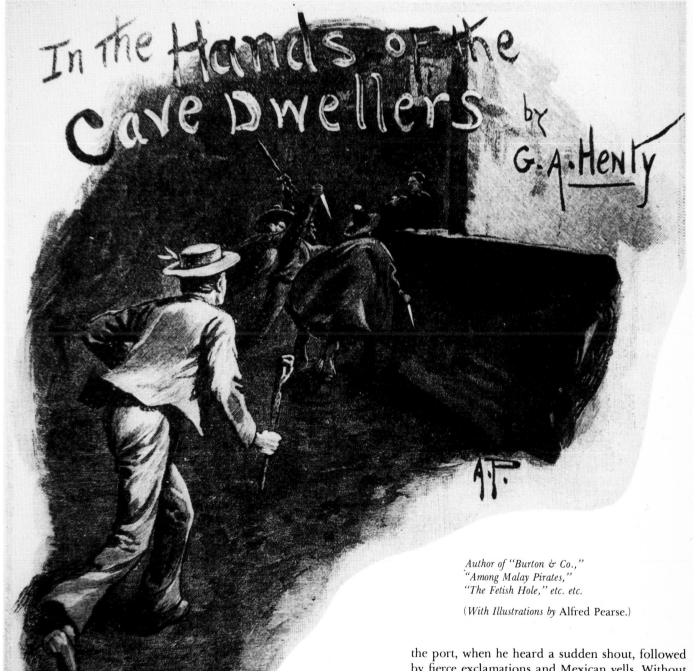

In the Hands of the Cave Dwellers by G.A. Henty

Author of "Burton & Co.,"
"Among Malay Pirates,"
"The Fetish Hole," etc. etc.

(*With Illustrations by* Alfred Pearse.)

CHAPTER I.

IT was late in the evening at San Diego, in the autumn of the year 1832. There was no moon, but the stars shone so brightly in the clear, dry atmosphere, that it was easy to distinguish objects at some little distance.

A young fellow in the dress of a sailor was making his way through the narrow streets that bordered the port, when he heard a sudden shout, followed by fierce exclamations and Mexican yells. Without pausing to consider whether it was prudent to interfere, the young fellow grasped tightly a cudgel he had that day cut, and ran to the spot where it was evident that a conflict was going on.

It was but some forty yards away, and as he approached he made out four figures who were dodging round a doorway, and were evidently attacking some one standing there.

The inequality of the combat was sufficient to appeal at once to the sailor's sympathies. The sand that lay thick in the street had deadened his footsteps, and his presence was unmarked till his stick descended with a sharp crack on the uplifted wrist of one of the assailants, eliciting a cry of pain, while the knife the would-be assassin held flew across the street.

One of the man's companions turned savagely upon the new-comer, but the sailor's arm was already raised and the cudgel alighted with such force on the man's head that he fell stunned to the ground. This unexpected assault caused the other two assailants to pause and look round, and in an instant the defender of the doorway bounded forward and hurled his knife into one of their bodies, while the other at once fled, followed by the man whose wrist had been disabled by the sailor's first blow.

"Carambo, senor!" the Mexican said; "you have rendered me a service indeed, and I tender you a thousand thanks. I could not have held out much longer, for I had been more than once wounded before you arrived."

"You are heartily welcome, senor. It was but a slight business; two blows with my stick and the matter was done."

"You are not a countryman of mine, senor," the other said, for the sailor spoke with a strong accent; "you are a stranger, and, as I can see now, a sailor."

"That is so. I am an American."

"Ah," the other said, speaking this time in English. "As you see, I know about as much of your tongue as you do of mine. I thought you must be a stranger even before I observed your dress, for street frays are not common in this town, whereas in other ports there are scores of men ready for any villainy, and few of my people would care to interfere in a fray in which they have no personal interest. But do not let us stay here; it is best to get out of this quarter."

"Shall we do anything with these fellows? The one I hit can only be stunned, and I should think we ought to give him in charge to the watch."

The other laughed. "You might wait some time before we found them, and besides it would give us a deal of trouble. No, leave them where they lie; the one I struck at least will not get up again in a hurry. Now, senor, may I ask the name of my preserver? Mine is Juan Sarasta."

THE LIFE OF A SPECIAL CORRESPONDENT

G. A. Henty.

FROM time to time I have received letters from boys asking me how they can best prepare themselves to become Special Correspondents; and it is hardly surprising that this should be so, for it may be doubted whether any profession whatever is so full of interest and excitement. However, there is no calling so limited and so difficult of access. If a boy made up his mind to become an Archbishop or a Lord Chancellor, he could at least be shown how to take the first steps in that direction; but this is not the case with regard to the calling of a Special Correspondent. Generally the qualifications may be stated as a familiarity with as many foreign languages as possible, the possession of a considerable amount of military knowledge, the gift of vivid description, a good constitution, a power of supporting hardships and fatigues, a certain amount of pluck, a good seat on a horse, and, lastly, the manners of a gentleman, and the knack of getting on well with people of all ranks and classes.

There are large numbers of men who possess all these requisites, and who yet have not the shadow of a chance of becoming Special Correspondents. In the first place, the number of such posts is extremely limited; and, putting aside the representatives of pictorial papers, who are of course artists and not writers, it is not too much to say that there are not more than a dozen men regularly engaged on the staff of the newspapers of Great Britain as Special War Correspondents. In the event of a great struggle such as the Franco-German War, where the scene of hostilities covered a very large area, the number of men employed as Special Correspondents is of course largely increased, as it is necessary that each newspaper represented should have Correspondents at all the points of special interest. These, however, are only appointed for the occasion, and are for the most part army officers whose object is rather to see the campaign than to obtain regular press work. It is, then, only with the dozen or so men permanently engaged as War Correspondents by the great London newspapers and the various press organisations that it is necessary to deal.

Some of these have been recruited from among the writers employed to do special descriptive work at home on the staff of their papers; still more perhaps have entered the profession by chance, or, perhaps it would be more correct to say, by availing themselves of some fortunate opportunity. If, for example, a serious struggle were to break out suddenly between the Dutch population in South Africa and the British colonists, and a man upon the spot were to send home a series of brilliant descrip-

THIS IS THE SECOND PART OF A NEW VOLUME.

PART 238.] DECEMBER, 1898. *Containing the November Nos., with Large Coloured Plate.* [Price 6d.

THE BOYS OWN PAPER

WITH WHICH ARE INCORPORATED

"BOYS" and "EVERY BOY'S MAGAZINE."

"*Quicquid agunt pueri nostri farrago libelli.*"

CONTENTS.

The Illustrations are by
ALFRED PEARSE, DAVID E. WILSON, J. FINNEMORE, A. RUSSELL,
G. E. ROBERTSON, B. BOESE, T. E. DONNISON, H. F. HOBDEN,
ELLEN A. BENNETT, H. OFFICER SMITH, and others.

Correspondence.   Poetry.   Chess.

LARGE COLOURED PLATE:

"*Still as Death.*"

By J. T. NETTLESHIP.

PUBLISHED AT 56 PATERNOSTER ROW, LONDON, E.C.

TWO NEW SERIAL STORIES BEGIN in THIS PART, by G. A. HENTY and J. T. MUGFORD.

SEE MORE NEW PRIZE COMPETITIONS: "FOOTBALL," ETC

tive letters or telegrams, he would not improbably receive a request by cable to continue to act as Special Correspondent to the paper to which he sent his letters, during the continuance of the war; and if his work turned out exceptionally good he might be asked to do other work, and finally, when a vacancy occurred, be put upon the permanent staff of the paper.

Another avenue of entrance to the profession is that of a special knowledge. For example, were a war to break out with Russia, and were it to become evident that Afghanistan would become the central point of the struggle, anyone, having travelled in that country and having a perfect knowledge of the language, together with that of some of the principal dialects of India, and who had by his published writings shown that he possessed descriptive powers, might obtain an engagement to act as Special Correspondent with the British army. His chances of so doing would be increased if he had served there and was personally acquainted with many of the principal officers of that army. The appointment would be only a temporary one, and his chance of obtaining a permanent appointment would depend entirely upon the character of the work he did there.

As an example of an entry into the limited circle by a fortunate opportunity my own case may be taken. I was in the Crimea on the Purveyor's staff—that is, the Hospital Commissariat. I possessed the knack of sketching, and sent home to a relative a number of sketches, and asked him to try whether any of the illustrated papers would take them. With them I sent home long descriptive letters. He failed to do anything with the sketches, as the illustrated papers had all made their arrangements; but he took the letters to the editor of the *Morning Advertiser*, who, on reading them, wrote at once to ask me to represent the paper, which I continued to do until invalided home; and being, when convalescent, sent out to Italy to organise the hospitals of the Legion we were then raising there, my connection with the press ceased for many years.

After leaving the army I was again in Italy for six or eight months, and acquired the knack of talking the language with some facility. In 1866, when Italy joined Prussia in her attack on Austria, I obtained the post of representative of the *Standard* in Italy, on the·strength of my letters to the *Advertiser* in the Crimea, and of my acquaintance with Italy and its language. This was my opportunity. Some half-dozen other gentlemen were at the same time sent to the Austrian and Prussian armies; but, as I suppose because my work gave most satisfaction, I was the one selected for the permanent post of Special Correspondent to the paper, and did all their foreign work for nearly twenty years.

Looking back upon the members of the profession whose names have been most familiar, Russell and Wood of the *Morning Post* were both connected with the press before being sent to the Crimea. Captains Hosier and the two brothers Brackenbury were all military men, and, although they did much and excellent war correspondentship, still continued in the army. Forbes had served for some years in a cavalry regiment, after leaving which he did some desultory press work, and went out with a sort of roving commission from the *Daily News* to the Franco-German war, where his splendid work at once placed him in the front line of War Correspondents. Beatty Kingston had represented the *Daily Telegraph* in Vienna and elsewhere, when he was sent as their correspondent with the German army, and did excellent service there. He did not, however, continue as War Correspondent, but for some years represented the paper at Berlin.

Cameron of the *Standard*, who was killed at the Nile campaign, gained his post by admirable letters from India, although having no connection whatever with the press when he began to send them; no man ever did better work for his paper than he did from the date of his appointment to his death. Of the present War Correspondents, Charles Williams of the *Daily Chronicle* had been for many years a descriptive writer on the press before he began work as a War Correspondent; and the same may be said of Pearce of the *Daily News*; while Knight of the *Times* first became known by his brilliant "Cruise of the *Falcon*," and it was his happy style of writing and his ardour for adventures that gained him his post; and Burleigh of the *Telegraph* knocked about the world for many years before he entered the ranks of War Correspondents.

As a rule, newspaper editors are very shy of accepting the offers of officers forming part of any British expeditionary force to send letters (although such offers are innumerable) because it is found that they are naturally soldiers first and Special Correspondents afterwards, and that the duties of the first position, and the fact that their regiment may not always be at the front, render them very inefficient in the latter capacity. They fail, too, to appreciate the absolute necessity for sending off news as soon as possible after any event; and may indeed be so occupied with their military duties after an engagement, that the despatch of the civilian correspondents gets off twenty-four hours before their own can be written.

Of late years the work of a Special·Correspondent has been very materially changed by the all but universal extension of the telegraph-wires. Instead of having to sit down to write two or three columns of description after his work is done, he has now to condense his matter into a few hundred words; for, if the scene of war is distant from England, letters are useless, for no one will trouble to read details of events whose main features have been published a month, or even a fortnight, previously. The consequence has been that the power of graphic descriptive writing is no longer a prime necessity in the case of a Special Correspondent, and the knack of terse and concise condensation, giving all the main features in the fewest possible words, has become all-important.

The cost of telegrams from distant countries is simply enormous—from China it is something like 7s. a word, 3s. 8d. to India, 5s. to Australasia, and from 3s. 6d. to 12s. to South America; thus, therefore, a telegram of three or four hundred words, which do not cover a very large space in a newspaper column, mounts up to a considerable sum when sent from the East, from South America, or the Cape, and the man who can the best condense his matter is the most highly prized. In some campaigns light weight and a good seat on a horse are most valuable qualifications: the nearest telegraph-station may be thirty or forty miles away, and after any important events an active Correspondent will, after writing his despatch, mount his horse and ride off at full speed, so as to get his message on the lines before those of any of his rivals, and will then, after a short rest, start for the front again.

In this way Forbes was the first to send home an account of the battle of Ulundi, taking down with him some of the general's despatches as well as his own report. Where the distance is much greater, it is of course necessary to entrust the report to the official post-bag, as a Correspondent dare not himself be absent long from the front; but in this case it is a mere matter of chance whether his message gets first or last on the wires. Not only for such service, but for general work, light weight is of advantage, as horses capable of carrying heavy weights are very difficult to obtain, and a horse lightly weighted is in any case likely to carry its rider farther and faster, and is less liable to knock up with continuous travelling in a rough country, than is one carrying a heavy rider. The general details of a Special Correspondent's life I will enter into more fully in another article.

THE BOER BOY

Ormond Lodge.

Right *In 1900 the* B.O.P. *takes a tolerant attitude to the Boers (perhaps a product of the classical education expounded in the succeeding article).*

AS SOON as he is old enough to walk about the Boer boy is left to his own devices. The Boer mother does not believe in "coddling up" her children—she believes that the harder they grow up the harder they will be in after-life; and she allows nature to look after them. In the glorious climate of South Africa nature fully repays the trust, for the boy, as a rule, grows up wonderfully sturdy, and by the time he is seven or eight years old is as hard as nails.

The Boer boy, like all other boys, is fond of companionship; but, unfortunately for himself, he is unable to obtain this. The Boer does not like to be crowded, he likes to have plenty of room, and he keeps apart from others, and his nearest neighbour may be ten or fifteen miles away; so the youngster has to find his comrades in his own home. His elder brothers are no company for him, so he turns to the Kaffir "boys" (every Kaffir who works on a Boer farm is called a boy, no matter if he is sixty years old), and the Kaffir takes this as a rare compliment, and goes out of his way to be civil and attentive to the young "Baas," so the two get along together capitally.

One advantage of this is that the white boy soon learns the Kaffir language, and this is of great use to him in after-life.

When the Kaffir "boys" go out in the morning to release the cattle and sheep from the kraals in which they have been penned up during the night, their little white friend accompanies them, and with a cutting sjambok assists in keeping the refractory calves away from their mothers whilst the latter are being milked, and, later on, in driving all the stock away to feed. After breakfast the lad will go into the fields with the Kaffirs and watch them work, and will listen whilst they tell those wonderful legends which every Kaffir learns from his parents, and which all implicitly believe in. In the evening the youngster assists the Kaffirs to bring the stock home.

The one ambition of every Boer boy is to possess a gun. At one time it was the custom for every father of a family to present his son with a new gun when he had reached the age of nine or ten; but of late years this practice has fallen off, and the youngster has to content himself with one of his father's cast-off guns; and then a new difficulty arises—where is he to obtain his ammunition?—for ammunition is expensive in the Transvaal, and the Boers have no money to waste in "luxuries." The way he manages is as follows: when a boy is born in a Boer family a certain number of cattle, sheep, and horses are put aside for him; these are his own individual property, and as soon as he has arrived at an age when he may be trusted with them, they are handed over to him, and when he finds that he cannot rest until he has obtained the ammunition he will take a sheep, and go over to the nearest store and will sell it and purchase enough ammunition to supply his immediate wants, and will hand the balance of the money over to his father to take care of for him.

Once he is supplied with a gun and ammunition, he considers himself a man—and the different style and manner of speech a youngster will put on, once he has armed himself, are amusing. He will then forsake his Kaffir friends, and will wander over the adjacent country in search of what he can kill. There

Two Strange Questions (Anxious).—Anxious, aged 13, has a pain inside his heel after running; it is probably cramp. Rub well with homocea. It costs, we think, a shilling a tin, but lasts a long time, and is a good thing for stiffness, pain, etc. 2. Referring to such expressions as kind-hearted, his heart is hardened, etc., Anxious asks does the heart really get affected in any way when we sympathise with a person? Is it the brain alone that controls the actions? You are no fool, Arthur, though but 13. There is a most intimate sympathy between the brain and the heart, and between mind and matter. The emotional heart is a feeble heart, and this is often *en rapport* with a somewhat excitable brain. As men grow older and the heart gets feebler, they become more sympathetic. It is the same when the heart is weakened by illness. It is the same in hysteria. But the heart never gets hardened, that is merely figurative. A coward never has a strong heart, so cowardice in boys or men is really a disease. If Dr. Gordon Stables gives further advice to boys in next Christmas Number, he will probably have something to say about cowardice, which is a more common complaint than is generally supposed, but in many cases a curable one.

are still a fair number of buck left in the Transvaal, and, besides these, there are wild turkey, pheasant, quail, plover, and other game, and the boy will for a time, after he has acquired his new possession, keep the family well supplied with game, for the Boer is a born "shot," and every boy seems able to handle a gun naturally. What game is not required in the family circle he sells to the store-keeper, and so purchases more cartridges.

This sort of life goes on until he gets about seventeen years old, and then he discards the gun, and sets his thoughts on more serious matters, for it is the custom of the country for people to marry whilst they are young, and the young man will now pass most of his time at some neighbouring farm, courting some fair Sanna, or Marta.

When a Boer youth goes away on a courting expedition he is a sight for the gods. He will be dressed up regardless of expense, his hair will be well oiled, and parted over his forehead, and his face will have been scrubbed until it shines again; his horse will be groomed to perfection, his saddle cleaned, and his stirrup-irons, bits, and spurs burnished to the consistency of silver, and he will mount, and, digging the spurs into his horse, will start off at a hand gallop to visit his inamorata.

After a three months' courtship the marriage will take place, and the neighbours, for fifty miles around, will drive over, and the quiet farm will be given over to riotous merriment for three days and nights, after which the guests will depart, and the young man will settle down to dream away the balance of his life in a placid calm, unless some unforseen circumstance, such as the present war, occurs to call him away to more stirring scenes.

A CLASSICAL EDUCATION

H. J. Lloyd, M.A.
(Trinity College, Cambridge).

I WONDER how many boys who are now engaged in puzzling over their Cæsar and Xenophon have ever seriously considered for themselves what are the advantages of a classical education. Why is it that the great majority of people competent to form an opinion have decided that the best and highest form of education that can be given to a boy consists of a prolonged study of two dead languages? It is strange at first sight, but there are reasons for this, as for any other fact, and good reasons too.

In the first place, the study of Latin, at all events, is useful, if not actually necessary, for success in all examinations connected with the higher professions—the Church, the Bar, the Army and Navy, as well as the examinations for the Indian and Home Civil Service. It is true that Latin is not now, as formerly, obligatory for entrance at Woolwich and Sandhurst; still, almost all candidates find Latin a "paying" subject. But, after all, the highest object of education is not to help a boy to pass this or that examination; and I think that in these days of fierce competition there is a danger of forgetting that, just as the real object of gymnastics is to increase the strength of the body, not merely to perform this or that exercise in the gymnasium, so the real object of education is to improve and expand the powers of the mind, to strengthen the reasoning powers.

If we take this broad view of education, it will at once be apparent how valuable is the study of Latin and Greek. Every boy knows that the Romans conquered, among other nations, Spain and Gaul. As a natural consequence, the language of the conqueror became, to a very large extent, the language of the conquered nations: hence a sound knowledge of Latin renders the knowledge of French and Spanish literature comparatively easy of acquisition. French is, in fact, Latin, changed, as all languages change after two thousand years have elapsed. Moreover, the language of the Romans has materially affected our own language, and the real meaning of a very great number of English words can be thoroughly appreciated only by a Latin scholar.

It is precisely because Latin *is* a dead language that it is far more valuable than French as a means of making a boy think. The character and structure of the language are so essentially different from French or English that it taxes the powers of the mind in the highest degree to translate, for example, a few lines of Macaulay's "History of England" into idiomatic Latin prose; and, just as we see the muscles of the gymnast grow larger and firmer by steady work; just as the oarsman, the runner, the boxer, the fencer, and the football player develop the muscles which they respectively call into play,—so we may be sure that, though unseen, the muscles of the mind—if I may be allowed to use such an expression—expand and grow as the result of puzzling out a piece of "unseen Thucydides," or translating a passage of Tacitus into good English. The reasoning faculties and the memory are alike improved.

It is, I think, true that Greek is superior even to Latin, from a high educational point of view: at all events, the mind becomes more refined by the study of Greek than of Latin authors. The student of Greek is brought into close contact with the master-pieces of the greatest geniuses that the world perhaps has ever seen. Rome, indeed, conquered Greece in war, but, as the poet said,

"Graecia capta feros victores cepit."

How truly "captured Greece took her conquerors captive" may be judged from the fact that, in the days of the Emperors, the education of a well-born

Roman youth consisted far more in the study of Grecian than of Roman "Classics."

THE "B.O.P." COMING-OF-AGE DINNER

By One Who Helped to Eat It.

THE completion of the twenty-first year of the "B.O.P." is in many ways a very notable event, and it was celebrated on the Editor's birthday, Tuesday, October 31, 1899, at the Holborn Restaurant.

Owing to the comparatively short time between the inception and the carrying out of the idea, it was impossible to get together all who would have liked to attend, but between 130 and 150 assembled to felicitate Mr. George Andrew Hutchison, and to wish him and the paper plenty of prosperity and an advancing circulation in each of the years to come.

The chair was occupied by the Ven. W. M. Sinclair, D.D., Archdeacon of London, and Past Chaplain to the Grand Lodge of Freemasons; and

no more kindly or genial occupant for the position could have been chosen. He was supported by the guests of the evening, Mr. and Mrs. G. A. Hutchison, with Rev. Prebendary White, Rev. Dr. Lansdell (the famous Asiatic explorer), Rev. Dr. A. N. Malan, Rev. Dr. Green, Mr. John Kirk (of the Ragged School Union), Mr. Cutliffe Hyne, Dr. T. J. Barnardo (the well-known philanthropist), Mr. W. J. Gordon, Mr. Paul Blake, Rev. C. H. Irwin, M.A., Mr. A. Devine (Headmaster of Claysmore School), Mr. Alfred Pearse, Mr. Harold Avery, Rev. W. J. Ferrar, M.A., Rev. J. P. Hobson, M.A., Mr. J. T. Nettleship, Mr. R. S. Warren Bell, Mr. J. Keble Bell, Dr. Stables, Rev. A. Colbeck, Rev. J. Bradford, Messrs. John Dawtrey, T. E. Donnison, T. Downey, G. H. Edwards, J. Finnemore, H. F. Hobden, J. Jellicoe, Coulson Kernahan, James Bowden, Elliot Stock, A. Lee Knight, Somerville Gibney, G. Manville Fenn, Ashmore Russian, Edward Step, J. Paul Taylor, C. Peters, Henry Frith, Louis Wain, F. G. Aflalo, J. T. Hawtrey, W. Richards, H. Walker, and many others.

The arrangements were in the hands of two honorary secretaries, Mr. W. J. Gordon and Mr. W. D. Lines; and when the moment came for the "happy despatch of the appetising viands," the seating of the guests was so expeditiously carried out that they found their places most comfortably. The *menu* was

Below 'B.O.P.-*ites at Dinner*'.

CORRESPONDENCE.

Bad Dreams, etc. (D. W.).
—Take the morning tub and plenty of healthful recreative exercise. Good plain food. If constipated take a pill or two at night (antibilious). Sleep on a hard mattress, with window open and not much bed clothing. Take a palatinoid twice a day of citrate of iron and quinine. Any chemist. Do all this very regularly for a month and see if you are not improved. 'Ware quacks.

Biting Nails (Dare D. Dick).—Better have the globe cleaned. Dip the points of the fingers in a strong solution of quassia.

Dogs (Antonio P. Fachiri).—1. Thorough good setter about five months about £10. If broken £15. 2. On board ship the cook takes charge of them. 3. Scotch terrier for country. 4. Fox terrier or any short-haired dog for town.

Seeing Black Spots (Spes).—It may be from debility, when iron and quinine, cod-liver oil, good food, change of air, and bathing would put you right; but it may be local mischief so you had better have your eyes examined by an oculist at once.

Worms (Strathblane).—She died of those most likely. Perhaps she had about a peck of them inside her. You ought to have taken it in time and given her Spratt's worm powder.

Calves and Fowls (Ray).—1. Yes, there is no necessity for knicker-bockers. 2. Want of exercise and good feeding will make fowls weak in legs, especially if kept on damp ground.

an excellent one; and the time allotted for the consumption of the dinner was pleasantly spent in renewing old friendships, or in beholding in the flesh those who had hitherto only known each other through the printed page.

Grace was said before and after the meal by the Rev. Prebendary White, D.D., of St. Paul's Cathedral.

The toast list was not a lengthy one, and was interspersed by vocal music. Dr. White proposed "The Queen," reminding the gathering that these were troublous times, and that the Sovereign was mindful of the sufferings of her brave soldiers in South Africa. They had read the messages of sympathy which that womanly heart had sent out, and they would devoutly pray that the war might soon be over, and that peace would be restored.

The National Anthem was at this point joined in most vigorously by all present.

The Chairman proposed "The Prince and Princess of Wales, and the rest of the Royal Family." "They," said Dr. Sinclair, "were popular with all sections of the people, and took a large share in the nation's life." The speaker alluded to the bright example to young men which the late Prince Consort's life was, and was sure that the whole of that illustrious family were deeply beloved by the English people. (Dr. Sinclair, himself an editor, was not aware that the Duke of York, with his lamented brother, was an old reader of the "B.O.P.," and, when informed of it, expressed regret that he had not known it in time to specially mention his name in the toast.) This toast was duly honoured, and then The Chairman proposed the "Boy's Own Paper," which was, of course, sufficient to bring the house down. Dr. Sinclair said that he was glad to have been permitted to preside, and that it had fallen to his lot to propose such a toast. He had a deep sympathy with boy life, and with all that appertained to it; and none knew better than clergy and ministers what a wholesome and healthy influence such a paper as the "B.O.P." exercised. Now, he had lately been reading Mr. Rudyard Kipling's story of schoolboy life, "Stalky & Co.," and, with all respect to the gifted author, he declined to accept that as a just and true picture of schoolboy life of to-day, or of any recent period. There was no school of importance in the land to-day where masters were all fools, or the boys quite as given over to wild escapades as "Stalky & Co." Then, too, those who had to educate the youth of England knew full well the danger of immoral literature permeating and poisoning the minds of lads. He was speaking to those who catered for boys—a company that included distinguished writers and artists— and he congratulated them on having been associated with a journal that had done such really splendid work. He congratulated their Editor, and he considered that the paper was filling, not only a literary but a national want, and he knew that it exercised a wonderful power for good in

raising the moral tone of the youth of our nation, both at home and abroad. Concluding, the Archdeacon said that he wished them in the next twenty-one years even greater success; and hoped that they would still be a factor in promoting the welfare of the boys of the English-speaking world. He gave them the toast. (Loud cheers.)

The toast having been drunk with full honours, Mr. E. Pontis Lines sang the "B.O.P." Song, composed by the Rev. Canon Foxell, M.A., B.MUS. The guests joined vigorously in the chorus. The opinion was very generally expressed by those near the present writer that it might well form the rallying song of our paper in future.

Mr. H. M. Paull ("Paul Blake") now proposed "Our Editor," in a capital and most eulogistic speech, and Mr. A. Pearse presented Mr. Hutchison with a beautifully illuminated and framed address, and a cheque. Rising to bow his acknowledgments, Mr. Hutchison was received, not only with loud applause, but with the assurance conveyed musically in the rousing words, "For he's a jolly good fellow."

Mr. Savage, before the Editor's response, recited the ever-popular piece, "The Bishop and the Caterpillar," which first saw the light in the pages of the "B.O.P." Then came the speech of the Editor, whose official reserve broke down at once, and who, when the cheers of welcome had died away, said, in reply, that he was sure they had given him the most difficult task of all that evening, to reply to so personal a toast so heartily responded to. It was a peculiar pleasure to meet so many friends, artists, and contributors around the festive board. He could only thank each one of them for the mark of their esteem, and he was deeply grateful from the bottom of his heart for such a recognition. The amount of the cheque considerably exceeded a hundred guineas, and it was only right that they should know it, as the collection of this, and the whole arrangements in connection with the testimonial, must have involved a great amount of trouble. The Editor then humorously alluded to the supposed ease with which writers produced their best work, and gave something of his own experience. But he had found his relations with the "B.O.P." writers and artists very pleasant indeed. He then briefly told the story of how the "B.O.P." was started, and why. For twenty-one years they had worked with a definite purpose to help boys to live straight. Often and often boys in trouble wrote frankly about themselves, and it had ever been his aim and joy to advise to the best of his ability—to aid in the making of manly, God-fearing citizens; and he had received many proofs from all parts of the English-speaking world that the work had not been in vain. (Loud cheers.)

The Rev. Dr. Lansdell then proposed "Our Contributors," and gave several illustrations of the out-of-the-way places to which their writings extended; and concluded by associating the names of the Rev.

CORRESPONDENCE.

In a Fix (T. E. F.)—There is some trifling difference in social position between a druggist and a surgeon in the Royal Navy. The former is a tradesman, the latter an officer holding Her Majesty's commission. Perhaps you are confounding dispenser with surgeon. Your having been a druggist would fit you for that, but you would not be an officer. Study for the navy by all means, if you can afford the time and have the funds. The position is honourable and the life a very jolly one.

Brain Asleep (Afflicted Scot).—It is usually the other way with Scotchmen. However, we think the confined state of the system may account for the disagreeable feelings. Try one or two Brandreth's pills every third night. Eat fruit in the morning and with dinner, take oatmeal for breakfast, and the juice of half a lemon before breakfast and before going to bed in a tumbler of cold water. Remember this constipation cannot be cured by medicine alone.

Languid (S. H. B.)—No, it is rest you want. Try cold bathing of a morning. Get the skin into good condition and keep the system free.

Obesity (Fat Subscriber). —The rule is to avoid sugar, fat, meats, and farinaceous food with the exception of toast. Take plenty of walking or cycling exercise.

Dr. Malan, Mr. G. Manville Fenn, and Mr. J. Finnemore, R.I., with the toast, which was heartily drunk. Madam Lizzie Owen now sang, and Mr. Fenn, for the writers, and Mr. Finnemore, for the artists, responded. "The Old Boys" was proposed by Mr. John Kirk, of the Ragged School Union, who recalled his early friendship with Mr. Hutchison, and spoke of the interest he had in boys and all that concerned them. He knew the journal in its early days, and when "Rob Roy" McGregor and Mr. Kingston were connected with it. This toast was replied to by Rev. T. C. Collings, who said Lord Aberdeen was unable to be present owing to pressing duties in Scotland, but wished them well, and the "B.O.P." too. Sir Edward Clarke, Q.C., M.P., greatly regretted he could not join them, but was represented by his son, while the Rev. F. B. Meyer, B.A., and many others, sent congratulations. Mr. Clement Hill and Mr. M. A. Noble, of the Australian Cricket Eleven, and Dr. Fitchett, the editor of the Australian "Review of Reviews," all regretted that their absence from England prevented them attending, and it was impossible to prolong their stay.

"Absent Friends" was the next toast, proposed by the Editor, who recalled the helpful and close association with the paper of many called away by death during the twenty-one years, including Sir Charles Reed, Talbot Baines Reed, Rev. J. G. Wood, M.A., Mr. Frank Buckland, Mr. Charles Jamrach, Mr. W. H. G. Kingston, Rev. Dr. Manning, Capt. Webb, Mr. R. M. Ballantyne, Mr. John McGregor ("Rob Roy"), Dr. Scoffern, Mr. Whitchurch-Sadler, R.N., Rev. J. Pycroft, M.A., Cuthbert Bede ("Verdant Green"), Rev. Dr. Stoughton, Mr. Gleeson White, Commander Lovett Cameron, C.B., General Sir Fredk. Middleton, C.B., General Sir Robert Phayre, K.C.B., Sir B. W. Richardson, Mr. W. H. Overend, Mr. Charles Cattermole, Mr. R. Bevis, Mr. Randolph Caldecott, etc.

A BOY'S ACCOUNT OF THE COMING-OF-AGE DINNER

I'M only a boy, and I haven't any swell togs, have I? I hardly knew where the Holborn Restaurant was; and if I tried to find out I should probably miss my last train home! Besides, I oughtn't to be out so late, ought I? Yet, I tell you, I MUST go to the "B.O.P." dinner.

And I did go, and thought you "B.O.P." fellows might like to hear how I got on. I guess there will be a rattling good account of the affair in the "B.O.P."; but I wouldn't mind staking my best Sunday topper that nothing will be said about the grub, and important things like that. So here goes!

I got there jolly early, there was only one old gentleman in the ante-room. I hitched down my cuffs, smoothed my hair, curled my moustache (oh, yes! I've got one coming), and strolled up. I had on a spanking new tie, green and purple, and stuck in it a fine scarf-pin (it only cost—ahem, well, never mind—but it looked worth an awful lot), so I felt fairly cocky. The old boy didn't speak for a bit, then he turned and said: "You've prepared for a good number this evening, I see."

Great Cæsar! he took me for a waiter. I felt—I felt—well, I don't know how I felt. "THEY have prepared for a good number, THEY have," I answered, almost shouting the word "they."

He stared and strolled off. Pheugh! it had got quite hot all of a sudden. The room was getting awfully full, so I kept in a corner: I don't like being taken for a waiter. I soon forgot this, though, for the Editor arrived.

"I'll speak to him or perish," I said to myself. Awful cheek, wasn't it? But he looked so jolly that I didn't feel a bit funky about it. There was a bit of a scrum round him, so I had a bother to get near. I wriggled in, and in two ticks should have shaken paws, when some wretched waiter yells out: "Gentlemen, the dinner is served." Everyone moved off to the dining-room, and my chance was gone. I could have pummelled that waiter! If ever any of you fellows go to the Holborn Restaurant, and see a waiter with a long nose, a cock eye, and a sickening grin, that's the man. Just kick him for me.

Now about the dinner itself. Well, everyone had placed before him a menu-card, a copy of the Coming-of-Age number, and a printed list of guests. There were an awful lot of swell writers and artists there—Manville Fenn, Dr. Gordon Stables, Harold Avery, Rev. A. N. Malan, J. T. Nettleship, Alfred Pearse, Louis Wain, T. E. Donnison, and tons of others who have written and drawn for our dear old paper. Grace was said, and then we started tucking in. We had soup first, but I was glad when they brought me something to eat. I had scarcely sampled it, though, when some wretched waiter whisked it off (you can kick him as well as the other chap). I held my plate tight after this, and had a go at fillet of sole, whitebait, mutton cutlet, roast turkey, and other fixtures. Then came such things as "abricots à la" something, "d'artist pallet" (that's not exactly right, but it's something like that. What rot it is using these outlandish double-Dutch names that no one can twig), "macédonne jelly" (I know that's right because I wrote it on my cuff), ice pudding—but I won't say any more about the grub because I have met people who say we boys think of nothing but eating. But really the ice pudding was ripping, and the abricots à la something were simply rattling, not to mention the what-you-may-call-it

CORRESPONDENCE.

Getting on Nicely (A Fish).—We are *so* glad. As long as you do what you mention it will not hurt you. To some extent it is natural, so long as you keep pure in thought and deed.

Epilepsy (Oxfordite). —No, you mustn't cycle at present. Walking exercise in moderation, but you ought to be under treatment.

Being a Sailor (J. Holland). —Measurements about right, but take daily exercise, especially dumb-bell or Indian club. No, we don't think the infantile rupture can have left any tendency to the complaint.

Stopping his Growth (T. I. G.).—No, Tom, we know how to stop cocks from crowing, but can't stop your growing. Fifteen years old, 6 feet 2 inches in height. Grows five inches a year. Oh! that will do famously. In five years' time you will be 8 feet and over. Try to grow broad also, and try to grow good.

Wants to Grow (Midget).—Nineteen, are you? It can't be done. You'll never be a T. I. G. Content yourself with remembering that little men are far more useful nowadays than giants.

Dog Licking a Sore (Tara).—No, not if the dog is healthy.

Dog's Eyes (Inquirer).—Bathe gently with warm water twice a day, and apply a little zinc ointment round the lids.

Swimming under Water, etc. (Smith).—It puts a strain on a weak heart, so, unless you are very strong, don't.

140

jelly; and as for the turkey it was awfully fine, and the whitebait was——but, there, I said I'd stop.

After the grub was all eaten a photo of us was taken—I don't know why, unless it was because we all looked so jolly happy. Then the speeches began. You may bet I kicked up a row when the toast of "The 'Boy's Own Paper'" was given. Don't I wish some of you fellows had been there, we would have made things hum. Then some chap sang "The Good Old 'B.O.P.'"—the song that was put in the Coming-of-Age number. Everyone joined in the chorus; but, really a dozen fourth-formers from any decent school would have made more row. Don't I wish some of you fellows had been there!

Then came the presentation to the Editor, and we all sang "For he's a jolly good fellow." We kicked up a decent row then—but don't I wish some of you fellows had been there! Our Editor made a rattling speech in reply—he's a *brick*, and if his hair *is* turning grey he's still a boy. I'm awfully sorry, but I forget what he said—oh, yes! I remember one thing, though. He said he always kept in mind that his boys (that's us) would be men some day, and he wanted to help make them strong, happy, brave, and pure. So, you fellows, the best thing we can do to repay our Editor for all his fag for us is to try to be MANLY.

There's heaps more I could tell you, but I've got a lot of swotting to do ("sapping," as some of you chaps call it), so I must shut up.

A.S.G.

PLAY UP AND PLAY THE GAME!

W. Cecil Laming, M.A.

I.

WHEN the match is going against you, that you've striven hard to win,
When the forwards rush the scrimmage, and the halves keep romping in,
When the score's three goals to one
With ten minutes more to run,
And victory seems hopeless, and you're very tired and lame,
  Remember, schoolboy pluck
  Will often turn the luck:
Play up! Play up! Play up! Play up and play the game!

II.

When the foes are closing round you, and the bullets whistle past,
And it's hard to keep your courage, with your comrades falling fast,
When fighting hand to hand
You make one desperate stand,
And home is distant, death is near, and glory seems a name,
  Remember, British pluck
  Has often turned the luck:
Play up! Play up! Play up! Play up and play the game!

DOINGS FOR THE MONTH

DECEMBER.

Dr. Gordon Stables, R.N.

The Boy Himself, Fowl Run, Aviary, Pigeon Loft, Rabbitry, and Garden.

Dr. Gordon Stables, R.N.

THE BOY HIMSELF.—Another "B.O.P." year gone, another year begun! How time does pass and go! When you take up your favourite paper to-day I really hope you'll glance backward as far as last November. It seems to me, at all events, that it was only just the day before yesterday. And yet there have been many ups and downs among our ranks, and to-day there may be some sighs and some sore hearts for things undone, and for sins and follies committed. And sins, lads, are like curses—they always come home to "roost." But there is good in

CORRESPONDENCE.

Dog Book (C. Owen).—Why, there isn't a dog book extant that doesn't give the Beddington. Don't let this breed of dog worry you however. Get a Manchester or fox terrier; you will have more fun and less fighting.

Palpitation (Funky).—You must *not* ride till well.

Teeth, etc. (L. M.).—1. Never saw the enamel you refer to; should be careful. 2. Beneficial. 3. Sulphur and cream of tartar.

Collie Ill (J. Stuart). —Have him examined by a skilled "vet," if a dose of castor-oil does not put him to rights.

Nervousness (Nil Desperandum and others).—Go in for manly open-air exercises, good food, and the bath. Leave off the habits, or they will kill you. It really is a question of life and death.

any boy who keeps his conscience soft and pliant, for if there be anything that could make sin less abhorrent to the angel eyes who watch us, it is our sorrow for them, and I guess that our guardian angels count every tear we shed. Mind, there is joy in heaven over every sinner who repents. And I know, too, from the letters I get that there are many among you who do repent; many who have been tempted and fallen, but tempted again and have resisted evil, as every British boy who is ever likely to become a man worthy of this great country ought to. I tell you what it is, boys; there are few truer texts than that which tells us that if we resist the devil he will flee from us; yes, and every attack he makes upon you after the first great victory will be feebler and feebler; and then, instead of feeling that you can't look a cat or a mouse in the face, you will be able to hold up your head among your fellows. Good food, fresh air, and pleasant exercise, with the morning tub, will so strengthen you after this that you will feel the very ground ring under your tread as if, like our ships of war, you were built of steel.

I hope that most of you have been fairly lucky with your fancies or fads this year. All I can tell you once a month in a few brief pars is nothing to what you should know, and that is the reason why I am constantly asking you to read back numbers and keep a note book of your special fancy, whether it be pigeons, rabbits, fowls, or whatever else your line may be. November is a good time to commence any fad, and don't you forget it; and now the hens are waiting, so I must say "Good-bye," and wish you all a happy and jolly new ("B.O.P.") year. And mind this, the "B.O.P." has come of age: One-and-twenty years old! Hooray!

THE WEST INDIAN CRICKET TEAM

P. F. Warner

(the well-known Rugby, Oxford University, and Middlesex Captain).

WE have grown accustomed to the visits of Australian, South African, American, and even Parsee cricket teams to this country, but the appearance of a West Indian eleven is quite a new departure. However, that they will receive a hearty welcome is as certain as anything can be, if only as some return for the unbounded hospitality that has always been shown to English teams in the West Indies. And that as cricketers they are not to be despised, they will, I feel sure, prove before their tour is brought to a conclusion. Of course they do not for a moment compare with the Australians—that is hardly to be expected; but that they will come, with satisfactory results to themselves, through the programme that has been arranged for them, I have little doubt.

As a member of Lord Hawke's team, which played in the West Indies in the early part of 1897, I may, perhaps, be allowed to say a few words on the prospects of the visitors. The team is composed as follows:

R. S. A. Warner (Capt.), L. S. D'Ade, L. Constantine and Woods (Trinidad); G. B. Cox, A. B. Bowring, H. Cole, P. Goodman, and F. Hinds (Barbadoes); S. W. Sproston, G. C. Learmond and Burton (Demerara); C. Ollivierre (St. Vincent); L. L. Kerr (Jamaica); W. H. Mignon (Grenada); and W. C. Nock (Trinidad), Manager.

The team were to arrive in England at the end of May, their first match being on June 11, at the Crystal Palace, against an eleven collected by Dr. W. G. Grace.

My brother, who is to captain the side, is the veteran of the team, being on the wrong side of forty, and, purely on his abilities as a cricketer, might not have been chosen; but he has done a great deal for cricket in the West Indies, and was really the only man to undertake the captaincy of the side. His selection for the post has met with the unanimous approval of the entire West Indies. A few years ago he was by no means a bad bat and scored 77 and 40 in two out of three innings against R. S. Lucas's team, while two or three times he batted fairly well against Lord Hawke's eleven.

The best batsmen on the side, in my opinion, are: D'Ade, Sproston, Cole, P. Goodman, G. B. Cox, and Learmond; and all are much of a muchness, though I think I should give the preference to D'Ade. He has a nice style, and some excellent off-side strokes. Sproston also did well against us, and an innings of 95 that he played at Demerara was the highest and best score hit against Lord Hawke's eleven during the tour. Cole is a determined bat—a good cutter and hard hitter; while P. Goodman can play for a slow wicket, and Learmond is a sound bat with a good style. All these men ought to get runs, and, in addition, there is Constantine, who is a black, and the best native bat in the West Indies. Against Mr. Priestley's side he distinguished himself on several occasions.

Constantine will be the wicket-keeper of the team, and in this position is fairly good, especially when standing back to Woods's fast bowling. He is particularly smart in gathering a return; but wicket-keeping generally in the West Indies is not by any means up to the high standard to which we are accustomed in this country. Kerr, who is by repute an excellent bat, and fair bowler, will be the other wicket-keeper, with Learmond as a third line of support if necessary. The batting, however, will prove the weak point of the side, as it rather lacks class. But if the batting is not strong, I fancy that the fielding and bowling will be up to a fairly high standard.

Woods, Ollivierre, and Burton, who are all black, are distinctly good bowlers, some of Woods's performance against English elevens in the West Indies being quite exceptional. Woods has a peculiar action. Taking only two or three steps, he bowls exceedingly fast, with rather a low and slinging action. Like most blacks, he can bowl all day, and apparently never tires. He is no bat, but can catch anything thrown over a hundred yards.

Burton is a bowler with a nice action, and varies his pace well. Ollivierre I have never seen perform, but he has a good reputation, and the members of Mr. Priestley's eleven thought him a distinctly useful bowler. Hinds I know nothing of. Mignon did uncommonly well against us at Grenada, and for him I venture to predict a successful season. He bowls medium pace right hand, with a nice easy action, and makes the ball come quickly off the pitch—the sort of man who gets you caught at the wicket. He clean bowled several of us on a hard true pitch, and I distinctly remember the ball with which he bowled Lord Hawke. It pitched just outside the offstump, "fined" off the pitch and knocked down the middle stump.

These four are the stock bowlers of the side, and as changes there are Kerr and P. Goodman, who bowls a difficult ball, to fall back on.

Goodman, by the way, is a nailing short slip, and, in fielding the team, on the form they showed in their own country, should be exceedingly smart. The black men are particularly strong throwers.

Of course it must be remembered that these criticisms of mine are based on the form shown in the West Indies, and that the different conditions and surroundings of first-class cricket in this country may affect the team adversely. Our somewhat dull light, as compared with the brilliant tropical sunshine, will possibly bother them considerably at first.

The visit of any new team to England is always an experiment attended with more or less possibilities of failure; but that they will be a failure I do not for a moment think, and in any case they are quite as capable of meeting the first-class counties as the Philadelphians, who, though victories did not often come their way, cannot be said to have done by any means badly during their tour in the summer of 1897.

As I was born in the West Indies, naturally I take more than ordinary interest in the team, and I sincerely hope that the tour may have the complete success it deserves.

THE NATAL OF TODAY: A LAND OF PROMISE FOR YOUNG MEN

A CHAT WITH THE AGENT-GENERAL —SIR WALTER PEACE.

"B.O.P." Special Correspondent.

Right A career article from 1900.

"NOW, Mr. 'B.O.P.' Commissioner, I shall be very glad to tell you all I can about Natal, but you must not ask me to pronounce any opinion as to the present situation, though, as you may imagine, it is a stirring time for a young colony!"

The speaker was the Agent-General for Natal, a remarkable man, who certainly had ample justification for what he said. It was only in 1893 that the colony became self-governing, and within the last quarter of a century the war spirit has been abroad no less than three times.

"The preparations for the Zulu war, the calling out of the volunteers, the constant arrival of troops of irregular cavalry, the organising and equipment

of Army Corps, the landing of troops from England, and their departure to the Zulu border occasioned great stir and excitement in Maritzburg and Durban. The dreadful news of the battle of Isandhlwana not only brought grief and desolation to many a colonist's home, but the towns had to be put into a state of defence. It was just after that, that the Prince Imperial of France fell, and the reception of his body was one of the most mournful and impressive pageants the city has ever witnessed. No sooner were hostilities in Zululand at an end, than the trouble in the Transvaal began, and the city was once more astir with the movement of troops to the Front. And once again, to-day, the young colony,

142

whose trade is very largely carried on with the adjoining republics, is greatly concerned and interested in the struggle which is going on.

"Maritzburg was, three-quarters of a century ago, the headquarters of a Kaffir tribe. About 1840, a party of emigrant Dutch entered Natal, and the trials and sufferings of this band of pioneers, whose central position was Pietermaritzburg, form a thrilling story. By the end of 1843 the district was constituted part of Cape Colony, and has gone on growing ever since, and in 1854 it was a borough, governed by a mayor and town council. It has large open spaces, recreation grounds for the people, a first-rate college, a cathedral, parliamentary buildings, town hall and market, with a hospital and botanical gardens. The town hall, recently destroyed by fire and rebuilt, cost over 40,000*l*., and that will give you some idea of the way in which it has progressed. At the present day it has a daily morning and evening paper, and also two other journals; and in the cathedral have been laid the remains of Dr. Colenso, the famous Bishop and the author of an arithmetic which has successfully plagued boys and girls who have not any keen interest in the subject."

"What would you say of the people, language, and the government?"

"There are about 70,000 whites, chiefly English, Dutch, and German. Coolies, under the apprenticeship system, and free Indians amount to 60,000, while the natives number over 700,000. The English and German settlers are engaged in agricultural and commercial pursuits; the Dutch are mainly the latter.

"In the first place it is necessary to rectify a curiously wrong impression which has got abroad with respect to the aborigines of Natal. There are many who think that these natives were the original lords of the soil, and that the whites are interlopers, who, by their aggressiveness and land hunger, are playing upon the birthright of the unsophisticated savage. But the fact is, that when the whites first arrived on the scene and established themselves, the natives were broken, defeated, and powerless to further oppose the might of the all-conquering Zulus, whose spears had reaped a rich harvest of blood over the now fertile and peaceful hills of Natal. Driven from their homes, unable to plant or reap, they were forced to take refuge in the bush, and it is asserted that, on occasions, they had resource to cannibalism in order to keep life in their miserable, war-ridden bodies. Under the fostering care of the colonists, and protected by treaties made between them and the Zulus, who, be it remembered, are the very aristocracy of the native races of South Africa, these scattered remnants of people were gradually formed into tribes. Under the same care, they have developed and had their number augmented by refugees from adjacent States, until they stand at the present time a splendid, stalwart nation, loyal to England and to their benefactors, the colonists, law-abiding, and in almost every respect desirable. The exception is, that life comes easy to them, their wants being few and simple, so that they scarcely need to toil for their livelihood. Their clothing at the kraals consist of the very scantiest garments or skins. They pay a tax of fourteen shillings annually, and this brings in over 80,000*l*. to the government a year; and if any of your readers are clergymen, and are likely to become missionaries, they may like to know that in marriage fees they pay 2,400*l*. per annum.

"The natives are under their own chieftains, who are, again, subject to the white magistrates; they follow the old patriarchal style of life. Cattle are used by them as currency, and they buy their wives in this way; but in such transactions there is nothing revolting—there is nothing of slavery about it; and the young girl has pretty well her choice. The amount of cattle given for a wife ranges, according to her station in life, from six to fifty head—the usual number is about fifteen. The Natal Zulu firmly believes in witchcraft, and the witch doctors are supposed to have power to bring rain, and to perform wonderful miracles. It should be said, also, that the Zulus are not great as workers in metal, but show an instinctive talent for wood and bone carving, mat making, tanning, and pottery. They make good soldiers and policemen, having a keen sense of the necessity of discipline; and their language is a very beautiful and musical one. As to education, a sum of 3*l*. is paid to parents on behalf of every child who resides five miles at least from a government school, and is found to have made good progress during the year. There are farmhouse schools for those in the scattered districts, and education is in every way very liberal."

"What are some of the best districts for the young man to go to?"

"The country between Maritzburg to Greytown and the Tugela valley offers great prospects to the colonist. It is one of the very finest stock-rearing and farming areas in the colony. The climate is superb, possessing as it does all the beauty of an English one with scarcely any of the drawbacks, and the air is very suited to invalids. Wheat, oats, potatoes, and other cereal crops, are plentifully grown, and thrive well. There is also a great deal of cultivation of wattle bark, and the development of this trade is of very great importance, as the British and Continental tanners need it for their goods. Ladysmith is also the centre of a good deal of progress, and perhaps your readers would like to know something about it. It is the third town in the colony, though, until after 1885, but little progress was made. To-day, however, it has a town hall, schools, public libraries, Wesleyan, Congregational, Lutheran, and Episcopalian Churches, and the railway authorities have very large repairing works there. The population is between five and six thousand, and it has a gas supply, and a very good water supply indeed. This district has seen a great deal of bloodshed, and it was near Colenso, on a hill called Rensburg Kop, that the early Dutch pioneers won the land literally through seas of blood. There are few more thrilling stories than the treachery of Dingaan, and the way he treated the Dutch settlers. After receiving their leaders, he ordered the slaughter of the men in the camps along the river. The story of how the impi or war party swept down on them in the night, and how they killed men, women, and children, cattle, goats, and sheep, is still remembered, and amongst those who escaped were the Pretorius and Rensburg families. This was about 1840, and there was much fighting until 3,000 Zulus perished in the final battle which broke the power of the great chief.

"Not very far away is Van Reenen's Station, which is situated on the western frontier of the colony. To the left of the pass and the station great isolated mountain masses are visible, each one standing like a palace of mystery, with summits swathed in clouds, and kloofs dark with impenetrable forests, amidsts whose almost untrodden solitudes are bushmen's caves containing on their rocky walls curious representations of beasts and birds. These bushmen, now almost extinct, are no doubt a branch of the pigmy tribe discovered by Sir H. M. Stanley in Central Africa. In almost every respect they are beyond the pale of the lowest class of humanity. Peaceful and kindly overtures meant no more to them apparently than to a tribe of those baboons to which they bear such a striking physical resemblance.

"In some parts of the colony the tea industry is very considerable; but the young man had better have some capital before he embarks in it, as it will be from three to five years before he gets very much return for his money. It would seem, however, that small capitalists can do very well, and there are many large estates owned by companies who are getting a very excellent return from them; but, like everything else, the measure of success likely to attend the planter or the farmer depends on the care, skill, and observation devoted to the task. The young man who wants to take things easy certainly should not come to Natal unless he has ample money. On the other hand, the climate is suited to invalids, and there is very much about it which makes it very tempting.

"Durban is a remarkable town, and contains an enormous number of public buildings, and as a health resort it is in winter as nearly perfect as possible. It is some sixty years old, and has the largest population of any town within the colony."

"You consider, then, that Natal is an excellent colony for our young people?"

"Yes, within the frontiers of Natal there is ample scope for the energies of the agriculturist, the trader, the miner, and the manufacturer. Zululand has been transformed from a wilderness to regions of untold treasure, and railway communication is well developed. Pondoland has been annexed to the Cape of Good Hope, and in every case the prospects are very bright. There are few parts of the world which offer more attractions to those self-reliant young men who find England too small for them, and who long to go into our Empire, and to play their part in consolidating and permeating the new country with the civilisation, the commerce, and the religion of the old. But they must be sober and enterprising. None of our colonies offer any facilities except to the hard worker. You may have capital—it is desirable that you should; but even capital will rapidly go, unless it is wisely used, in any part of the Empire. The spring and autumn are the best times for emigrants, and young men will find not a very long period elapse before there are openings for them, if they are willing, and not very particular as to what they put their hand to. A few years in the colony will enable the hard worker to gain sufficient to come home, if he wish it. The free life, the ample room, the perfect climatic conditions, and the beneficence of nature, may be trusted to bring ample contentment and satisfaction to the settler."

Coming of Age of the " B.O.P."—The World's Congratulations.
(*Drawn by* THOMAS DOWNEY.)

THE GOOD OLD "B.O.P."

CHAPTER FOUR
AFTER VICTORIA AND INTO THE 20th CENTURY

When Queen Victoria died in January 1901 the *B.O.P.* made no mention of the fact; presumably the Editor thought the event was adequately reported elsewhere. The *B.O.P.* was well aware of the new mechanical age. There were colour prints of trains appearing between pictures of animals and lifeboats, and there was an article on how to make a 'grammaphone'. Gordon Stables was now taking us cruising in the *Arctic Fox* in 'Icy Seas around the Pole', and C. J. B. Marriot was discussing rugby football rather more coherently and constructively than his predecessors had done. A page of public school cricket captains shows that short back-and-sides were now the current vogue for haircuts; collars do not look very comfortable. There was an article on how to collect and preserve flies and another on how to get rid of bugs – if you happened to be abroad.

In 1902 there were four articles on 'When I was at School' by George A. Wade. Wade, mentioned in the Introduction, had a dedicated knowledge of public schools unlikely ever to be exceeded. But there were runners-up. York Hopewell (a pen name) was another devotee. In 1904 he wrote an article on 'Famous Flogging Masters' and followed with 'Fags and Fagging' and 'Trades that Princes work at' and so on. A. Podmore and C. W. Alcock also became regular contributors. In 1905 'T.C.C.' (the Rev. T. C. Collings) interviewed M. A. Noble, the Australian cricketer, on 'swerve' bowling. In the later 1920s E. H. D. Sewell was still saying swerve bowling was impossible. The other side was not forgotten. In 1902 there was an article on 'A Boy's Life in a Workhouse School'.

Percy F. Westerman joined the ranks of *B.O.P.* writers in 1902, but his best stories – all about the sea – came later. A different sort of story – with a significant though misleading title to modern ears – is 'Queer Mr Quern'. Quern had once been a prosperous schoolmaster but had become mentally deranged. His wife and daughter died on the same day, the school was sold up, and Quern retired to a hermit's life in an old cottage. There were flashbacks into the past, but the insane dodderings of an old man seem an unusual subject for a boy's paper, even though the Rev. A. N. Malan did contrive to make it all end happily.

Wade's great saga of details about public schools began in 1904 with 'Some Famous Tuck Shops'. In the same year he wrote an article on 'Old Friends We Never Knew' about the writers (and characters) of school text-books. He noted that they only become 'friends' in misty reminiscence.

Wade's enthusiasm for public schools was almost matched by H. B. Philpott's for elementary schools; he was given plenty of space by the *B.O.P.*

In 1904 a newcomer to the team, G. G. Blake, described 'How to Make a Wireless Telegraph' and subsequently supplied many more articles on the same theme. Gordon Stables and George Manville Fenn were still searching the world for fictional adventure, and there was the same quantity of true-life stories as before.

In 1906 T. C. Bridges, later to acquire a fine reputation as a writer of adventure stories, was writing about 'Brave if Humble Lives', starting with the sewer man and the stoker.

Gordon Stables produced a serial 'From the Slum to the Quarter-Deck' in 1907, but it differed somewhat from Kingston's on a similar theme in the first volume. A new writer, Tom Bevan, contributed an excellent serial in 1907. This was 'The Goldsmith of Chepe: a tale of the Plague Year'; it lacked nothing in atmosphere. Gordon Stables continued in 1909 with 'From Fisher Lad to Fleet Surgeon'. Another future stalwart, Raymond Raife, was making his appearance at this time. Raife would become as versatile as Stables and contribute not only serials but nature notes. J. Claverdon Wood made his first appearance in 1910 with 'Sinclair of the Scouts'. He was destined to write for many years and was the author of 'Jeffrey of the White Wolf Trail' and 'When Nicholson kept the Border'. 1910 also saw the arrival of Gunby Hadath, who would prove to be the equal of Talbot Baines Reed as a school story writer and the equal of David Ker for illegibility. Even now, after thirty-one years of editing the *B.O.P.*, Hutchison had not lost his touch for finding the right authors. Captain Charles Gilson came in, as did W. E. Cule, Argyll Saxby, various writers who could talk knowledgeably about flying, J. B. Hobbs, soon to be cricket's world record holder for scoring centuries, and Wilfred Rhodes, whose articles were entitled 'Do you Wish to play for your country?' Hutchison died in 1913 and the new Editor was A. L. Haydon. It was the end of an era, of course – the last year before the War of 1914–18 changed the world for ever. But had Hutchison lived on and edited the paper there can be little doubt that he would have coped admirably with changing conditions.

A BOY'S LIFE
IN A WORKHOUSE SCHOOL

Hugh B. Philpott.

READERS of Dickens's "Oliver Twist" will remember the grim picture given by the great novelist of the life of a boy who had the misfortune to be left to the tender mercies of the poor-law authorities. And no doubt many people's ideas of the English poor law and the officials who administer it are derived in great measure from that book.

Happily things have changed a great deal since the time when a little workhouse boy could be beaten and bullied and starved in the way related to the luckless Oliver. Although it is not to be denied that there are still poor-law guardians and officials who seem to be animated by the spirit of Mr. Bumble, yet there are others—and, happily, an increasing number—who are intelligent and kind, and sincerely anxious to do their best for the boys and girls committed to their charge.

Prominent amongst the schools conducted on these more enlightened and humane lines is the Poplar Training School at Forest Gate, in which are educated the poor children of the great London parish of Poplar. The Poplar guardians have said, in effect: "It is not fair that a boy should be handicapped all his life owing to the sins or misfortunes of his parents; because a boy is poor and friendless is no reason why he should not have his chance like the rest; we don't admit that our boys are more stupid or more wicked than other boys, and we intend to give them as good a start in life as we can." This is an attitude of which, I think, all fair-minded boys will heartily approve.

The life of a boy at the Poplar Training School is in many respects not unlike that of a boy at a public school. The education given is, of course, more elementary, as the boys leave school when they are fourteen or fifteen years of age. It is similar to that given in a London Board school, only more time is devoted to manual and technical training. It is the spirit of the public school rather than of the workhouse or the charity institute that is cultivated amongst these Poplar boys. They are not for ever having the fact of their poverty flung in their teeth;

they wear no uniform, and so are not to be distinguished out of doors from other boys, and being treated with respect they learn the virtue of self-respect.

I daresay the school has its mean side, and that not every one of the three or four hundred boys is filled with the *esprit de corps* which is one of the glories of British school life. But that the spirit really exists you cannot doubt when you have heard, on some special occasion, the singing by the whole school of their school song, "The Poplar Tree"—as appropriate and inspiring a song as any school could desire; or when you have watched a keenly contested football match, and noted the energetic and unselfish play of the eleven, and the eager enthusiasm of the onlookers; or, again, when in private chat with the boys who have heard proud stories of the doings of old boys at the war, or the hardly less noteworthy achievements of Jones the half-back, and Brown the champion sprinter.

All kinds of manly sports are not only tolerated but encouraged at this school. You would not get this healthy tone were it not so. Behind the school building is an extensive playing-field where cricket or football, according to the season, is diligently practised, and where matches are played on Wednesday and Saturday afternoons. The school has its own swimming-bath, and nearly every boy can swim. The sixpence with which a boy is rewarded when he first succeeds in swimming two lengths no doubt acts as a stimulus to learners. The bath is too small to be of much use for racing purposes, but many of the boys are evidently adepts at life-saving, diving, and various aquatic tricks.

The annual sports day is a great occasion in the school year. I don't know whether any startling "records" have been made, but it is certain that the day is looked forward to with as much zest as in any public school. Musical drill is carried to a high pitch of excellence; but as that comes into the school curriculum, it would perhaps be regarded by the boys as work rather than recreation. However that may be, it has an undoubtedly beneficial effect in keeping them in good physical condition. . . .

WHEN I WAS AT SCHOOL

George A. Wade, B.A.

PART I.—THE "BURIAL" OF RICHARD II.

DO boys nowadays have as much fun and as many frolics at school as we used to have when I spent my days trying to imbibe the spirit of knowledge from clever and painstaking masters? I sometimes wonder if they have, when I am sitting over the fire and thinking of the incidents of those "happy days of long ago." I suppose you boys *do* have your fun and jokes in your own ways, just as we had. But perhaps you will not be averse to hearing of a few escapades of the early eighties—escapades connected with the schools that the writer had the honour of attending.

I think you will certainly pardon my omitting to mention the names of the institutions where the incidents occurred, though I may venture to tell you that nothing will be set down to their credit in this matter which is not substantially true.

There were about one hundred and thirty boys, all boarders, in the school where the following occurred, and some of my companions at that date—school chums, I mean—were about as daring and lively as any men I have met with since.

We had been utterly sickened for two or three months past, at the date of which I speak, by the preparation of "Richard II" for a reading-examination. The "Head" always took us for the reading, and he himself was quite a character in his own way, of which more later. As a reader or elocutionist he was great, and I fear we must have often caused him much bitterness of spirit by our attempts to do justice to Shakespeare. Even now I can recall poor Pilky's tragic style of reading, in broad Lancashire dialect:

> "Nought shall make us rue
> If England to herself remain but true!"

whilst the "Head" would look at Pilky with a withering glance, and blandly inquire if he (Pilky) ever supposed Shakespeare would have written such lines had he dreamt for a minute that they could be so rendered?

Well, we were sick of the whole business of this annual reading-exam.; but there, it was over at last! And it was whilst we breathed sighs of relief in our own assembly-room that Heavyfoot, one of our school wits, suggested that it would be both a fitting and a graceful act to complete perfectly the "burial" of the defunct Richard by holding a midnight service, and consigning him and all our copies of the play to the dust-bin that stood at the far end

150

The Picturesque Present ; or, the Reign of the Motor-car.

ALGIE: "Hurry up, my deah chap, the motor's waiting."

EDWIN: "Coming, Algie, but it just struck me, as I was looking at your old ancestor boundahs, that it's an awfully good job we don't have to turn out in such silly costumes as those nowadays !"

of the upper corridor. Heavyfoot proposed that the school-band should manfully do its part in the business by marching at the head of the funeral procession, and performing the Dead March in *Saul* during the ceremony.

Loud shouts of approval greeted Heavyfoot's suggestion, mingled with the not unusual cries of "Good old Heavy," "Ripping," etc. The arrangements for the carrying-out of the affair were left in the hands of a small committee, and it was two days afterwards that the whole school received its first instructions in the matter. It appeared that a night had been chosen when, owing to a chance remark of the "Head," it had been gathered that he would be away from the school for a day or two, and thus only "Ralph" would be on guard. Ralph was one of the junior tutors, and was much liked by most of the boys, since he had either the good sense not to see more of such pranks than he was obliged to, or usually forgot to report what he did see. On this occasion, however, it was certain that even Ralph would interfere and stop the affair if he had the chance, so it was resolved that he had better not be allowed that chance!

Accordingly, when it was ascertained on the evening in question that Ralph had retired for the night to his bedroom on the first long corridor, Heavyfoot, Pilky, and Landwater deftly screwed up his door on the outside without attracting his attention, so that egress for the junior tutor was out of the question until the screwing was undone again. Having thus secured the only superior who was likely to interfere with the proposed "burial" of Richard, the coast was clear for the ceremony. The signal had been given for half-past eleven.

Precisely at that hour some 110 youths met at the far end of corridor number two, and filled the adjacent rooms (kindly lent for the occasion by Ward, Lucky & Co.). The procession was put into proper order by "Billy," who had a genius for such things. First came the "choir" of twenty members. They all had their white night-shirts hanging over their ordinary dress, and in their hands they carried open books, in reality the "Gallic Wars" of J. C. Esq.! After the choir came the "band." I remember that Hampton played the flute, and "Cocky" had a cornet, whilst several fellows brought their violins into requisition. As the most available substitute for a drum Pilky had obtained from the servants an old tea-tray, and this certainly made a noise loud enough to satisfy even his musical soul.

Behind the band followed the rank and file, each boy carrying his own copy of Richard II. The procession set out at a slow and well-regulated pace; the tread of over a hundred boys, marching in regular step, making a peculiarly strange effect in the silent night as they went along the wooden floors of the corridors.

First the choir performed a most doleful ditty, "specially written for this occasion" by "the poet"—a wight who rejoiced in the name of Cowper, and slid now and then into poetry without being able to help it! Personally I always felt that it was a pity he was so afflicted; but "the poet" seemed rather proud of his failing, as he did of his historic name!

The funeral song was a strange poem, and was sung to a strange tune. Maurice, our precentor, was responsible for the latter—an original one of his. I can certainly testify to its being quite original, as no other composer ever composed such tunes as Maurice's! This one seemed to be what is known, I believe, in some circles as "Peculiar Metre." It rose in some places to the top G, and went down in others to the E below the middle C. As for melody, if you can imagine sixteen cats trying to sing at once on a dark winter's night, you will be getting something near what Maurice's tune sounded like as we heard it sung by the choir on that memorable occasion!

After the choir, the band chipped in with the Dead March in *Saul*. At least that is what the programme said it was. Every instrument played its own key and tune, regardless of the rest; and several of the violins were perceptibly two semitones flat or sharp. But nobody cared one bit; and I am sure the bandsmen, especially Hampton with the flute, thought the performance would have done credit to Hallé's orchestra at its best! The music sounded weird and strange along the silent corridors, as the procession passed first on one of them, then on another.

When we at length reached Ralph's door we heard his voice inside the room asking "What is all that noise about?" and we heard him trying to open the door. But we knew Landwater's work too well to have any fear of the screwing not having been effectively done, so we simply burst into a shriek of unearthly laughter and resumed our march. It was coming to a close, for the dust-bin loomed in sight. Then Carter, who had always been the "cleric" of the boys during my school career there, stepped forward, attired as much like a clergyman as could be managed, and advanced to the front of the procession. He began to read from a book of mock burial service, which regretted the death from old age and infirmities of his Most Noble Majesty King Richard II., and consigned his remains to the grave amidst the best wishes of his numerous admirers!

After this each man in turn advanced to the dust-bin and, having torn his copy of the play into several pieces, threw the fragments into that receptacle, whilst uttering an ear-splitting yell of delight that would have turned a Red Indian green with envy had he heard it. Carter then "improved the occasion" by making a few remarks upon kings in general, and Richard II. in particular, with sundry hints on "How to Read Well and Effectively," *à la* the "Head." Finally, with one universal shout of "God save the Queen!" we dispersed to our rooms, and the ceremony was over.

Ralph's room was unscrewed at 5.30 a.m. by

Landwater, whilst its occupant was yet asleep. And to have seen the look of astonishment on the faces of one hundred and twenty boys next morning, when that tutor, at breakfast, declared that there had been a terrible "row" the night before—("Which must not be repeated again!")—would have done you good. As to the door-screwing never a word was said. Ralph was a tutor in a thousand; he knew when to know and when to appear ignorant. But we all were aware that, like the weasel, he had generally one eye open when he seemed to be asleep!

CHRISTMASTIDE ON THE AFGHAN FRONTIER

Dr. R. T. Halliday,

Author of "With the Red Cross to Kassala,"
"A Filibustering Adventure," etc. etc.

MIR ALI KHEL is a small demi-bastion fort situated close to the river Zhob, in a widened part of an otherwise narrow valley, and but four miles, as the crow flies, from the nearest point of the Afghan boundary-line. Though designated a "fort," its position is bad from every point of view. It is commanded by a hill four hundred yards distant, from which an enemy could enfilade two faces of the fort and take a third side in reverse; while from the surrounding hillsides the whole place could be swept by modern rifle fire. The approaches could be rendered impassable by a very small force. The water supply is a well in the open three hundred yards distant, and for this reason alone the place would inevitably capitulate after a three days' siege. It has no artillery, and as a frontier military station seems almost a colossal joke. Its walls are thirty feet high and of immense thickness; but its magazine in the barrack square, with two or more barrels of gunpowder and over 100,000 rounds of reserve ammunition, is not even provided with a lightning conductor. . . .

I had not been long resident at Mir Ali Khel when I tired of my unvarying diet. With fowl for breakfast, fowl for tiffin, and fowl again for dinner, I grew sick at the very idea of fowl. The culinary accomplishments, moreover, of my apology for a khansama were not of a sufficiently high order to enable him to hit the happy medium between a tough indigestible leather and an orthodox cinder. And my own education, alack! had been sadly neglected so far as cookery was concerned. My initial attempt at boiling a bird brought such a sarcastic grin to the face of the khansama, that I at once appreciated the predicament of the diner who ordered a hammer and chisel in the determination to "see this thing to a finish." I had therefore every

reason to forgo fowls, and when I reached my fiftieth I struck. These fowls are sold by the villagers at two annas (about three halfpence) per head, and are about the most miserable specimens of barndoor game-cocks one could conceive. And when the feathers are removed ——!!

I had recourse then to native diet, mostly chupatties. These consist of a paste made with flour and water, baked for about three minutes over a fire. The result is a rather indigestible kind of dough, of which the first mouthful generally suffices for the amateur. When baked some minutes longer they are much improved, becoming like a biscuit, and when I began to suspect my khansama of mixing the flour with sand to enhance the crispness, I took to cooking them myself and soon became quite an expert. This servant, I may note *en passant*, was a veritable heart-breaker. I took him out in the belief that he was a first-rate cook, and I had to learn my error by a bitter experience. I did not know till later that he had been ignominiously dismissed from his previous situation for straining his master's morning coffee through his socks, and I then promptly sent him about his business.

I secured in his place a naick who proved a perfect gem. This boy, on my next visit to Mir Ali Khel, varied my fowl to a surprising degree. I had broiled fowl and fricasseed fowl, roast fowl, and hashed fowl, curried fowl, and fowl in every conceivable form and dress, many of which I should never have recognised as fowl had I not been aware that there was absolutely nothing else to be had. A true Indian khansama can turn out quite a varied and luxurious meal out of the barest and most unpromising materials, and this man seemed a born cook. That, however, by the way.

When I began my chupattie diet, I might indeed

View of Fort Mir Ali Khel.

have had variations of a sort, for our varied company had varied tastes. The Sikhs were most troublesome in their desire to oblige me in this respect. They seemed to have innumerable festivals—about two feast-days per week, and, on each occasion, out of kindly courtesy, presented me with a princely share of some odious concoction which they apparently relish, but which I never had courage to sample. I was for ever in a dilemma with regard to the disposal of this periodical gift. Neither my dog nor cat would assist me out of the difficulty, and I dared not offer it to my servants or orderlies in fear of offending the donors, which I was very loth to do. I had, therefore, to stroll round the ramparts after dark and carefully scatter the gift to the winds!

The news that relief was practically impossible, even at the end of four weeks, was received with feelings akin to dismay. All hope of spending Christmas among white men even was rudely dispelled, and I began to realise that my Christmas dinner would probably consist of an overboiled or underboiled fowl, with chupatties as usual and sardines by way of a luxury, all washed down by the peasoup liquid from our well. But ere that memorable morning dawned I found that I had earned the deep commiseration of my brother officers, and I was provided with the wherewithal to dine right royally, with a store for future feasting in reserve.

My extra supplies came by instalments, as opportunity offered, and the first was somewhat disconcerting. One day the postal escort brought me a gift from our colonel's wife. Ladies were at that time permitted to accompany their husbands to Fort Sandeman, a privilege since by regulation withdrawn. The gift consisted of a fancy cake and a couple of loaves of bread. The Zhob levy sowar to whom it was entrusted was, like the rest of his kind,

indescribably filthy. Most of these frontier tribesmen allow their hair as well as beard to grow until it hangs in long matted ringlets over their shoulders, and they neither comb nor clean it from one year to another. Their turbans are of the most primitive kind, and are usually soaked with the greasy concoction with which they besmear and gloss the hair.

This messenger on arrival proceeded, to my surprise, to unwind his turban in my presence, a turban which resembled an engineer's oil-rag on an extensive scale. He then presented me with the cake, which had lain for security among his filthy hair. The loaves were produced from an equally disreputable haversack. I could not afford to be particular, however, when I had seen no fresh bread for a month, so after a few cursory remarks to the sowar, which I will here omit, I proceeded to cut off a thick layer all round the loaves, and utilised the interior. My dog, not gifted with the same fastidiousness, finished the cake in a trice, and beyond a little extra somnolence seemed nothing the worse for his feast. Each post, thereafter, brought some little addition to my store, and several days before Christmas a party of sipahis arrived with ammunition, and some hampers for me which the officers had seized the opportunity to send.

I then discovered that I had accumulated a princely stock. In one hamper were two huge plum-puddings and a jar of sauce, and the wherewithal to set alight the former in old-fashioned British style. A Christmas cake with icing, two plum-cakes, a dozen of mince pies, two chicken-rolls, several tins of preserved fruit, five loaves, and two small jars of cream. The odd spaces were filled in with oranges, and some tins of pepper, mustard, and salt. This hamper came from the colonel's wife. Our major sent an ammunition-box containing a round of beef, some preserved ginger, and a bottle of chutney, with packages of ground rice and other dainties. Other cases contained eggs, tinned meats and fruits, a variety of meat rolls, and pastries, not to mention sundry little boxes of pills. The adjutant forwarded a horse's nosebag full of vegetables and a box of cheroots, while the regimental doctor included in his parcel a small square bottle which looked like fortified cough-mixture, but which was labelled, in glaring red-ink characters, "SOOTHING SYRUP FOR INDIGESTION, SPECIAL."

Finally, there was a parcel of some size, from which we unwound layer after layer of stout wrapping, each securely fastened with cord or wire. At last we reached the kernel and found *a lean and shrivelled fowl!* I threw it at once across my room, and the dog carried it outside in a twinkling in fear that I should regret the donation. But I could afford now to be generous with such a gift, having had a surfeit of its kind.

My excitement, however, was nothing compared with that of the wily khansama. Each package unwrapped seemed to give him an additional spasm of delight at the prospect of trying his 'prentice hand on something new. He was ravenous for "experience." I foolishly did allow him on Christmas eve to cook my beef, and when I saw it reduced to a cinder I felt inclined to kick him round the fort by way of working up an appetite. The remainder of the viands I cooked myself, and escaped with a scalding over the vegetables. But I had the satisfaction, after dressing my wounds, of sitting down to a regal Christmas feast, such as I had not experienced since my arrival in the Orient.

THE BOYHOOD OF DR. W. G. GRACE

JULY 1848 was the red-letter day of the Graces' calendar. Our cricket champion was, it is said, a big baby, and was born in the quiet village of Down-end, Bristol.

W. G. had two brothers—E. M., who is still alive, and G. F., the youngest and pet of the family, with bright laughing eyes and cheery musical voice. Straight as an arrow, genial and gentle of manner, with a hearty word for everybody, it was a breath of life to watch him, and a deep stimulating draught to know him. He died in 1880.

The home of the Graces was a very remarkable one. The father was the inventor of a kite-carriage (fully described and illustrated in an early volume of the "B.O.P."), with which he was continually experimenting, now and then trying a race with Father Time, and making it hot for him. He once did two miles under five minutes, repeatedly fifteen within the hour, and when life became a trifle dreary within the provinces, rode to London for a change. On one occasion the Graces overtook the Duke of York's carriage, and yelled at the postillions for permission to pass. Royalty was not to be treated in that way, and the Grace boys vainly shouted and sought for an opening. The pace grew exciting, the youngsters lost all sense of the fitness of things, and when the common was reached, seized the opportunity of a wide bit of road to pass. They had gained their point, and showed it in a variety of playful ways to the postillions; then, their native politeness returning, they fell behind again, doffing their caps.

Their uncle taught them cricket, and the boys were apt pupils. On the lawn, at all hours of the day, they could be seen playing. The Grace family soon earned the reputation of being earnest and thorough in play and in work.

The uncle was coach, and proved an able one. He was a good bat, and scored many useful innings for West Gloucestershire. As a bowler, he could hit a single stump thirty times out of a hundred with a good length ball. The Grace pitch faced the front of the house, and a stretch of canvas, supported by three poles, was fixed behind the wicket. The elder members were allowed fifteen minutes' batting each, but the younger had to content themselves with five, until they grew in years and were worthy of more attention. W. G. and G. F. were thus kept in the background, and considered it very hard indeed. Still, they were not going to be crushed, and set about for some means of supplementing the family allowance. W. G. enlisted the aid of the boot-boy, and had quiet times to himself. It was anything but a pleasant time for the boy.

A great difficulty lay in the scarcity of fielders. There was no side canvas in those days, and a leg hit of any force went over the fence into the wood or deep pool. Seeking for the ball made a big hole in the batsman's innings, and human aid was not always procurable.

Animal aid was at hand, however, and with a little painstaking the difficulty was surmounted. Don, an intelligent pointer, was initiated into the science of fielding, and did it gracefully. Ponto, of the same breed, followed; and between them the game proceeded merrily, but neither would take to water. Noble, a retriever, appeared in his intelligence and might. For general proficiency he was far and away the best of the wonderful three, and feared neither land nor water, so long as he could minister to the wants and pleasures of his masters. Sad to say, they had their weaknesses, and that in the form not uncommon to strictly human nature. Strongly lacking in sympathy for weak performers, they insisted on the game being played in the straightforward orthodox way. Their position was right behind the bowler, watching his movements and following the pitch of the ball. If pitched on one side, they tarried not for the batsman to hit, but made for the spot that custom and scientific training had taught them it ought to go. Imagine their disgust to see it placed or hit to leg!

E. M. was an occasional offender, but in slight form. His uncle says, in his early days most balls to the off he hit there; but everything on the leg stump, good, bad, or indifferent, was mowed all over the county. Well, he had to pay for it in dog respect. Strangers were violent offenders, and received unmitigated contempt—Noble invariably turning tail and taking holiday for the rest of the day with a dirty Skye. W. G. speaks feelingly yet of their smartness in stopping balls with their chest, and catching with their mouth first bound. Peace to their memory—they helped the good cause.

It will be seen from the arrangements of the Grace house that W. G. had example and precept to

CORRESPONDENCE.

C. A. Carter and G. Woodville.—Making fireworks without a licence is now against the law, and no licences are granted for making them at home whether for sale or not.

H. J. Taylor.—Neither a coin nor a medal but a worthless piece of brass, as the inscription, "in memory of the good old days," should have told you at a glance. These so-called coins of George the Third were used as counters in certain games and have been frequently referred to in these columns.

An Ever Faithful Reader. —You will be told what book on navigation is required when you join the training-ship; in the meantime improve your mathematics and become quick at logarithms.

L. Toulson.—Motor-scooters are classed as motor-bicycles and are subject to the same regulations. Apply for particulars to the local post-office or police station.

S. W. Randall.—The boat was designed for sailing and should not be altered. You require quite a different design for a motor-boat.

B. J. Brooks.—Value depends on date, but Queen Elizabeth shillings are usually worth eighteenpence when hammered and six shillings when milled.

A. Davidson.—Have nothing to do with tattooing; you will regret it afterwards if you do.

enable him to become a cricketer, and Mr. Pocock soon noticed and encouraged the straight defence and wonderful placing that were to elicit the admiration of everyone who knew anything of the game. At nine years of age his play was as correct as at twenty. He had the courage and judgment to resist the temptation to pull, that often brought down the gallery with a big hit, but more often cost a wicket. Unwearying patience and coolness were characteristic of him then as they were later, when making his great scores.

What was W. G. like at school? Well, he went to the village seminary, kept by Miss Trotman. He earned the reputation of being a steady lad, good at arithmetic, and with no mischief about him, though very fond of collecting birds' eggs and snakes—and this latter practice did not altogether conduce to harmony in the house. Snakes, of course, were a terror to mother and sisters, and had a most inconvenient way of appearing when not wanted.

Signs of prowess were not lacking at this school. Here he became champion at marbles. Cricket and football had their share of attention, and he was also an excellent shot. He was very fond, too, of hunting, and once the talk of taking the harriers away troubled both W. G. and his brothers, so they determined to remedy the scarcity of game. The boys and their uncle one morning laid a drag of aniseed over a ploughed field or two, then through a belt of wood, a cottage garden, meadow land and wood again, till they completed the circle.

At the meet that day, the scent was strong an

At the meet that day, the scent was strong and the dogs wild to begin. Round they went for over an hour, and only when commencing the circle for the third time did glimmerings of a sell dawn in the minds of the huntsmen. The boys had disappeared, leaving their uncle to explain.

In his twelfth year W. G. was playing for West Gloucestershire against Clifton, and scored fifty-one; and by the time he was fifteen had established himself as a fine cricketer. In 1864 W. G. played at the Oval against Surrey. It was for South Wales, in the same year, that he made his first century, and it was a curious coincidence that he was only asked to play as a substitute. He made, however, 170 in his first innings, and was not out in the second. He scored in that season 1,179, and the next year was chosen for Gentlemen and Players. In the following year, five times he scored over a century, and his 224 not out for England *versus* Surrey at the Oval on the 30th of July simply electrified all who saw it. It was the largest score that had ever been made.

His boyhood drew to a close, and by the time he was nineteen he was a magnificent bowler as well as a batsman. His defence and hitting powers were second to none, and his scoring for three years was marvellous. From that day he has gone on improving, and at fifty-three years of age still makes the highest score on the Gentlemen's side.

W. G. never smoked, and his advice to boys to-

day is not to begin the habit, as it will spoil their eyesight, and they will lose their power of judging.

T. C. C.

Left *Dr William Gordon Stables, who contributed for over thirty years to the B.O.P., seen in later life* (right) *sketching near his caravan 'The Wanderer'.* Above *Jack Hobbs, from an article on 'How to improve your cricket' in 1912.* Above right *A famous advertisement from the B.O.P., 1910.*

[NO. 36 OF CURRENT VOLUME.]
Full No. 1638.—Vol. XXXII.

SATURDAY, JUNE 4, 1910.

Price One Penny.
[ALL RIGHTS RESERVED.]

A Smashing Hit.
(*Drawn for the "Boy's Own Paper" by* T. Lemark.)

CORRESPONDENCE.

Icarus.—Under the scheme for the training of apprentices for the Royal Air Force, introduced by the Air Ministry, the Air Force co-operates with the local education authorities throughout the country, who nominate suitable boys to sit for the entrance examination. The examinations take place twice a year and candidates for them must be between 15 and 16½ years of age. The subjects are English, history, geography and mathematics. Those who pass are attested for ten years' service in the R.A.F., and two years in the Reserve; they receive a three-years' apprenticeship, at the end of which, if qualified, they are promoted to leading aircraftmen.

S. V. Stone.—Not a coin but a medal or counter. British coins are not struck at Nürnberg.

W. A. Bennett.—There is no coin with "Rule Britannia" on it.

SELF-DEFENCE TIPS

Percy Longhurst.

FIG. 1 represents an effective defence against a round-arm swinging hitter—as are most individuals who have never had boxing instruction. The position of the hands shows whether the blow will come from right or left, and when it is avoided by a step back the force of the delivery will whirl the striker round, when instant and successful retaliation may be made as depicted.

Or you may strike down the arm as in fig. 2 with one hand, following this up with a flooring blow with the other.

The next drawing, fig. 3, shows a perculiarly efficient defence. It is simplicity itself, but can only be employed when the aggressor is standing with his feet fairly close together. One simply drops on one knee and seizes the assailant round the ankles with one's head between his legs. Pressure with the shoulders on the shins combined with a quick forward jerk of the feet will send the would-be assaulter flat on his back.

The defence is one I well recollect being employed with great success by an acquaintance of mine against a huge bully who attempted to assault him one afternoon in an East London street.

Do not forget that it is necessary to go down exactly as illustrated, with the chest bent along the left thigh and the right knee a few inches to the rear of the left heel. This requires a forward step with the left foot before ducking down. The lower the hand holds the better.

A Modern Martyr (Drawn by Tom Browne)
THE BOY: *"Don't you get awful tired doin' nothin', mister?"*
THE MAN: *"Terrible; but I never complains. Everybody has troubles!"*

A Rugby Incident. – 'Nearly In'.

A Try! – 'Took the pass and dived over'.

Above *Illustrations to a rugby football article in 1904.*

FACE-READING

Written and Illustrated
by Percy V. Bradshaw.

PRESENTED "B.O.P." readers, a short time ago, with much useful and reliable information about dreams and their meanings, giving, however, full credit for a lot of my expert knowledge to the author of a penny handbook which I was lucky enough to pick up on one of my travels!

During a train journey recently I was able to delve into the mysteries of that wonderful science, Physiognomy, with the aid of a similar authority!

The style of this physoginomy—I mean Physiognomy—handbook suggests that it was produced by the dream-expert, and once again that distinguished personage gives the reader excellent value for the penny expended.

When I obtain, for one solitary copper, a wealth of scientific information, enclosed in a highly decorated cover—which bears the alluring title, "The Revelations of a Gipsy Queen"—I don't think "B.O.P." readers are likely to upbraid me for reckless extravagance, especially as I intend to share with them the really wonderful. information contained in this most exciting volume.

The early part of the book contains many valuable hints to the youthful lover on the language of flowers. I do not propose to spend much time just now over youthful lovers, but, being possessed of a kindly and sympathetic disposition, I feel compelled to tell the Romeo of fourteen that, if he wears

160

a white camellia in his buttonhole, he personifies "loveliness," while a pot of fern placed conspicuously upon his person means "fascination." In a country ramble with a pretty cousin, therefore, if you don't happen to be wearing a flower-pot in your buttonhole, it would be an act of gallantry to tear up a large fern by the roots and present it to the lady as an indication of your enthusiasm for her. It's so much more original than pressing a forget-me-not or ivy-leaf into her palm—though it might be advisable to shake a little of the superfluous dirt from the fern-roots before you place them in the lady's lap!

Don't hand her mignonette, if she understands the language of flowers, for you're politely informing her that her qualities far surpass her charms of beauty—and no girl wants to be told that!

Following the flower information we come to the language of precious stones, which won't interest the average "B.O.P." reader for many years to come—until, in fact, he thinks of sporting a saucy tie-pin—but the next "Revelation of the Gipsy Queen" must surely appeal to everyone, dealing as it does with the language of postage-stamps!

Having thoroughly digested these useful hints, you will be ready to devote what is left of your leisure to the study of that important and beautiful subject, physiognomy.

This is "the art or science of discerning the character of the mind from the features of the face," says Lavater, the greatest authority on the subject. According to the expert who discusses the question in the book under consideration, "some people are so gifted in thus reading character, and can form

Original ideas as to Beauty

such rapid and sound judgment, as to be of great service to them in their various walks of life, and, by studying the following indications, a fair amount of proficiency may soon be obtained."

Then follows some fascinating details—which I have supplemented here by elaborate il-

lustrations—for the guidance of the beginner in the art of physiognomy. (You'll be able to pronounce the word quite satisfactorily after the third or fourth attempt, if you make a plucky dash at it.)

"When the face," our expert remarks, "is even and well balanced, and the general appearance smooth and free from angularity, a natural, good, and loving disposition, though somewhat distrustful, is indicated, fond of pleasure, and agreeable in social life.'

Is your face fairly well balanced, reader dear?—or do you favour the lop-sided, twirly, "new art" style of countenance? Perhaps you have original ideas as to beauty, and have permitted your features to run riot and develop into rather quaint

'Allowed his chin to be elongated'.

shapes, in the hope that you may one day be adopted as a design for a door-knocker, a carpet, or a decorative jug! If so, it is obvious that you do *not* possess "a natural, good, and loving disposition." I'm sorry for you, and your only consolation will be that you avoid being "somewhat distrustful."

Mayhap your lines are cast in a generous mould, and your face is "full, fleshy, and bright in colour." If that is so, it's a bit of luck for you and your friends, showing, as it does, that you are reliable in friendship, faithful in love, and amiable of temper—in fact, your disposition is so beautiful that you are likely to be imposed upon by the unscrupulous. It would seem, therefore, that you should do your best to combine your features with those of the first-mentioned type, so as to acquire a touch or two of "distrust."

I'm afraid I have very few crumbs of comfort to offer the youth whose face is "angular in contour, with the cheek-bones projecting and conspicuous" (in fact, plenty of cheek), the temperament served out with such faces being one that anticipates trouble, is restless, complaining, and generally dissatisfied with life—though possibly without cause.

The best thing to be done for such a face is either to take it out for a long walk, and lose it, or to cultivate a cheery outlook on things in general—keep smiling—when the colour will come back to the cheeks, which will grow plump and cover the bony bits, and, in short, everything in the garden will be absolutely lovely.

When a careless youth has allowed his chin to be "elongated in disproportion to the upper portion of the physiognomy" (d'you know what that means in English?), he is giving his nasty disposition away completely, for the abnormal length of chin indicates a "cruel propensity, with indiscreet talk and slander."

Now you can see how carefully we ought to watch our features—and train them. Chins are especially dangerous things to neglect. If you let them slip about recklessly, they are bound, in time, to monopolise too much of your face, and you become branded as an undesirable personage by the physiognomist.

Don't allow your chin too much breadth, for, if it becomes too broad, square, and prominent, very bad character is indicated, among your other horrid failings being faithlessness in love and friendship, deceit, ingratitude, and thorough all-round selfishness.

Which of you fellows has a dimple in his chin? The boy with such an ornament is, as a rule, rather sorry for himself, and regrets the pretty little depression, thinking that it makes him appear rather girlish. He must think nothing of the kind, in

'The boy with the noble brow'.

future, for the dimple denotes all sorts of good qualities in the person who owns it. He is a devoted lover, good-hearted, generous, sincere, steadfast, and extremely intelligent. I envy and congratulate you, my dimpled reader! I haven't—alas!—a dimple to bless myself with, and I suppose I'm too old to start cultivating one.

And now we come to the boy with the noble brow. A full smooth forehead indicates good mental capacity—especially business ability—but, these valuable possessions are considerably modified by the length of the face.

If the forehead takes up too much of the face, you're an extremely naughty person.

If your chin is small, it denotes meanness, spite, and a weak revengeful disposition. Furthermore, if there is "a depression or channel where the jaws unite, great quarrelsomeness, villainy, callous relentlessness, and hard-heartedness is indicated."

I have just been examining, in fear and trembling, my own face, to see if there's a channel hiding itself away anywhere; with a sigh of relief I've found that there isn't. Had it been there, I suppose the only remedy would have been to grow a beard—and I should look *so* horrid as a whiskery person!

I will now proceed, after expressing the hope that all my readers are channel-less.

There are, of course, very many other types of face familiar to the student of English beauty, which my penny physiognomist has not touched upon, and I should like to have been able to give you information as to the temperament of the "pudden-faced perisher," "the kite-face," "the onion-head," "the turnip-face," and other interesting types we have heard mentioned in playgrounds, but, in the excitement of his work, my expert has switched off on to a consideration of separate features.

A face that is merely plain and fat "without any rising" (whatever that may mean) indicates that the person who has to trot it about always is "very wise, faithful to his friend, and patient in adversity." He must find the last quality very useful and comforting.

Finally, the owner of another mysterious type—"the face inclining to leanness, sinking down a little, with crosses in it," doesn't necessarily show that its owner has had a rough time at footer, or that he has been trying to stop a train, *or* that a horse has kicked him; it merely denotes a very laborious, vain, quarrelsome, and silly person. I've never met such a face, but if the description tallies to the appearance of any of my readers, I'd be most delighted to have his photograph, and would promise to stick it in an honoured place among my curios.

Next we come to the consideration of eyes, hair, noses, and moles as important indications of character; but on these I cannot long linger.

The eyes convey considerable information as to the inner feelings of the owner—and here's a small specimen of the careful manner in which our expert discusses the subject. "If able to meet your gaze naturally (without a brazen stare forced into them)," he says, "and to remain calmly expressive under your constant (but not rude) inquiry, you may add this impression as a favourable one to assist or qualify those you have already found in the features of the face; but always distrust a person who constantly averts the eyes or looks down when so scrutinised—of course assuming that you do not assault by your gaze and so abash or terrorise a timid but honest nature."

THE BOY'S OWN PAPER

No. 1238.—Vol. XXV.
[No. 1 of New Vol.]

SATURDAY, OCTOBER 4, 1902.

Price One Penny.
[ALL RIGHTS RESERVED.]

QUEER Mr QUERN.

"A shuddering fear seized him."

By the Rev. A. N. Malan, D.D.,

Author of "The Belgian Hare," "The Wallaby Man," etc., etc.

(With Illustrations by Alfred Pearse.)

CHAPTER I.—A NOVEMBER EVENING.

"Grand! Magnificent! Superb! Garlands of dried flowers from the coffin of Rameses II.! Imagination is awed in attempting to bridge over the interval of two thousand years since that far-off morning in the childhood of the world, when those dried petals were fresh-gathered flowers of the beautiful blue lotus of the Nile! Empires have risen and flourished, have tottered and decayed meanwhile! Those withered blossoms are more wonderful than thy pyramids and obelisks, O Egypt! Time's corroding tooth has gnawed the solid stone, but it has had no power to hurt those frail daughters of the river. The flower still lives, and the fair relics of its imperishable beauty defy the tooth of time!"

Public-School Cricket Captains, 1901.

1. F. G. WHATELY, *Eton.*
2. V. H. CARTWRIGHT, *Rugby.*
3. F. W. MANN, *Harrow.*
4. DONALD BROMFIELD, *St. Aloysius College.*
5. H. C. McDONELL, *Winchester.*
6. W. SMITH, *Hurstpierpoint.*
7. N. C. D. ROSS, *Uppingham.*
8. D. BURTON, *Fettes.*
9. GEOFFREY M. GILL, *Lancing.*
10. G. A. EDE SMITH, *Bedford Modern.*
11. F. BROOKS, *Bedford Grammar School.*
12. H. WRIGHT, *Mill Hill.*

You see, you *must* be careful. It's absurd to go cruising about abashing harmless youths till they are half hysterical, and then triumphantly stating that they are sneaking rascals.

It's not at all a fair test to suddenly grip hold of a

'There are many other types'.

lower-former, freeze him with the baleful glare in your brazen orbits, and then, because he simply can't stand it, assure him that he is not a fit person to be on the earth with you. It won't do. If you want to be a successful face-reader you must not abash or terrorise.

"They whose eyes are neither too little nor big, and inclined to be black, denotes them to be mild, peaceable, honest, witty, and of good understanding."

There are very many varieties of eye discussed, but they all show their owners to be undesirable personages, except the above, which is the only type of eye worth having. And mine are not a bit like the

description! It's a shame!

Then we have some valuable information, in our volume, which will enable you to make a good start in life, reading character by the hair; but the nose—ah, there's the rub!

A long and thin nose denotes a man bold, furious, angry, vain, and credulous. A long nose, "extended unduly," shows the person to be wise, discreet, honest, and faithful. A "bottle nose" denotes a man to be vain, false, luxurious, weak and uncertain. A nose broad in the middle and less towards the end denotes a vain, talkative person, a liar, and one of bad fortune, and so on, and on. But our space is precious, and my little body is a-weary.

So you'll forgive me—won't you?—if I lay down my pen, wash the ink from my fingers, and,

"With a pleasure that's emphatic,
    Retire unto my attic
With the gratifying feeling that my duty has been done."

THE VANISHING REDSKINS

Algernon Blackwood.

PART I.

THE Red Indians of the north-eastern portion of Canada and the United States are so fast disappearing before the march of modern life that before very long they will be nothing more than a name and a memory. This is a very striking fact when you think how it seems so short a time since the settlers and backwoodsmen of Canada were never safe from scalping raids and midnight attacks; how the deep woods constantly echoed the dreaded war-whoops; and the blue lakes and rivers

of that wild country were often covered with great war canoes, loaded with prisoners and stained with the blood of red and white men alike.

But conditions change very rapidly in these days of discovery and education, and the old races are bound to keep up with the march, or else to die out. And the old Red Indians are dying out—fast!

I have travelled a great deal in Canada, especially in the eastern parts, and the first time I saw a Red Indian I experienced a dreadful shock—of disappointment. It was in Toronto. The man was undersized and walked with a shuffling gait. He was dressed—I hardly like to tell you—in a faded old frock-coat and a top-hat, with baggy striped trousers and brown boots, and he was selling grass hand-made articles such as mats for teapots, little work-baskets, and needle-cases. I went up close and looked at him, and he turned up a weak and half-tipsy face into mine, and gazed at me out of rather bleary eyes, and asked me in his broken English if I would buy a mat or a needle-case. It was a pathetic sight, and all day I was haunted by the apparition, and kept thinking of the tall, strong, eagle-eyed men who only a few years before had the scent of a fox and the speed of a deer and the endurance and courage of the wolf. It was, as I said, a great shock!

This particular Indian had come down from the great Government Reservation among the Lake-and-Island region a hundred miles north of Toronto, where the Indians have large tracts of land reserved for their special use, and where they live, fishing, hunting, making canoes, paddles and the like, and where the women make knick-knacks out of the sweet-scented grass called *abaznoda* and send down the "braves" in summer to sell what they can among the white folk of the towns. It is a crime punishable with very heavy fines indeed for anyone to sell whisky or intoxicating liquor to the Reser-

AWKWARD VERY! (*Drawn by Tom Browne*)
SPANISH GUIDE: *"Will the señor please pay my fee?"*
TOURIST: *"But I paid you a sovereign—what you asked for—before we started."*
SPANISH GUIDE: *"Yes, señor but don't you think this beautiful view is worth another five pounds?"* (*The tourist thinks it is and pays up.*)

vations, but once the Redskins get into the demoralising atmosphere of the towns they are not so easy to look after, and they drink the "firewater" whenever they can get it.

The main body of Indians who still dwell in this eastern part of the American continent are the Wabanaki branch of the once great Algonquin stock, and they consist of tribes known as the Passamaquoddies (meaning "Spearers of Pollock fish"), Penobscots, Abenaki (Land of the Dawn), Micmacs, and Delawares. They are disappearing so quickly now before the white men that, as Professor Prince of New York says, they are a race "which fifty years from now will have hardly a single living representative." Some of their lesser tribes number now but a mere handful of twenty or thirty men, and when the last of these are dead there will have passed away an entire race of men whose memory will always live on to stir the thoughts and imaginations of readers and thinkers for centuries.

CHAPTER FIVE
FROM THE FIRST WORLD WAR
TO THE FINAL ISSUE

In 1914 the *B.O.P.* adopted a format that scarcely changed for the next thirty years. It was less crowded than in the previous decade, and infinitely less so than in the nineteenth century. This was partly due to the fact that pages now had two columns instead of three. The 1914 volume contained a Jules Verne serial, 'The Master of the World', although Verne himself had died in 1905. An invader had built a spacecraft which was so powerful and unusual that it enabled him to defy the world. The Great Powers offered him money for the secret, but the offer was contemptuously refused. As the inventor was a megalomaniac there was widespread concern – but fortuitously the machine was destroyed by lightning; its inventor and secrets perished with it. Other writers were not slow to copy such a promising theme.

Like many people the Editor of the *B.O.P.* probably hoped the war would soon be over and there would be time enough to discuss it afterwards. This view was soon dispelled; and in the 1915 *B.O.P.*'s there were articles on gun-making, submarines, mine-laying etcetera, and a serial by the new Editor (A. L. Haydon) 'For England and the Right: A Tale of the War in Belgium'.

Jules Verne appeared again in 1915 in 'Kongre the Wrecker'. Captain Talbot Reed, 67th Punjabis, second son of the author, was killed in action in 1915, at the age of 28.

Gilson contributed 'In the Power of the Pygmies', 'Submarine U93', 'At the Call of the Tsar' (in which an English boy went to fight for the Russians) and 'The Mystery of Ah Jim' during the war years. The Editor no doubt felt that romantic adventure fiction was preferable to everyday reality. George Soper illustrated Gilson, but the artist who really made the reader take notice was Stanley L. Wood, who drew for a variety of authors. Wood had spent his early life in California, Texas and other American states. Every detail of dress and equipment in his vigorous drawings was correct.

1917 saw the arrival at the *B.O.P.* of Kent Carr, a female writer of boys' school stories. She was held in high esteem by many. The Western Front killed off many writers, proven or potential, and it was principally the old favourites, such as Gilson, Argyll Saxby and Claverdon Wood, who kept the serials going. George A. Wade was still churning out articles on every aspect of public-school life, but there was a newcomer in 1917 called F. Bayford Harrison, who contributed a series on 'School Etiquette: Customs that are unwritten laws at Winchester, Eton, Harrow etc.' There was also an article on 'Mr Arthur Feather, Ventriloquist to the British Army'.

The old weekly parts had been dropped in 1913 – never to be revived – but otherwise the *B.O.P.* stood the war well. Paper, of course, deteriorated in quality, but the coloured plates continued without great loss of clarity. The Editor reported in 1918 that numbers of old readers, now soldiers, had called in at his office during the war to tell him how much they enjoyed the paper. He had visitors from Australia and letters from Salonica, and other theatres of war. It was, someone said, very cheering to find your copy in the trenches when you returned from a bombing raid. It is not difficult to understand such statements. In the Second World War, for instance, the drowsy cathedral-close atmosphere of Anthony Trollope's novels made them extremely popular. In a world which has clearly gone mad anything savouring of normal placid life is eagerly sought.

One of the most compelling serials of the war years was W. E. Cule's 'In the Secret Sea'. It began in an atmosphere of naval warfare but soon moved into an extraordinary fantasy of an explorer's ship which had vanished on a small island some thirty years before.

The Rev. A. N. Malan was still alive, though no longer writing. He had been headmaster of Eagle House, Crowthorne, a prep school for Wellington College.

After 1918 the *B.O.P.* seemed as keen to forget the war as everyone else, though there were a few articles on individual acts of heroism. Gilson contributed 'The Lost City' about Egypt and 'The Wizard King' about Africa, and there was a series of 'straight talks' to boys on such topics as boys 'starting to bowl in life's match'.

Gordon Browne, R.I., was still drawing pictures. His father had drawn for Dickens as 'Phiz'. In 1921–22 the *B.O.P.* produced what many considered to be its finest volume in this century. It contained the memorable 'Treasure of Kings' (about Peru) by Major Charles Gilson; 'The Red Flag', a school story by Richard Bird; 'A Fifth-Form Mystery' by Harold Avery; 'In the Realm of the Arctic Poppy', a convincing fantasy by Raymond Raife; and 'The Secret of Canute's Island' by G. Godfrey Sellick, a story set in the eighteenth century. The last was illustrated by R. H. Brock. T. M. R. Whitwell illustrated Avery's serial: both Brock and Whitwell gave their characters very strong faces.

In 1922 Gilson's biography was summarised. After a successful sporting career at Dulwich College he became a county rugby player and scratch golfer. He served in the Boer War with the Sherwood Foresters and was badly wounded at Vlakfontein. While recovering he started to write. He was subsequently able to serve in many Far Eastern stations, notably in China. He was invalided out with the rank of Captain but contrived to serve again in the 1914–18 war in spite of early rejections. Eventually he left the army as a Major, and continued to contribute to the *B.O.P.* until his death in 1944.

Almost unbelievably Alfred Pearse, who had contributed since the first volume in 1879, was still doing so in 1924.

G. R. Pocklington took over the editorship from A. L. Haydon in the mid-1920s. The *B.O.P.* now seemed to have settled into being a middle-class paper rather than one for boys of all ages and classes. There were articles on motor cycling, foreign travel, ski-ing and yachting. There were still excellent 'how-to-make' articles but they involved a substantial outlay of money. A particularly good series was by 'Adsum' (A. D. Stubbs) whose radio-building articles were authoritative, simple and clear. Major J. T. Gorman contributed a series of articles on how to pass Certificate 'A' (the basic exam in the Officers' Training Corps), and it was clear that the *B.O.P.*'s future now depended on the readership it obtained in the public and grammar schools. Even so there were worries about circulation, and new fountain pens were offered to boys who could introduce new readers.

A number of the articles seem of very limited interest, such as 'Some Canadian Schools' and 'Scouting in other Lands'. In 1927 one of the competitions involved writing down the twelve leading public schools in the British Isles in order of their importance. Popular vote gave Eton and Harrow equal, then Rugby, Charterhouse, Winchester, Marlborough, Westminster, Uppingham, Repton, Shrewsbury, Cheltenham and Haileybury all equal. No definition was given of 'importance', but presumably the term did not include either academic or athletic qualities.

The price was still one shilling (which it had become in 1918), except for Christmas numbers which cost 1s 6d. The price was held at this figure till the 1960s, when it doubled.

A considerable fillip was given to the *B.O.P.* in the late 1920s by four serials from Geo E. Rochester, who had an interesting airman hero called 'The Flying Beetle'. Rochester had been a Flight-Lieutenant in the First World War; he was shot down over German lines. After the war he became a golf caddy (in the land fit for heroes to live in). His first story in the *B.O.P.* launched him on a career of seventy books. He also wrote for many other papers, including women's magazines. Ill-health prevented him keeping up his output and he died in poverty in the 1960s. Not only did the *B.O.P.* owe him a debt but so also no doubt did the R.A.F. and its volunteer forces. Few boys could read his stories and not wish to become a flier.

An amusing writer of the inter-war years was John L. Roberts, who had a schoolboy character called Blundell. Roberts was never heard of after the Second World War and was believed to have been killed in an air raid.

Percy Longhurst, Sid G. Hedges, H. G. H. Chandley and Captain F. A. M. Webster all wrote good sense about various sports. Webster's keenness came through his articles and he was a pioneer of systematic athletic coaching and training ('Secrets of Success in Athletics'). Frank Elias, Harold Avery, Gunby Hadath, Richard Bird (school stories), Sercombe Griffin and Robert Harding, Argyll Saxby, A. Lloyd-Owen, S. T. James, Percy F. Westerman and K. McLure were the mainstay of the fiction writers.

In 1933 G. J. H. Northcroft became Editor for a short time before handing over to Robert Harding. In 1939 the Lutterworth Press (owned by the United Society for Christian Literature) took over the *B.O.P.*

The paper held on little-changed till the end of 1940, but after that a drastic slimming process began despite the appearance of W. E. Johns of 'Biggles' fame. In 1941 the *B.O.P.* was so much smaller that the price had temporarily gone down to ninepence. In an advertisement Ovaltine was recommended because 'many war time pilots drink Ovaltine every night on retiring'. Conditions might be hard and paper scarce but standards were maintained, as the Editor's severe comments on the jokes page show. The *B.O.P.* had been very much aware of the war from the beginning – before much of the rest of the country had seemed to be. Even school stories were about schools which had or had not been evacuated. Paper shortages made its existence precarious but somehow it managed to struggle through.

It fell to Jack Cox to try to revive the former glories, and he made a great fight of it. In 1963 the paper was taken over by Purnells and doubled in size and price. It seemed as if it might achieve its century, but in 1967 Volume 89 saw the end of a very gallant innings. *The Boy's Companion* would appear as an annual publication but the *Boy's Own Paper* was no more. The cause was not that it was losing readers but that it could no longer attract the necessary advertising revenue.

But what a mark it had made, particularly in its heyday!

WAR NOTES AND PICTURES

New Features of Fighting on Sea and Land.

A SILENT GUN.

IN France and in Belgium the Germans have been using some guns that make no noise when they are fired: that is to say, these are guns that make no sound sufficiently loud to reach the ears of the Allies, and so assist them to locate the position of

The Silencer.

the enemy's batteries by hearing. This circumstance has been freely commented upon in newspaper accounts and letters home from our troops at the Front.

As a matter of fact, all armies are ready to adopt a noiseless gun if one of quite satisfactory pattern can be found, and, in addition to the Germans, the British and the French army authorities have been experimenting with weapons of the kind. Our illustration shows a French silent gun that is reported to be in every way effective.

This gun is a quick-firer, capable of discharging twenty-five shrapnel projectiles a minute. Each shell contains 250 bullets; so that in sixty seconds the gun fires 6,250 bullets, capable of killing men at a distance of between four and five miles.

The silencer or cut-off is an attachment that is fixed at the muzzle of the gun, and this contrivance is seen in section in the small diagram. Briefly explained, it may be said that B is a hinged shutter which is drawn up by the passing out of the gun of the emerging shell A. The shutter thus closes the bore of the gun, preventing the passage out of flame and smoke, and also eliminating the sound of loud explosion by stopping air from rushing into the barrel. The gases that are produced by the explosion of the charge pass out rearwards through the two escape channels CC, with the result that the sound of firing is restricted to a distance of a hundred yards or so.

Usually, the provision of silencing devices of any kind is found to have a retarding effect upon the shell; but with this French gun it is claimed that the velocity of the projectile is in no way impaired.

"THE ALLIES' TINDER-BOX."

"MATCHES have been selling for a halfpenny each in the fighting-line."

That item of information sent home from the seat of war shows that, as Tommy himself has also said, "pence may be less precious than pipelights." But matches are readily rendered useless when campaigning; they are spoilt even by the damp of the trenches. That is why extensive supplies of the old-fashioned flint-and-tinder boxes have been urgently called for by our gallant troops. The Navy, too, wants these boxes badly. Smouldering tinder is fanned into ruddier glow by the wind that would at once extinguish a match. And ashore or afloat the tinder-box in use reveals no flame to serve as a mark for the foe.

By special request of many naval and military officers, Mr. Haden Crawford, of Marlow, Bucks, has organised a fund for sending out to our Tommies and Tars consignments of the water-tight tinder-box that he has prepared. Small and compact as is the box, only a half-inch deep, it contains a $7\frac{1}{2}$-inch fuse or length of prepared tinder, a shaped section of flint, and a handy steel. Within the close-fitting lid of the box are printed these instructions for obtaining a light:

"Hold flint flat side up in left hand, hold fuse with left thumb on top of flint, level with edge. Strike flint vertically. When spark on fuse, blow gently into flame."

The operation calls for a certain amount of knack; but that once acquired the soldier or sailor has with him at all times what may be truly described as a perpetual light box that does not require refilling. Various others kinds of lighters have been sent out to the Front, but for one reason or another none proves so useful to our fighting men as the flint, steel, and tinder. Petrol-lighters, for instance, are of service only to motor-drivers, etc., who have petrol handy for refilling.

Since the men began to write home enthusiastically about these lighters, donations large and small have been flowing to the fund. Five pounds pay for a hundred lighters delivered on the Continent; some subscribers furnish enough for a whole battalion, that is, fifty pounds for a thousand men; others pay for lighters for the entire crew of a particular torpedo-boat, submarine, or cruiser. One lady, who has seven sons at the Front, sent £250 for lighters for five whole battalions—5,000 men.

This World's War is being waged with wireless, with aeroplanes and sea-planes, submarines, explosive mines, giant howitzers, machine-guns, motor transport, and all the other very latest products of man's ingenuity. Strange, then, that our soldiers and sailors strongly appeal for such old-time products as these flint, steel, and tinder-boxes! Yesterday, one had to look for specimens as curios in museums. To-day, the manufacturers of them are working overtime to cope with the demand.

MILITARY FOLDING BICYCLES.

BICYCLES that are made to fold up, so that on occasion they can be carried upon a man's back, have been in use for years in Continental armies. In this war the French, Russian, Belgian, German, and Austrian troops have used them in great numbers. The top tube and the lower tube of the machine are hinged in their centres, and by simple manipulation with only the fingers these hinges are freed and the cycle can then be folded wheel beside wheel, as shown.

In military cycling our gallant ally, France, took the lead—a few cyclists being used in the French manœuvres of 1894. The following year, permanent regulations for the employment of cyclists were issued; and at the manœuvres one of the two cyclist detachments engaged was commanded by Captain Gérard, who by some of his compatriots has been quaintly enough termed the Father of the Folding Bicycle. In those manœuvres Captain Gérard's now well-known folding bicycle was adequately tested for the first time, and it came triumphantly through the ordeal. Laden with the soldier's full kit, the machines covered 1,250 miles of give-and-take country, and they were folded up and carried more than 300 times. So successful was the experiment that the machine was at once adopted as the standard pattern for the French army, and it is the type of machine upon which all other military folding bicycles have since been modelled.

General Galliffet, Colonel Denfert, and Captain Gérard were the pioneers of military cycling in France, and the latter's folding bicycle set the fashion in such machines to at least six armies.

Bicycles of this kind can be folded or unfolded in approximately ten seconds, and when the machine is ready for use it is as rigid as any non-folding bicycle. In some types handle bars are fitted that can be collapsed into position parallel with the steering-tube by simply pressing a button; all are provided, within the diamond frame, with a stout strap, by means of which the cyclist soldier can sling the machine on his shoulders.

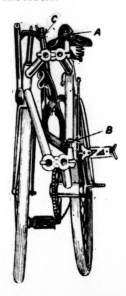

Overleaf Two illustrations from Jules Verne's last story in the B.O.P., 'The Master of the World' (1914), which appeared nine years after his death.

**WAR TYPES—
A BELGIAN CAVALRYMAN**

The Lancers, Hussars, and Chasseurs of Belgium have ·done splendid service in the field against the enemy. Our picture shows a typical mounted patrol.

DISCIPLINE

DISCIPLINE is the difference between an army and a mob. We have lately had an example of a cable which became a rope of sand—in the case of a portion of the Russian army: instead of every man being subject to law, every man became a law to himself, and the result was anarchy, disintegration, defeat. Without discipline, concerted action is impossible and the attainment of great ends unthinkable. The moment obedience is forgotten, oppression becomes possible. The man who thinks to be a law to himself becomes subject to mob law, which is lawlessness.

Freedom without discipline is licence, and therefore no freedom in any proper sense. I was reading a book of astronomy the other day, and I was struck with wondering awe in contemplation of the divine order of the universe. Every planet moves in its own orbit with an exquisite regularity which no mechanism of man can even remotely copy. Even the return of those seemingly erratic wanderers of the sky—the comets—can be reckoned almost to a day or an hour. We speak of sidereal time, which is star time, because it is the absolute standard of regularity and precision.

That is Nature's object lesson in discipline, in order, in regularity, in co-operation. Even the stars and the suns obey orders—the orders of the great Ruler of the universe who "calleth the stars by name"; and in their order and discipline, as well as in their majesty and beauty, "the heavens declare the glory of God, and the firmament showeth His handiwork."

If a school is not a school of discipline it misses its first and best lesson. Indeed, discipline is essential to the learning and the teaching of all other lessons. A class which is in an uproar—where paper pellets fly about, where nuts are cracked, where pert answers are given, where the teacher is the butt of the scholar—is a class where the dunce remains a dunce, and where the willing boy is wasting his time. It is the class which does everything promptly, which obeys the word of command, which respects and bows to the rules of the school, which produces wranglers in the university sense, and makes men who make nations great and strong.

You remember what St. Paul said about "enduring hardness as good soldiers"? Namby-pamby molly-coddling never made a soldier and never will. Many an anæmic youth, who had never carried anything heavier than a cane, has become a man in camp and trench. When we hear of the hardships which our splendid lads have to endure, and do endure cheerfully, we are apt to think that their health will suffer. The opposite is the case. They come home bronzed and healthy and hard, and scornful of ease and softness. The discipline of suffering has made them strong.

That is what our old word "grit" means. I was using some soap the other day, after I had been gardening and had got my hands covered with soil. I had picked it up unthinkingly; but I was surprised to see the dirt fly, leaving my hands clean as before. Then I found that I had used soap with grit in it. It was harsh to the touch, but very effective as a cleanser.

Last spring we were all grumbling more or less at the east wind. We quoted rhymes about its being neither good for man nor beast. We were wrong. It is like chastisement of which the Bible tells: grievous while it lasts, but working for lasting good.

"A nasty east wind to-day, Farmer Hayseed. Bad for the land, I reckon. It goes through me like——"

"Bless you, sir, it's just what we want!"

"You don't mean to tell me that!"

"Indeed, I do, sir! You know what a wet winter we have had. I couldn't get the plough through the sodden earth. It was so soft and sticky there was no doing anything with it."

"Well, what had the east wind to do with that?"

"Why, everything, sir! The dry, hard, biting, piercing wind came along and took all the softness out of the land—all its spongy, sodden, heavy un-workableness—and made it a real pleasure to get the furrows turned over and the seed in."

Yes, the very wind which cracks your lips dries the farmer's field and makes the autumn laugh with golden corn. It is more of Nature's discipline. The chastisement of the east wind produces good soil and rich harvests.

No, do not imagine that war is the only thing that requires discipline. Peace requires it still more. The terror of war draws men together in a common purpose. Peace sometimes brings slackness. Yet it ought not to do so. Peace has her victories as well as war. Are there no great ends to attain by peaceful means as well as by warlike weapons? Supposing that this Britain of ours were to work as hard and as zealously in making cutlery, and cotton, and woollen, and scientific instruments, and in research, and invention, and the attainment of useful and uplifting knowledge, and in the pursuit of all the best things of life, as it has worked at the making of munitions of war, what a difference it would make to this empire!

Nothing great was ever done easily. The way of the Cross is still the way to the Crown. Even Jesus of Nazareth was called the Man of Sorrows—yes, with reverence, the Man of Self-Discipline, the Man who never shirked the hard road and took the primrose path, the Man who ever chose the trench of hardship to the dug-out of safety and ease.

Yet out of His determination to face everything, to shirk nothing that lay in the path of duty—which is only another word for true discipline—came all that we hold dear. Life came out of death, victory out of seeming defeat, good out of ill, hope out of despair. And thus, if we are true to our highest ideals, will peace and blessing come out of the hardness of war.

After the war flying was of great interest to boys, many of whom would become pilots in the next world war.

INSTRUCTING PUPILS AT THE GRAHAME-WHITE SCHOOL.

SHADOW ON THE SCHOOL

A Story of Public School Life.

Frank Elias.

Author of "The Mystery of the 'Mayflower,'" "A Boy's Adventures in the South Seas," "The Mine Detector," etc.

(Illustrated by T. M. R. Whitwell.)

CHAPTER I.

A Council of Three.

IN a study on the second floor three boys sat looking into the fireless grate. The centre figure, which appeared to be that of the room's proprietor, was dark and seemingly, in spite of a somewhat bent back, tall. He had the quick, rather idle manner of a boy who could cheerfully let others pass him in a race because he was confident of recovering his position in the last lap. That would have been a true enough description of Tom Hemingway, Hemingway major—or, as the school preferred in modern days of war to call him, "Major Hemingway." He was perfectly aware that his powers were greater than those of most boys—he was a year the junior of his two companions, yet was above them in form. Whether he really was as lazy as he professed to be and even liked to be considered, there were boys higher up in the school who had begun to doubt. His extraordinarily bright eyes seemed to supply the element appropriate to, but on this early summer evening missing from, the empty grate to which, whether it was glowing or dead, he had a habit of drawing himself.

The boy on his right was fair-haired, very straight, with the air of a sportsman. And Sole was what he appeared. He had won his cricket cap in his first term—a thing never known in the history of the school before. Called sometimes "Lemon" Sole because of his pale-yellow hair, he was the quickest creature in the field between cover and long slip

that Grange thought possible. The third boy was shortish and stout. George Lily—"Airy Fairy Lilian" in school terms—was declared to be the easiest-natured animal that ever walked on two legs. Yet in spite of his amiability there was obvious decision in the mouth and general aspect, as well as evidence of thought in the wide forehead, rather high for one of his age.

The relations between him and Hemingway were understood to be those of close, though for some reason, scarcely acknowledged friendship.

The talk was being carried on by Lily with Sole to interject remarks. From Hemingway not a word had fallen for ten minutes.

"I've never understood how Blackburn got his success. The little beggar was never any sport. And yet from all one hears he's been the biggest hit as captain of the school that there's been. I remember Davidson when he was captain—fine big chap he was—I was his fag for a bit. You'd have said he really was a skipper for a school. Old Berry prophesied he'd get a fellowship when he'd gone through Balliol. Dunno whether he did or not—and he got into the nineties twice against Crossford. And yet I shouldn't say he was the captain that Blackburn is. And what is Blackburn? He's an ugly little brute, and though he works hard and might have got some kind of a schol. I suppose, he's not brilliant. And he's no bat. They couldn't honestly play him for the school. And he plays for the second! I wonder if you'd find a parallel for that in any other school—the skipper of the whole place playing with the middle-aged skuts in the second eleven."

"That's *why* he's succeeded."

It was Hemingway who spoke, though his eyes looked into the fire grate.

IN A LIGHTER MOOD

Not Quite the Same

A professor of biology at a large university was notorious far and wide for one thing, an absent mind. One day he entered his class-room, and, after clearing his throat, said:

"Now, gentlemen, pay particular attention to what I say. I have, in this parcel, a very fine specimen of a dissected frog—very interesting."

Slowly he opened the wrappers, and disclosed to view were a few sandwiches and some fruit.

The professor seemed transfixed; then he said:

"But—good gracious— surely I ate my lunch!"

•   •   •

The Question

The moving-picture producer was giving his final instructions for the production of Part Nineteen of "The Adventures of Annie."

"Mr. Dareall," he addressed the curly-haired hero, "for realism purposes I have borrowed a live lion for this act. The animal will pursue you for five hundred feet."

Mr. Dareall interrupted him. "For five hundred feet?"

"Yes," replied the producer, "no more than that. Understand?"

The hero nodded dubiously. "Yes, I understand; but—does the lion?"

•   •   •

"I wonder?" said Sole.

"You well may!" cried Lily. "An old man playing with the middle-aged—he might as well play with the kids—get buckets and spades out."

The "middle-aged" at Grange, it should be explained, were merely the boys of the Middle school, to distinguish them from their seniors or "old men" on the one side and the "kids" on the other.

"Still," went on Lily, "I own he's made a success of his job—a howling success. There was a lot of bullying—the quiet sort which is the nastiest—when Davidson was here, and one used to hear a good deal of low talk. Little Blackburn somehow got rid of it. I don't know how—I think there's something funny about his eyes that chaps get frightened of—that is, the rotters do. I've felt it myself sometimes."

"Though you're but a simple, innocent Fairy," said Hemingway.

"Exactly, Major. Well, we've got to lose Blackburn, that's what we've got to remember."

"It's fixed, is it?" asked Sole.

"Sure thing. His father's crocked up and he's got to go right into the business. He's going at half term and then—well, there's no doubt who'll succeed."

This seemed to be a climax towards which the minds of the three were working, but a curious pause now succeeded. Three pairs of eyes seemed to seek the grate; and an onlooker might easily have said that there was a general evasion of the very point to which the talk was moving.

It was the quick-firing Lily who broke the silence.

"There's no doubt who gets the job."

"Yes?" said Sole, though perhaps less with curiosity than by way of encouragement to utter something he preferred not to say himself.

"It will of course be Sharp." It was Hemingway who now spoke.

"And equally, of course," added Lily quickly, "the school will go down."

Hemingway still looked gratewards. "Not necessarily," he said slowly.

"I don't know . . ." Lily was speaking more carefully now as if much less certain of his way. "But frankly I don't feel too sure myself, Major. I wish I did. But they won't give it to anybody else. Think what he is. Old Gorgon loves him—thinks he's no end of a chap."

"And he is, isn't he?" Sole, speaking now, was a little tentative.

"Is he?" inquired Lily.

"Well, what is he?" Sole continued. "He's senior classic. That's something, though not everything. But he's the finest bat we've ever had. Why, when Davidson saw him playing against Tunsby at Lords he practically promised him his blue if he came up to Cambridge before Davidson went down. The whole school knows it."

"We don't need to ask *how* the school knows," said Lily.

"Well, perhaps not. But the fact remains. Gorgon Graham wants him to take over from Blackburn and the school, as a whole, will think it a jolly good arrangement."

"Yes," said Hemingway, "except a few disgruntled beasts like poor old Lilian here, who never did like people who played games too well—they reminded him too much that he was a heavier-than-air machine himself didn't they, Fairy?"

He looked up affectionately at the only boy in the school regarded by this curious and independent character with any confessed liking.

"Still," said Sole, "I don't see that we're called on to do anything."

"Oh, we're not called on to do anything," said Hemingway. "We're not the three tailors of Tooley Street—we don't think we're the people of England."

"And I don't think we'd be entirely alone, Major," said Lily. "I doubt whether Ross or Gresford will be overjoyed. Of course they're not Gorgon. And Gorgon's a bit bat-eyed. Still, he deserves the credit for appointing Blackburn, though he did that more as a compromise than anything else. There was Dickinson top of the school, but whom the chaps wouldn't take seriously, and there was Simmons who said the job of being captain of the eleven was as much as any man ought to be expected to carry on. I've always had a notion that it was he who put up Blackburn's name to Gorgon, and he's certainly supported the old thing like a trump ever since. If he wasn't certain to leave at the end of the term—he may, they say, go earlier—he ought to be jolly well kicked into the job. But as he's going I really sympathise with old Graham to the extent that I'd say he's really got a beastly narrow choice."

"Well," said Hemingway, getting up and stretching himself, his eyes on certain beloved books on a black oak shelf in a corner, "what can't be cured must be endured."

"As the customer said to the grocer about the bacon," finished Lily.

"What a quick wit you have, Fairy," said Hemingway. "I do like to see a man profiting by his reading, and though I always found *Funny Chunks* a little advanced myself . . ."

"And what a superior person you are, Major. I often wonder whether you can see me at all. We must, in any case, look like ants from that pedestal of yours."

"Ants? Well, you do look rather like old women sometimes. But it's time I had some toast. Where's that batman of mine?"

Since the war Grange was beginning to prefer "batmen" to "fags," especially if one's elder brother had held a commission.

Hemingway went to the door, opened it, and called "Fork!"

There being no reply, after a very brief pause, he called out again.

This time a scrambling footstep could be heard from below, then came the answer "Coming!" and the master returned to his room. A minute later a loutish figure presented itself, its dull eyes regarding Hemingway with the devotion, if with less than the intelligence, of a dog.

"Stove and then—toast, Fork!" said Hemingway. The clumsy youth, who appeared to be about thirteen or fourteen, nodded and began opening the door first of one cupboard and then of another. Hemingway watched him impatiently for a moment and was about to call out a sharp word, when he checked himself in the way he was accustomed to do in the case of this maladroit fag of his.

"Fork," he said slowly, "try to remember: stove under table; bread—food—in right-hand cupboard; boots, clothes, in left-hand; bats and things of that kind in window cupboard. Got it?"

"Yes, Hemingway. Very sorry I forgot so quickly."

"That's all right. But buck up with the stove and the toast, and put the kettle on and—well, I think that's all."

The clumsy Falk, or "Fork" or "Toasting Fork," as he was called, having lighted the stove—when he

'Like hungry wolves the school fought for the dish set before it.'

had allowed one piece of bread to fall into it—at last, with his master's help, succeeded in providing four slices of bread sufficiently burnt to pass for toast. These, having been plentifully smeared with a mixture of butter and margarine, were laid out for the delectation of Hemingway's visitors, and then, the kettle being on, Falk stood balancing himself first on one foot and then on the other.

"Is that—is that all, Hemingway?"

"Yes, that's all," said Hemingway, not looking up.

The younger boy turned to withdraw, stumbled against a chair, recovered himself, and finally succeeded in conveying away his ungainly person.

"Poor old Toasting Fork," sighed Hemingway.

"I wonder why you keep the chap?" said Sole, looking a little ruefully at the toast which he was supposed to help consume.

Hemingway shrugged his shoulders. "One gets used to him."

"But you could have had the choice of a dozen good workers, regular lot of little gluttons for work."

"Oh well, I took him really through Blackburn; he and that silly little idiot Hopkinson were having a fearful life of it. It's always the way with these big clumsy fellows who've outgrown their strength. It doesn't look like bullying if a smaller, stronger boy, helped by some filthy little friend, gives the bigger chap a hiding. That, as you were saying, Fairy, was the kind of thing that was common when Davidson hadn't enough vision to see his hand before him. I believe he thought Fork and Hopkinson were bullies who were kept in their place. And in any case Bruce, who used to lead the pack, was his fag as well as being the kind of smart self-reliant fellow he liked. But when old Blackburn came to his job he went round seeing things for himself. He took Hopkinson for his new fag; his old one had got his remove—and, well, he asked me to take poor old Fork. He said he was going to stop the active kind of bullying, but that it was impossible to protect mugs completely and that I might go halves with him in his little enterprise. Well, I did, and I don't think there's been *very* much misery suffered by that pair of faithful asses since. As for Bruce, I don't know what Blackburn said to him, but that amiable youth was quite off his feed for a week or more."

"And now that he's got up into the Fifth," put in Lily. "I expect he's looking forward to the departure of Blackburn almost as much as—well, as another person is."

Hemingway made no answer.

The scratch meal to which Hemingway's guests had been invited being at last ended, and the toast, to Sole's satisfaction, being mostly eaten by his host, Lily looked at his watch. Then slowly he rose, stretched himself, and moved towards the door, Sole following him. At the door Lily turned.

"Well, cheerio, old bird," he said in his slow, idle way.

IN A LIGHTER MOOD

Good Links

The man in the rainbow stockings was trying to play golf. The difficulty was, of course, to hit the ball. It was so much easier to hit the ground. He hit that every time. The turf flew in all directions. Swish! Swosh! Plop! More excavations. Something was wrong somewhere. It couldn't be his stockings. It must be the links. He turned helplessly to his opponent.

"What do you think of these links?" he exclaimed.

"What do I think of 'em?" gasped his opponent, wiping a bit of soil from his lips. "Pouf. Best I ever tasted!"

* * *

Not Enough Flags

A certain admiral tells an amusing story of an explosive old seaman under whom he served many years ago.

During some tactical operations one of the ships of the squadron had made some bad blunders, and at last the admiral lost his temper. He stormed about the quarter-deck, and informed his hearers of his opinion of the officer in command of the erring ship.

When he paused at last for want of breath, he turned to the signaller and said, "And you can tell him that!"

The man scratched his head meditatively. "I beg your pardon, sir," he ventured, "but I don't think we have enough flags for your messages."

Hemingway nodded but did not look up. His eyes were studying the imaginary flames again.

Lily went out, closed the door in a way that seemed oddly silent after the clatter of his departure.

"What an odd bird he is," he said, and the tone, half admiring, half puzzled, was marked by the same curious hush as had been exhibited in his exit. Then suddenly he stopped. "Look here, Lemon," he said, "If only we could have seen him follow Blackburn!"

"Yes?" It was the way of both boys to encourage others to speak rather than to speak themselves. Sole would not answer now for a moment. But then he spoke.

"Yes," he said, "you're right."

Lily smiled. And then he did a thing Sole had never known this amiable untalkative boy do before, he thrust his arm inside the other's. The pair moved off down the corridor.

* * *

While speaking they had gone by a half-open door, but they did not notice the figure that withdrew into shadow and that did not emerge until they had begun to descend the stairs.

The boy who now came into the passage watched their disappearing heads for a moment.

"Sharp might very well like to hear how some people try to queer his pitch for him before even he's got started."

His was a shortish figure but extraordinarily muscular. The face too, was curiously lined for a person of this boy's age, which was about seventeen. The feature that one noticed most, however, was his eye. It was dark, quick in movement, very passionate. But the instinct to turn away from it that some people had when they met the glance of George Bruce was due to the odd remote, but distinguishable quality of cruelty—cruelty for its own sake, which harboured there. One wondered what, in years to come, this dark, relentless face would signify for those on whom it turned.

The Astronomer Royal of Mars (as a game of football shows up):—"I am bound to confess that there are times when I almost wish that I'd been born an inhabitant of that inferior planet, the Earth!"

PROOF POSITIVE

AN old-time blue jacket was at the mast before Captain Evans of the U.S.A. battleship, "Indiana," charged with getting food out of a mess chest outside of meal hours. This getting food for night watches was a common and strong desire on the part of most men aboard ship.

Captain Evans asked the man what he had to say, and the man, sizing up the delicate situation, said:

"Captain, I didn't take no food outer that chest. Why, captain, there weren't no food in that chest! I looked in that chest, and, captain, I met a cockroach coming outer that chest with tears in his eyes."

A LOW DIET.

THE hospital was well known for not giving its patients sufficient to eat. Meal-times came and went, and convalescent Tommy found himself just as hungry as ever. One day the commanding officer was visiting the wards. He came up to the bedside of a patient and asked him what was his complaint.

Now, this man was particularly "fed-up," so his reply was very curt.

"Trench fever."

"What's the diet?" asked the commanding officer in solicitous tones.

The man had been aching for this opportunity. Now he could get a little of his own back, so he replied:

"Two sucks of the thermometer daily!"

ANSWERED.

THE young cyclist was fighting hard against a strong head wind and wondering what unhappy thought had prompted him to venture so far from the school. It was growing darker every minute, and to crown his misery rain began to fall.

Soon the rain came down in the best style, and the poor fellow got wet to the skin. Then a piece of glass laid his tyre open. With a moan he flung himself from the saddle and commenced to repair the damage.

Presently there approached from the opposite direction a benevolent old gentleman. Gazing at the upturned bicycle, the perspiring youth, and the repairing outfit which he had dropped in the mud, the old gentleman inquired:

"Had a puncture, my friend?"

The boy looked up and swallowed his feelings with a huge gulp.

"No, sir," he replied, with a magnificent effort at sarcasm. "I'm just changing the air in the tyres. The other lot's worn out, you know."

HAD TO LAST OUT.

A VERY good story is being told about a certain two-days' cricket match organised by a local club. Great preparations were made, and the services of a local man were requisitioned as umpire.

Everything went very well, but unfortunately the game seemed likely to finish on the first day, as by luncheon-time each team had concluded an innings. On resuming play, one of the bowlers made several unsuccessful appeals for "leg before."

"How's that, then?" asked the bowler triumphantly as a swift ball scattered the stumps far and wide.

"No ball!" roared the umpire. "And look here, it ain't no use you bothering! This 'ere match has got to last out two days. I own that refreshment tent over there!"

Below A 1922 advertisement for two very popular B.O.P. writers; and a Stanley L. Wood illustration to a story about Mexico.

Author of "The Wizard King," "The Lost City,"
"In the Power of the Pygmies," etc., etc.

Being the Story of the Discovery of the "*Big Fish*," or the Quest of the Greater Treasure of the Incas of Peru.

(*Illustrated by R. Caton Woodville.*)

CHAPTER XXI.

I am made a ghost, and then a fool.

 SPRANG at him with my sword, the rusty blade that I had stolen from those grim and whitened bones.

The man was at my mercy. He was unarmed, having laid aside his rifle before he approached the Tomb. He trembled in every limb as he fled before my onslaught and cried out aloud for pity as I jabbed at him in a kind of vicious frenzy.

In the twilight his face looked pale-green in colouring, and his little pig-like eyes seemed in danger of springing from his head. It would be difficult to conceive an expression upon which abject terror was more strongly marked.

Amos Baverstock was an evil man in many ways, and a brave man in others; else, he had never risked his life so often amid the dangers of the tropic wilderness. Courage of a sort he had in plenty, but, because he was evil in his nature, he feared death and all connected with the grave, though I had never thought to find him as superstitious as he was.

He had always struck me as a hard, calculating man, who looked upon the practical side of all things. And yet without a doubt he now took me for a ghost.

And after all—when the full facts are considered—his mistake was excusable; even to-day, when I call to mind that scene that was enacted in the half-light of the woods, I am inclined to laugh at it all, for there was something ludicrous about it. I wore the helmet of the dead man, and had sprung at Amos out of the Tomb, without giving him time to think. Assuredly, in his eyes, what else could I have been but an infuriated ghost, dangerous and active because my solitude had been disturbed.

I thrust at him savagely in the darkness, whilst he hurried here and there, in and out among the trees, yelling like a fiend. How hideous he was! I can see him now, with his hunchback, his green face, his staring eyes, his mouth contorted in terror. For all that, he was quick and agile, and once or twice eluded a sword-thrust that would have pierced him to the heart.

And then, at last, I had him. I carried my sword in my right hand, and, as I lunged, he jumped

'"No ghost," said he. "No ghost." And he went on repeating the words as if he were a parrot.'

aside, towards the left. As quick as thought I caught him by the throat. Whereat he fell down before me on his knees and clasped his hands in the attitude of one who pleads for mercy.

He was in my power. I said not a word, but clenched my teeth, and looked into those eyes that even then I feared. I drew back my sword, and then paused a moment; for I had no liking for the work, which was the hangman's job.

"Mercy!" he groaned again.

I took in a deep breath, like a man about to dive. I felt that I must brace myself for this red task of common justice. I looked at his body, clothed in tatters, to select a spot most vulnerable where I might plunge my sword.

"Amos Baverstock," said I, "you die."

"You know my name!" he stammered.

"You die, here and now. And may the good God forgive you for your sins."

And as the words left my lips, I was felled by someone who had crept upon me from behind. I was felled like an ox. A single blow upon the back of the head sent me over like a ninepin, and I lay stretched upon the ground, but half-conscious, with a singing sensation in my head.

Presently, I sat up, and looked about me. There was Amos, still upon his knees, as green as ever. And immediately above me stood one whom I did well to recognise as Mr. Gilbert Forsyth.

That place was dimly illuminated by the white light of the newly-risen moon, turning the leaves upon the trees above us to a glistening silver.

Forsyth was wearing the remnants of a pair of trousers the legs of which ended in a tattered fringe a little below his knees. He was naked to the waist, around which was a belt, crammed with knives and pistols.

I remembered his curled whiskers and his pomaded moustache on the morning when I had first set eyes upon him, when I lay hidden in the gorse-bush. His fair hair now had grown so long that it reached to his shoulders; and his whiskers had spread into a short, shaggy beard, which was divided somewhat in the middle like that of a Frenchman or a Sikh. I had thought of him always as a very immaculate gentleman; but here was a desperate, piratical blade who, one might easily believe, chewed glass and compelled his unhappy victims to walk the plank.

He looked at me, and folded his arms; and then spoke in a voice quite calm.

"And who the blazes are you?" he asked.

I was wise enough not to answer. Ghosts—so far as I knew—could never speak. And was I not a ghost?

If I had been a fool to go down into the Tomb, I showed at least a little wisdom in now holding my tongue. For this, however, I take no credit. I could not foresee the course that events would take. I had been surprised and mastered, and cursed myself because I had not killed Amos out of hand, when the man was in my power. Disappointed, disgusted with myself, I was stubborn as a mule. They might do what they would, they might torture me, but still I would not speak.

Forsyth repeated his question; and for answer I rushed again at Amos, and even then would have killed him had not the other caught me in his arms and held me fast.

The man was stronger than I thought; for, though I kicked and struggled, I could not free myself. Amos, as he watched us, regained a little of his commonsense, and got slowly upon his feet.

"No ghost," said he. "No ghost." And he went on repeating the words as if he were a parrot.

"Ghost!" laughed Forsyth. "If this is a ghost, he is a warm-blooded one, and as vicious as they make 'em."

"Then, who is he?" asked Baverstock. "I swear to you, he came out of the Tomb, as I'm a living man."

"And he's another," added Forsyth. "Who he is, or what business he has in such a place as this, I can no more say than you can. None the less, the circumstantial evidence is all against mortality. I am reminded, my friend, of the Carthaginian Queen: 'Exoriare aliquis nostris ex ossibus ultor'—(May some avenger arise from my bones). I call this individual 'Hannibal,' on that account."

"Who wants your Latin gibberish!" cried Amos. "Look plain facts in the face; call a spade a spade."

"Also," said Forsyth, in his usual sing-song voice, "call a man a man, and not a ghost."

"If he's alive," said Amos, coming even nearer, "then, who is he? I tell you, when I lifted the tombstone, he sprang forth like a Jack-in-the-box,

and, had it not been for you, I would never have escaped with life."

"I have told you already," said the other, "I know no more of him than you do." . . .

The opening chapter of Geo E. Rochester's 'The Flying Beetle' (October 1926). This was the first of four excellent serials by this author.

THE FLYING BEETLE
BY GEO · E · ROCHESTER

(Illustrated by H. L. Shindler.)

CHAPTER I.

"GENTLEMEN!"

The five men thus addressed turned from their low-toned, desultory conversation to watch in silence as a tall man who occupied the chair at the head of the table rose slowly to his feet.

He wore a black silk mask, as did the five who remained seated. The hush that followed his quietly spoken word was broken only by the faint rustle of the trees outside the heavily curtained windows.

"Gentlemen," he continued, in a soft, quiet voice, "this is our first meeting. I have chosen this isolated house near Wallington so as to be reasonably safe from prying eyes and over-curious ears. Each one of you knows the events which have culminated in his being here to-night, and before you leave this room I trust that I shall be the means of putting you all on the high road to wealth and fortune. But——"

He paused and wiped his lips with a small spotlessly white handkerchief.

"But what?" growled one of the men.

"But the work will not be easy and death will be ever at your elbow," replied the other. His gaze swept the masked faces turned towards him and he continued harshly:

"You do not know me, and you do not know each other. But during the years that have passed since this cursed England emerged triumphant from the World War, you have been watched by those on whose behalf I am here to night. I do not think that we have chosen amiss in selecting you for the work there is to be done. You hate this England, *yes?*"

The last word came on a high note of interrogation. The five others mumbled an assent and for a moment the lips of the speaker twisted into a faint smile.

"Before I say anything further," he went on, "I want any one of you who has the slightest doubts as to his courage in the face of danger or death to stand up and say so. He will be allowed to depart now. I warn you, gentlemen, that the risks which you will be called upon to take will be great. Furthermore, your duties will take you to the farthest corners of the earth and to the ends of the seven seas. A powerful nation is seeking your aid, but I want it to be clearly understood that she cannot raise a finger to help you in any danger you may encounter!"

"Why?" demanded one of the five sharply.

"Because," snapped the other, "by so doing she must of necessity show her hand, and the time is not yet ripe for her to declare an antagonistic attitude towards Britain and her Empire. No," he went on steadily, "any hurt you do to England will be regarded by us with horror, but you will be cogs, and important cogs, in the great machine which we are steadily building, and which, when complete, will crush this England to the dust. But, you understand, we cannot associate ourselves with you in any manner whatsoever if you happen to run foul of the British authorities when carrying out our orders."

He was silent for a moment, then said sharply:

"Will any one of you who feels he is not prepared to go on, please stand up."

The five men stirred uneasily.

"Can't you tell us more before we decide?" asked one, suddenly.

"I cannot."

Again silence settled on the room. The rustling of the trees outside became more pronounced. The man at the head of the table waited motionless.

"Then I am to understand," he said, after a long minute had passed, "that you are all prepared to accept service with us?"

A man nodded and the other four followed suit.

"Good! I will not tell you all that I may, but remember, when once your ears have heard that which I am about to say, you stand committed to us and our cause for all time. There is only one way in which you may draw back. That way is death!"

A man coughed nervously and demanded, hoarsely:

"What about payment for our services?"

"You will all receive generous expenses, very generous expenses, and when the work is completed you will each receive the sum of fifty thousand pounds—provided that you are still alive. Are those terms satisfactory?"

"Yes!" grunted one of the five men and the others also signified their approval.

"Very well, we will now get to business," said the man at the head of the table, briskly. "Two days ago you all received the following letter."

He unfolded a thin sheet of paper which lay on the table in front of him and read:

"DEAR SIR,—If you care to undertake work of a somewhat hazardous and dangerous nature—but amply recompensed by excellent pay—then it will be to your advantage to be present at 'The Larches,' near Wallington, at seven o'clock in the evening of the eighth inst.!"

He paused and the watching men saw his thin lips curl into a mirthless smile.

"In order to prevent you from communicating the contents of that letter to any other person," he went on, "and also to make more certain of your attendance here this evening, I think you will remember that enclosed in each envelope was a brief *résumé* of the past of the person to whom it was addressed. Further to that there was also a short note informing you that failure to attend would mean the forwarding of a copy of that *résumé* to the police. How far that fact has influenced you in deciding to throw in your lot with us I neither know nor care. However, as long as you keep faith with us your secrets are safe. I give you my word on that. But every one of you is wanted by the police and we know it!"

From behind their masks the five glowered at him sullenly, and, throwing back his head, the speaker laughed and spread out his hands with a gesture.

"But what would you," he said, "we all kick over the traces now and again. Well, we can find a better and more profitable field for your activities. But let us get on."

From the pocket of his dinner-jacket he produced a small silk Union Jack.

"I have here a piece of highly coloured rag," he said with a snarl. "Strange as it may seem, to some people this rag is sacred—a thing to honour and even to die for. But to me, and to those behind me, it is the emblem of all that is hateful. You boast, you English, that you have an Empire on which the sun never sets. But the day will come when that Empire will be rent asunder. The day will come when her Colonies will have broken away." The speaker's voice became vibrant with suppressed passion and his lips twisted evilly. "And that day is fast approaching. Bowed, broken and beaten, her glories gone for ever, then this filthy rag will be a thing for the nations of the world to mock at and to jeer!"

With the words he savagely tore the Union Jack across and again across and threw the pieces to the floor.

"My friends," he resumed more quietly, "you and I will work together to bring that great day about: the day when the British flag comes fluttering down from the last seat of power. Then will come your reward from my own grateful country, and you will rest content in the knowledge of work well done. But between now and then there is much that is dangerous to be done. There is only one man from whom you will take your orders. That is myself, and you will address me as Chief."

He turned to the masked man sitting on his right:

"You know the East well? You have spent a great part of your life there?"

"Yes."

"You will be Number One, and as such you will be addressed. We have work ready for you in the East!"

He turned to another.

"You know the great shipyards of England and Scotland well?"

"I do."

"You will be Number Two," replied the Chief.

He went round the table with his questions, and each man was allotted a number.

"And now, gentlemen," he said, when the ceremony was finished, "you will each receive your orders secretly. From now onwards you are in our pay and you will hold yourselves in readiness to depart for any corner of the world at a moment's notice. Ask no questions and keep your mouths shut. We shall always be in touch with you, no matter where you are!"

He broke off and inclined his head in a listening attitude. In the silence the distant drone of an aeroplane engine was plainly heard. It grew louder every moment till with a deafening roar it swept over the house.

"He's very low!" muttered one of the men, and another mumbled an assent.

"Attention, gentlemen, please!" snapped the Chief. "I wish to impress on you for the last time the absolute necessity of secrecy. Let any one of you think to betray us and he will die suddenly and—painfully. You will find betrayal exceptionally difficult, as no man will have any knowledge except that of his own allotted task. Do your work according to your instructions and *ask no questions*. And now I am going to ask you to drink a toast with me."

He pressed a bell concealed under the table near his hand, and a few moments later a foreign-looking manservant shuffled into the room. He was a big swarthy fellow, clad in an ill-fitting lounge suit.

"You rang, master?" he said gutturally.

"Yes, Carl. Bring glasses and wine!"

Carl withdrew, to return in a few minutes with a well-laden tray. When each man had been served with a glass of wine, the Chief dismissed the man and rose to his feet.

"Gentlemen," he said, "the toast I give you is this: Success to our venture, and may the day soon come when the might of England is but a memory, when her flag is torn and——"

"Interesting!" cut in a cold, calm voice from the door-way. "How extremely interesting!"

The six men wheeled round, then stood as though frozen.

For, standing with his back to the closed door of the room, was a slim boyish figure clad from head to heels in black. His face was covered with a black flying helmet and face mask. His body was encased in a tight-fitting black flying suit and tight black

flying boots came to his knees. But what riveted the attention of the six conspirators was the short, deadly-looking revolver that flickered first at this one, then at that.

The Chief was the first to recover himself. His fingers groped under the table for the bell-push and his lips moved inaudibly in a language that was not English.

"You!" snapped the stranger. "Put your hands up!" The Chief hesitated.

"I'll give you three seconds!"

The stranger's voice was icy, and with an oath the Chief raised his hands slowly above his head.

"All of you," went on the cold voice, "turn your backs to the table and put your hands up!"

They obeyed and glared in angry silence at the black-clad figure.

The latter laughed slowly, mirthlessly.

"Really," he said, a hint of mockery in his voice, "for six pledged and desperate conspirators, you are ridiculously easy to handle. A line of Kipling occurs to me, about the curs that yelped at the English flag. He doubtless had in mind you and your kind!"

Then in a tone tense with the deadly menace it held he continued:

"But you are serious and, like rats that gnaw in the darkness, lacking the courage to come out into the open, you can do a lot of damage. Well, I am serious, too, and I tell you, each and every one of you, that this venture on which you have embarked to-night will have one end for you, and that is—*death!* One by one you will die. These are no idle words of mine. England may have her enemies, but she has also her sons. They did not all die on the battlefields of Flanders!"

The Chief's lips parted in a shrill cackle of laughter, but it died on his lips as the stranger took a short step towards him.

One of the five shuddered visibly, whilst the others glowered in sullen and helpless rage.

"Come here!" snapped the stranger, and with a slight inclination of the head he indicated the man nearest to him.

The man hesitated, and the other snapped:

"I shall not ask you again!"

With his hands above his head the man walked unsteadily till he was within a yard of the black-clad, motionless figure. Then, without warning, the latter stepped quickly forward and wrenched off the silk mask that covered the other's face.

Earnestly, intently, he studied the pale, strained features for a long moment, then barked:

"Your number?"

"Number Five?"

"Very good, Number Five. Return to your place!"

Number Five backed to the table, and the stranger treated the other four men in a similar manner. He scrutinised each face before sending its owner back to the table.

"'Really,' he said. . . . . 'for six pledged and desperate conspirators, you are ridiculously easy to handle'."

It was the Chief's turn now, and a look of interest crept into the eyes of the five men.

"Now you!" snapped the stranger.

"And what if I refuse?"

"You will not refuse!"

"You seem remarkably well informed!"

The words were courageous enough, but, try as he would, the Chief could not hide the quiver in his voice.

The stranger laughed coldly.

"One may be forgiven," he replied, "for presuming that you have some claim to being an intelligent man. An intelligent man knows when he is at the wrong end of a gun!"

"You would not shoot!"

"I shall give you just five seconds to cross the floor to me. If you refuse, I shall shoot, and shoot to kill!"

And, be it said, every man in the room knew that it would be so.

For the fractional part of a second the Chief hesitated, then slowly he left the table, and slowly he advanced towards the figure by the door.

"I believe you're bluffing," he snarled; "you'd never get out of here alive if you did shoot!"

"Obviously neither would you!" was the response.

Three yards of carpet only separated the two men. The five at the table watched with bated breath. Then the Chief stopped. Quietly, conversationally, he said:

Illustration by T. M. R. Whitwell in 1923 in 'A Sixth Form Feud' by Harold Avery.

"No, Carl, don't brain him. I want him alive."

It was excellently done, and for a brief instant the revolver in the stranger's hand flickered away as he half turned his head to glance over his shoulder.

With a roar of triumph the Chief was upon him. The other five sprang to the assistance of their leader. In a heaving, struggling mass they surged around the door. The black-clad stranger struggled frantically, but the odds were too great, and he was borne down and overpowered. At the same moment the door burst open and Carl and another man dashed into the room.

They grasped the stranger and held him securely, whilst the others dusted themselves and removed traces of the struggle as best they could.

Stooping, the Chief picked up the revolver, which had slid along the floor during the struggle, and with it in his hand, he resumed his seat at the table, motioning his companions to do likewise.

"So, my friend," he laughed, "my bluff worked. I must confess to a feeling of surprise that so clever a fellow as yourself was taken in by so simple a trick!"

"I must confess to some surprise myself," replied the stranger coolly. "I must also congratulate you on the high standard of your acting. It was well done. I have, if anything, underrated your courage and intelligence. I did not conceive that you had the wit to bluff when so close to death."

The Chief stared at him in silence.

"You talk glibly of death," he sneered after a moment, "but to you it will be stark reality before morning. I will deal with you later."

Again he paused and stared at the stranger curiously.

"I know you, of that I am certain, but I will reserve the pleasure of tearing that mask from your face till later in the evening. Carl, take him and lock him up in the room that I am occupying to-night. Tie him up well and remain on guard. If he escapes, you know the penalty I shall mete out to you!"

It was evident by the terror that leapt for a moment to Carl's eyes that he did.

"He—he shall not escape, master!" he whined.

"I trust not, Carl, for your sake," purred the Chief.

"Wait a minute," broke in the man known as Number One, "let's have his mask off now. He's threatened the lot of us and it's only fair that we should see just who he is."

A murmur of assent rose from his companions. The effect on the Chief was remarkable. Leaping to his feet and, crashing his fist on the bar mahogany of the table top, he screamed:

"Dogs that you are, would you thus early in our service dare question an order of mine. You soon forget that all that is required of you is obedience and nothing more. What is it to you what I do with my prisoner? What is it to you? *Answer my question?*"

But they shrank from the torrent of wrath in silence, and turning to the two servants, he snarled:

"*Go!*"

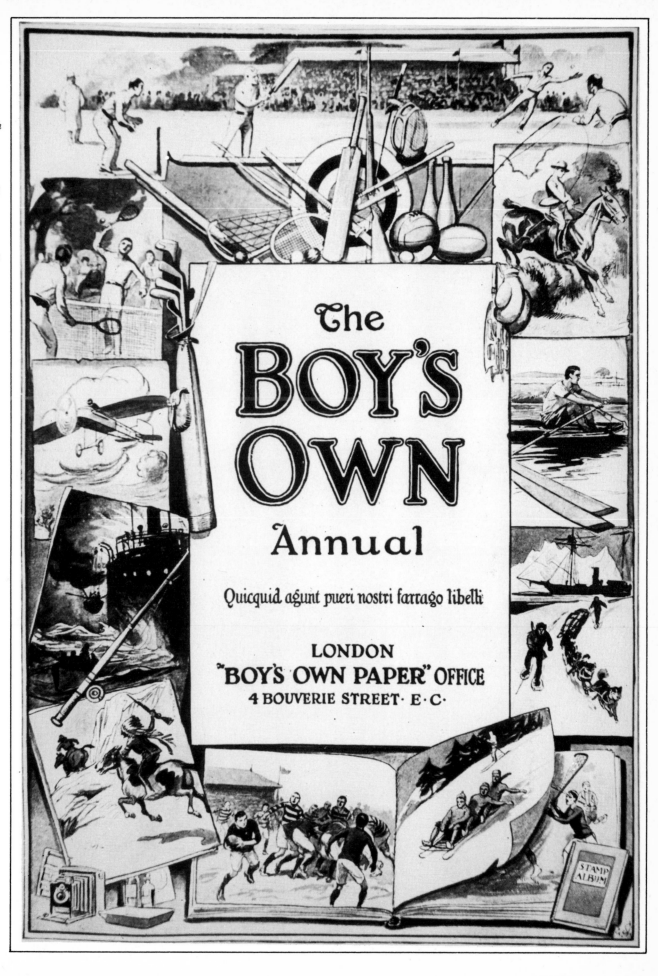

The
BOY'S
OWN
Annual

Quicquid agunt pueri nostri farrago libelli

LONDON
"BOY'S OWN PAPER" OFFICE
4 BOUVERIE STREET · E·C·

WRESTED from the DEEP by Percy F. Westerman

CHAPTER I

The Case of the S.S. "Euralia"

A Percy F. Westerman serial, November 1935.

"WELL?" enquired Mr. Findon, senior partner of the marine salvage company of Messrs. Findon & Rayse, Ltd. "What d'ye make of it, Bob? Bit of a hard nut to crack, eh?"

Robert Wroxall, chief engineer of the company although still in his twenties, did not hesitate in his reply.

"I think we ought to tackle it," he declared. "We've been successful with wrecks in greater depths."

"We have, my boy," agreed the self-made, hard-headed Mr. Findon. "But it's not the depth that's going to worry us; it's the artificial conditions."

"Artificial conditions, sir?"

"That's what I said and what I mean, Bob. Let me explain. That chart you're looking at doesn't. Furioso Harbour is, I think, unique. It is the only large harbour in South America that is divided by an imaginary line. East of that line is Socilian territory, although it sounds funny to describe water as territory. The part west of it belongs to Condalia. Although these two republics haven't had a proper dog-fight during the last twenty years, their relations cannot be exactly described as cordial. Almost on the boundary, but in Condalian waters, lies the wreck of the *Euralia del Sol* in fifteen fathoms."

"And in a little over her own length to the east-'ard is a hole shown on the chart as having a depth of seventy-five fathoms," observed Wroxall. "If she'd sunk there, that would have been the end of her."

"It would," agreed Mr. Rayse grimly. "And, if report speaks truly, that's where the Socilian Government wanted her to sink!"

"What's that, sir?"

"Thought that would make you sit up and take notice, Bob. The *Euralia*, as you know, was a Condalian-owned liner of a gross tonnage of 18,000. Her length is 580 feet."

Wroxall nodded. He knew these particulars and the circumstances under which the *Euralia* was supposed to have been lost.

It was in June of last year. She was proceeding from San Tomé, the principal seaport of Condalia, to Marco Paz, the capital of Socilia. Both ports are in the harbour of Furioso, and about thirty miles apart, or about an hour's run. She carried a consignment of half a million in gold for New York and had about ninety first-class and two hundred steerage passengers on board, mostly Condalian subjects. She was embarking more passengers and bullion at Marco Paz before proceeding to sea. But she never made that thirty miles' run, let alone the voyage to New York. According to official reports, there was a terrific explosion in her starboard engine-room. She took a heavy list and sank in twenty minutes. All the passengers and most of the crew were saved, the loss of life being heavy amongst the engine-room staff. In fact, there were no survivors from either the starboard engine-room or stokehold to give any information as to what had occurred below.

So much Wroxall knew, but his chief was about to throw startling light upon the matter.

"The Condalian authorities, although they have publicly expressed their views, are of opinion that the sinking was caused by an internal explosion brought about by a delayed-action infernal machine, and hint that the outrage was either planned or encouraged by the Socilian Government," explained Mr. Rayse. "Naturally the Socilians would deny such a charge; but the funny thing about it is that the Condalians want the wreck to be salved and the Socilians are putting every obstacle in the way. They don't want her to be brought to the surface."

"For what reasons?" asked Wroxall.

"For several. The loss of the ship together with half a million in gold, which was insured by Condalian underwriters is a severe loss, not only to the owners, but to the country, and a corresponding gain as far as Socilian interests are concerned. The only liner that can use Furioso Harbour—they bar those under the Stars and Stripes and European flags—is Socilian owned, so she now has the monopoly. But the chief reason, I take it, is Socilia's reluctance for direct evidence of the sinking to be found; that is, if she were guilty of an outrage in the form of a bomb hidden in the ship."

"If that's the case, salvage operations are likely to be more exciting than usual," observed Wroxall.

"I hear that German, Dutch, Italian and American salvage firms have been invited to tender," continued Mr. Rayse. "It'll mean a cut price and probably not more than ten per cent profit if the operations are successful. If they aren't, then the firm concerned is out to lose a big sum. However," he added briskly, "I'll be glad of your opinion, Bob, after you've run through these papers. We've three weeks before the tender is to be handed in to the Condalian Embassy in London."

Bob Wroxall worked all the afternoon on the documents, making notes, calculating pressures, volumes and weights of various substances in water and in air. Then, upon returning to the rooms which he occupied during his short and infrequent visits to London—salvage operations all over the world kept him out of England for eleven months of every twelve—he resumed his study of the problem until past midnight.

Amongst other papers, that containing the report of an Argentine diver—called in as an independent authority—was interesting. He described the *Euralia del Sol* as lying on her starboard side with her bows in six fathoms less water than her stern, which was within fifty metres of the "deep" which on the chart was called the Devil's Cauldron. There was an enormous rock close to her keel-plates that would prove an almost insurmountable obstacle to righting her. The obstruction could, of course, be removed by blasting, but it would be a long and expensive business, in the course of which the explosions might seriously damage the already badly injured hull. Another serious factor was a strong submarine current that set constantly in an easterly direction. If the wreck were to be filled with compressed air and raised that way, there was always the possibility of it being moved over the Devil's Cauldron during the operation. Then, should any of the airtight compartments "blow" and the hull lose buoyancy in consequence, the wreck would fall into the seventy-fathom hole and be lost beyond hope of salvage.

Another document, that of the report of the captain of the ill-fated vessel, threw a certain amount of light upon the situation. As soon as the explosion occurred and the ship began to take a heavy list, he ordered the wheel to be put hard to port. Aided by the port engine, which, unlike the starboard one, was still going ahead, the *Euralia del Sol* made a sixteen-point turn and was heading in the reverse direction to that before the explosion when she sank, although she had lost way for the boats to be lowered.

But for this action on the part of her captain the vessel would have sunk in the Devil's Cauldron instead of in the fifteen-fathom patch adjoining.

"I wonder why he did that?" thought Wroxall. "Was it to avoid sinking in seventy-five fathoms or to let her recross the imaginary boundary and settle in Condalian waters?"

Next morning Wroxall was in consultation with his chief.

"I've made a covering estimate," he announced. "Every item has been cut down to a bare minimum, to allow a profit of ten per cent if the job is successful."

"If the job is successful," echoed Mr. Findon.

"It should be—it must be," declared Wroxall confidently. "They want the hull raised. They say nothing about the ship being brought to the surface in such a state that she can be reconditioned. It's evidence of the cause of the disaster *and* the gold that they want."

The two men went into figures and other details. They brought in the other partner, Mr. Rayse, who, being of a cautious nature and prone to tackle only jobs that might reasonably be considered certainties, was inclined to let the *Euralia del Sol* severely alone.

"But, dash it all, Rayse!" exclaimed Mr. Findon. "If we don't tender, you bet your bottom dollar the foreigners will."

"Then let 'em," rejoined his partner. "They'll lose money on it and probably chuck their hands in."

"Do you think we would abandon the job once we started?" asked Mr. Findon. "Look here, I'm with Wroxall on this business. He says he can pull it off. He's prepared estimates. I've been through them, and, of course, you can examine them. It's not a question of beating foreign competitors over the work, but undercutting 'em on the contract. We can afford that as things are at present."

As a matter of fact, there was a mild slump in marine salvage work. The large stock of tools and plant owned by Findon & Rayse was almost idle. Expert divers and mechanics had to be kept on against an emergency job. There seemed no reason why some of them should not be employed to solve the problem that was a source of irritation between the republics of Condalia and Socilia.

That night the tender was signed, sealed and delivered.

A month passed. The Condalian Embassy in London had dealt with the tender and had cabled its contents to San Tomé. Dutch, German and Italian tenders were put through similar channels. No United States firm tendered, possibly because the American plan of reconstruction had given them all the work they wanted.

Meanwhile Wroxall had gone to supervise a small

Right-hand column *'I saw that dreadful assegai pass clean through the Arab's body, as if he had been but a man of slender straw'—from 'In the Land of Shame' by Major Charles Gilson.*

salvage job at Lowestoft. He was recalled to London by telephone.

"We've got it, Bob!" announced Mr. Findon gleefully. "And against eleven foreign firms, too. Ours wasn't the lowest tender, so I've been informed."

"Then why did we get the contract, sir?"

"Because, acting upon your suggestion, young man, we gave an all-in quotation. Our rivals put in a price for compensation in case of failure. We didn't. It's all or nothing as far as we are concerned—and we're going to pull it off!"

"I'm glad," said Bob Wroxall sincerely.

"You'll direct operations?"

"Of course."

"By the by," broke in Mr. Rayse, "you carry a life insurance, I hope?"

"Yes," replied Wroxall. "Have done so for several years."

"Then," continued the junior partner, "you might examine your policy and see if you're covered against civil war, civil commotion and acts of the king's enemies. I think I ought to warn you."

"Is it as bad as that?" asked Wroxall cheerfully. "Nothing like a little excitement to liven up the trivial round, the common task of salvage-work!"

A firm line from the editor about jokes in bad taste, even in wartime (October 1941).

The Editor will be glad to receive jokes and humorous stories from his readers for this page. When these are not original, the source from which they are taken must be stated for the Editor's information. Small prizes will be given by way of acknowledgment, for any that are accepted and used. No contributions of this sort can be returned, nor can any correspondence be entered into in connexion with them. Jokes on sacred subjects, or intoxication, or involving the use of bad language, are not wanted and will not be accepted.

All Clear.

After he had told the old lady a number of hints for use during the raids, the warden asked her if everything was quite clear. "Oh yes, sir," she replied. "But it'll be a bit sticky using a syrup pump!"

(*John Taylor, Sutherland.*)

Penny Wise.

"Why are you crying?" asked the old gentleman of the small boy.

"I've lost my penny," was the tearful reply.

"Well, cheer up, and here's another," said the gentleman. But upon this the boy began yelling louder than ever.

"What's the matter now?" asked the puzzled donor.

"If I hadn't lost my penny, I'd have twopence now," wailed the boy.

(*A. Cornwall, London.*)

No Black-out.

A party of soldiers were being troubled with mosquitoes while fighting in a swampy district of Central Africa. One night a few fireflies appeared on the scene.

"It's no use fighting them," said Private Johnstone. "The wretches are looking for us with lanterns."

(*W. H. Drake, Nailsworth.*)

Both Hogs.

A yokel in a country lane was knocked into the hedge by a high-speeding car that passed. He got out slowly and turned to the driver who had turned back. "Roadhog!" he said bitterly.

The driver thought this over for a bit. Then, "Hedgehog," he replied.

(*John Hindle, Bradford.*)

GRIM and GAY

The Story of a School that stayed put

Gunby Hadath.

CHAPTER I

What Feversham Felt

Right *The B.O.P. in October 1941 was thinner, but holding on: a Gunby Hadath story with a war setting.*

ONE of the August bombs had gone crashing through the roof of the Old Library, which, replaced just before the war started by the more spacious new one at the corner between Terry's House and the Armoury, had already been earmarked for demolition. Accordingly it was decent of Hitler, the School said, as soon as it returned for the September term, to save them the cost and trouble of breaking it up.

To be exact, this irreverent comment was passed by the early birds who hurried back on the first of the three coming-back days. And when these early birds discovered as well a crater or two in the middle of the cricket ground, they said, "sold again, Adolph! You ought to have gone for the rugger ground. For in England, you twerp, we don't play cricket in winter!"

But Warburton of Terry's House, the Captain of the School, looked grave when discussing it with some of his cronies that evening. There was Dollinger there, "old Dolly", the skipper of rugger, and Broomfield, a man of few words; and Cruden who looked half asleep but rarely missed much; and Feversham with his sandy hair and pale face.

When they had squeezed themselves into his study, Warburton began by reminding them that that which had happened once can happen again. He stopped for a long moment there, with so much significance that they taxed him with having some bad news up his sleeve. "So out with it!" uttered

Dollinger, scowling at Cruden, who kept imploring him to give him more room. For when old Dolly shared a chair with a man, the latter's half made anything but good arithmetic.

"Confound you, Dolly," spluttered Cruden, like a fish gasping. "Do keep your abominable shoulders out of my mouth."

Old Dolly yielded an inch. "That better?" he grunted. "Sorry, Warburton, old boy, if I dried up your eloquence. You were saying that what happens once might happen again. That's your opinion, is it?"

"Mine!" scoffed Warburton. "My opinion doesn't matter a hoot. It's the opinion of the Board of Governors that matters."

"Oh!" ejaculated Feversham. "Then you know something!"

Warburton leaned forward. "Yes, I know something. I'm going to tell you what the Head has confided to me with permission to pass it on to you if I like. But it isn't to be generally mentioned, I warn you." He rose and stationed himself in front of the mantelpiece, and Cruden seized in a flash on the chance of a chair to himself.

Then standing there, thus facing them, hands in his pockets, and his grey eyes travelling from one to the other in turn, Warburton said, "Well, I take it you give me your words that what I'm going to tell you won't travel further?" He paused for their assent. "That being so," he resumed, "the Head has informed me that the Governors will be holding a meeting any day now to decide whether or not the School had better stay put!"

It was Dollinger who managed to find his voice first. "Had better what?" he cried, glaring. "Had better what?"

"Had better," repeated Warburton, quietly, "stay put."

"And why ever not?" shouted Dollinger.

"Because of the air raids."

"Because of the air raids! By gosh! And what's the alternative?"

"To evacuate," drawled Broomfield.

"And where in blue blazes should we evacuate to?"

"All right! Keep your hair on," they bade Dolly. "What's the idea, Warbler?"

Warburton, who had told them again and again how strongly he objected to being called Warbler—"just as if I was some perishing siren," he'd protest—explained that during the vac, as the Head had disclosed to him, the Governors had discovered a place in the heart of the country to which the School might be removed if they liked. "And they've paid something down for an option upon it," he added.

"An option?"

"Yes. The right to refuse it or take it."

"But they're still undecided!"

"I said they were, didn't I, Cruden? But I said, as well, they were meeting to make up their minds. And now that the Old Library has caught such a packet——"

"And the cricket ground. Don't forget that," Dolly struck in again. "But all the same it's too late to evacuate now. We've missed the boat. The fellows are on their way back!"

"Not being totally blind," remarked Warburton, drawling a little, "I am able to distinguish your gorilla-like form, Dolly, and also that of most of the present company. And not being altogether devoid of intelligence——"

"Sarcasm doesn't suit you. Warbler, old son!"

"No, Dolly, I don't think it does," agreed Warburton heartily. "So cancelling the bit about 'void of intelligence' we'll say that I know just as well as you know yourself that the rest of the people are jolly well due back to-morrow. Followed on the day after that by the new kids."

"Accordingly I'm right about missing the boat, Warbler!"

"I wish you were. For the fact remains nevertheless that the Governors mean to decide when the whole school's assembled whether or no to remove us lock, stock, and barrel!"

"You'd have thought that they'd have made up their minds before that!"

"You might. But they haven't."

"Because they are not all unanimous."

"Exactly. That's why they're calling a full, special meeting. But they've given the new kids notice already to stand by."

"Which looks ominous."

"Yes, I admit it does."

"The idea being that if we do decide to evacuate the new kids can toddle straight off from their homes to the new place?"

"Precisely. While the rest of us are packed off from here in a body."

Then Feversham turned to Dollinger, with a mischievous glance. "Well, since," he began, "you would like my honest opinion——"

"We shouldn't," growled Dolly, rising at once to the bait.

"Never mind. You shall have it. Here it is Dolly. We're in for the wickedest rugger season on record!"

"Wickedest?" queried Cruden.

"Leanest, I mean."

"But haven't you strayed from the point, Feversham?"

"You think so? Not a bit. It's all in the picture."

"Oh, hang your pictures," roared Dolly. "What are you driving at?"

"I'm softening the blow for yourself and your miserable rugger. Unless we evacuate lots of the fellows will leave. 'Who's going back to be bombed?' their people will say. Sad disappearance of much of your heftiest material!"

"You seem pleased?"

"No. Prophetic," droned Feversham.

"And if we evacuate?"

"The same thing," said Feversham. "You see, lots of seniors are due to leave next year in any case. So their people will say, 'Jimmy hasn't got more than a year to run, so what's the good of sending him into the wilds?'"

"Is *your* Christian name by any chance James?" demanded another voice of remarkable huskiness, which came from Elkin, of School House, who had just slipped into the study in time to catch the gist of these gloomy predictions.

"No. It's John Arthur Augustus," smiled Feversham. "Any objection? But I didn't know you were back, Elkin! How's your poor throat?"

This stung Elkin, as intended. It wasn't his fault that he always spoke like a person with a sore throat. "Feversham, I believe you're a ratter," he answered. "Unless we evacuate you mean to clear out!"

"And if I do, is it any business of yours, Elkin?"

"Do you? Or don't you?"

"Do I what?"

"Intend to leave if we stay put?"

"Well, stranger things have happened," said Feversham, blandly. And then his face changed and the flippancy went from his air and he sat there, with all their eyes on him, feeling for words in which to express the thoughts that were busy inside him. At last he uttered, uncomfortably rather, and slowly.

"Cliffeborough has had a long innings. A jolly

long innings. I haven't."

Perhaps only Warburton glimpsed the application immediately. He gave Feversham a nod of the head, without speaking.

But Feversham had finished. "That's all," he said, while a little spot of colour showed in his cheeks.

He had turned his face to the window, and now he flung round again with the colour in his cheeks as hot as a flame. "But what right has Elkin to cross-examine me on my intentions and virtually to accuse me of funking?" he flared.

Elkin was throwing back a furious retort and an angry general argument looked like beginning, when Warburton brought them sharply to their senses. "Easy on!" he commanded, "that does no good. And it's exactly what the senior chaps must avoid. Whether we stay put or whether we move, for goodness sake let's have no barging about it."

"But surely a fellow is free to express his opinion?"

"Not he, Elkin! He must keep his opinion to himself unless it agrees with the Governors'. You see; whatever our individual opinions may be on the question of evacuating or staying put, it's up to us to back up the Governors' decision. You see, don't you?" Warburton repeated, appealing to all

of them. "We don't want people arguing and disputing. We've got to jump on that sort of thing, one and all of us. And that's one of the reasons why I collected you chaps. To warn you that we must show a common front."

"Horse sense," said Broomfield.

"United we stand, divided we fall," grinned old Dolly. "All right. That goes with me, as they say in America."

"And if you hear any grousers, clout them," bade Warburton.

"Then it looks as if Grummett is in for a packet," laughed Cruden, alluding to that pillar of the Upper Fifth whose gift for grousing had never been equalled at Cliffeborough.

Smoothed down, but looking dubious still, Elkin persisted. "About the rest of the fellows who come back tomorrow?" he asked. "Are they to be told that probably we'll evacuate? For if so, how can you stop their chins wagging?"

Warburton said, "They are not to be told—till it's necessary. Except the few of us here, no one else is to know yet."

Then he swooped upon Cruden, turned him out of his chair, and on this intimation the party broke up.

NOVEMBER 1953 · ONE SHILLING

Boy's Own
PAPER

In this issue
MOON WRECK!
THRILLING SPACE STORY

B.O.P

JAN 1967 2/-

BOY'S OWN PAPER

SCOUT CANOE PLANS

3 EXCITING STORIES

CARTOON COMPETITION

POPS—PETS—PUZZLES

THIS ISSUE

onte Carlo Rally Diary